The Messages of Light

The Journey of an Empath
in the Discovery of Miracles

Christi Conde

BALBOA.PRESS
A DIVISION OF HAY HOUSE

Copyright © 2022 Christi Conde.

All rights reserved. No part of this book may be used or reproduced by any means, graphic, electronic, or mechanical, including photocopying, recording, taping or by any information storage retrieval system without the written permission of the author except in the case of brief quotations embodied in critical articles and reviews.

All Bible scriptures per the Holy Bible, New International Version, NIV. Copyright 1973, 1978, 1984, 2011 by Biblica Inc. Used by permission. All rights reserved worldwide.

Balboa Press books may be ordered through booksellers or by contacting:

Balboa Press
A Division of Hay House
1663 Liberty Drive
Bloomington, IN 47403
www.balboapress.com
844-682-1282

Because of the dynamic nature of the Internet, any web addresses or links contained in this book may have changed since publication and may no longer be valid. The views expressed in this work are solely those of the author and do not necessarily reflect the views of the publisher, and the publisher hereby disclaims any responsibility for them.

The author of this book does not dispense medical advice or prescribe the use of any technique as a form of treatment for physical, emotional, or medical problems without the advice of a physician, either directly or indirectly. The intent of the author is only to offer information of a general nature to help you in your quest for emotional and spiritual well-being. In the event you use any of the information in this book for yourself, which is your constitutional right, the author and the publisher assume no responsibility for your actions.

Any people depicted in stock imagery provided by Getty Images are models, and such images are being used for illustrative purposes only.
Certain stock imagery © Getty Images.

Print information available on the last page.

ISBN: 979-8-7652-3015-2 (sc)
ISBN: 979-8-7652-3016-9 (hc)
ISBN: 979-8-7652-3017-6 (e)

Library of Congress Control Number: 2022913133

Balboa Press rev. date: 07/26/2022

To my husband for loving me even when I wasn't willing to love myself.

To my daughters for your wisdom, love, and compassion. You three inspire me daily.

To my mom for loving me and guiding me in this world and for continuing to do so from beyond.

To all the messengers of light in these pages. You have helped me and inspired me in ways you may never truly know.

I love you all!

Contents

Acknowledgments ix
Introduction xiii

Part 1: Concept: Understanding the Gift of the Empath

Chapter 1   The Whisper 1
Chapter 2   The Early Experiences of an Empath 11
Chapter 3   Shaped by Society 28
Chapter 4   The Wonder of a New World 37
Chapter 5   Enter the Teenage Years 48
Chapter 6   Finding Myself 54
Chapter 7   Life-Changing Choices 59
Chapter 8   A New Trajectory 66
Chapter 9   Designing Dreams 79
Chapter 10   Domestic Bliss 88

Part 2: Application: Using the Gifts of the Empath

Chapter 11   The Messages of Light 105
Chapter 12   Wait—Is This Real? 123
Chapter 13   Growth and Expansion 130
Chapter 14   Discovering New Opportunities and Abilities 147
Chapter 15   Love, Fear, and the Unhealthy Ego 175
Chapter 16   Embracing and Understanding My Gifts 197
Chapter 17   Concept versus Application 237
Chapter 18   Recurring Themes and Lessons Learned 273
Chapter 19   Finding My Stride 299
Chapter 20   Magic and Miracles Abound 314
Chapter 21   Coming Full Circle 339

Acknowledgments

This book would not have been possible without my husband and daughters; my mom; my dad and my other mother, Mary; and all those I am honored to call friends, as well as every other angel on earth who helped me along my way—my messengers of light.

Starting with my daughters, I want to acknowledge and thank Riane for her wisdom. Thank you for reminding me that I had to do the work to begin to heal. You were right. Kira, your fierce love held me to the highest standards. I love you more than you know. You inspire me daily. Aja, through your unconditional love, you helped me to see myself in a better light. Thank you for believing in me and encouraging me to believe in myself.

I want to especially thank and acknowledge the love of my life, Ron. You taught me about true love and sacrifice by standing by me even when you couldn't protect me from myself. You did the most important thing you could: you supported me until I could find the strength to save myself.

Thank you to everyone in these pages—you know who you are. Thank you for the amazing gifts you've given me. Thank you for sharing your miracles with me.

Thank you to my extended family: Tony, Lodi, Yvonne, Kathy, Tony, Conrad, Becca, Tony III, Sandy, Diane, Marcus, Alex, Laneige, Phoenix, Barrett, Breeann, Maya, Conrad, Sammy, and Manny. You all bring color and wonder to my life. I love you all so much. I am blessed to call you family.

I want to thank my Happy Healthy Whole World business partners: Stacey, Tina, Erica, Rocio, and Kathy. What we did together was nothing short of magic! Thank you, Kathy, for constantly pushing me outside my comfort zone and more or less forcing me to answer the higher call to service. You have changed my life, and I trust you will see just how much in the pages that follow. Stacey, thank you for being my friend and for seeing my mom in the picture of the clouds. I saw the butterfly, but you saw more. Your insight and intuition are truly remarkable. Happy Healthy Whole World would never have happened without you. Tina, thank you for your energy and enthusiasm. Your willingness to explore and absorb new and different information is inspiring. Thank you also for your support in the editing of this book in the initial stages. Your input and support were invaluable. Erica, thank you for being awesome. Thank you for courageously following your guidance regardless of societal expectations. Your example is paving the way for the future. Micah Sol has an amazing life ahead of her thanks to you. She shines so brightly you can see nothing but love and feel only the freedom and ease of divine flow in her presence. Thank you also for being one of the first readers of this text. You inspired me to keep going. Rocio, thank you for being the voice of reason for me many times when I failed to access my own. You have helped so many, and I am honored to call you my friend.

Thank you to my Chi Omega sisters: Alexis, Camille, Chelsea, Claudia, Leslie, Lisa, and Merri. Your kindness and positive examples helped me decide who I wanted to be.

Tina, Lina, Kelly, Angie, Corrina, Yvette, Michelle, Becky, Wendy, Chelsea, Pam, Priscilla, Joseph, Michelle, Patricia, Marc, Julie, Rosa, Valerie, DeAnna, Veronica, Tricia, Chris, Isabelle, Parker, Jackie, Ana, Sofia, Araceli, Erika, Lidia, Tracy, Lorenzo, Norma, Paramdayal, Julie, Rachel, Megan, Nydia, Kat, Christina, Suzie, Hannah, Yvonne, Josie, Nicole, Mandy, Laura, Chris, Esme, John, Brenda, Paul, Dora, Clarissa, Em, Ruby, Annmarie, Taylor, Kim, Heather, Neese, Jaime, Michelle, Nell, and Brandi, thank you for your friendship. It has meant the world to me. I adore you all.

Thank you to Deb, Nydia, Lina, and Paramdayal for teaching me the beauty in yoga.

I also want to thank Deb for being my friend. Thank you for reading my book and sharing your insights. You reminded me why I began this journey in the first place. Thanks to you and Chris also for sharing little Elia Marie with me and for letting me be her fairy godmother. The light in her eyes is God. She's got his playbook, and she's here to teach us. Let's all have fun learning from her!

Thank you to Lidia, for all you do for me and others. You are truly an angel on earth.

Laneige, thank you so much for your help in the editing of this book in preparation for publication. Your insights and expertise have helped me to feel confident and excited about what I am offering to the world.

A special thank-you and deep appreciation for all my clients and students, then and now. Working with you has helped me to grow, learn, and become the best version of myself so far. You not only have helped me to believe in miracles but also have reminded me that we can be part of them too.

Thank you to Tricia for being the backbone of our troop. We never would have done half the cool things we did if not for you. Thank you for everything. Thank you to DeAnna and Rosa for being awesome co-leaders. You made it fun. Thank you also to Rosa for taking over the troop at the perfect time. Thank you to the girls in the troop, and I thank your parents for supporting you. Hannah, Sara, Katie, Alina, Bella, Camilla, Jessica, Janey, Sammy, Rose, Taylor, Marissa, Analisa, Amely, Esme, Olivia, Anabelle, Madison, Georgia, Tiffany, Gabi, Simona, and, of course, my own Kira and Aja, I learned so much from you girls, and I love you all. Thank you for making those years so special for me.

Thank you to the students in Kathy's Father Yermo classes—you know who you are. Spending time with you reminded me that miracles are real and that we can help them along when we try.

I can't forget to thank Jerry and Esther Hicks and the Abraham entity of teachers for sharing wisdom of the ages that I continue to use as a guide along the path of prosperity.

Thank you to the people at Balboa Press for your professionalism and dedication in helping me in this endeavor.

Thank you, Marcus, for sending me the perfect Bible scripture that tied this book together in the end.

Thank you to everyone who is in this book, whether you are mentioned by name or not. You are a messenger of light, and you made my life better. Thank you.

Last, most importantly, I want to thank God, the Creator of all things and the divine Source of all beauty and light, for bringing the messages and the messengers of light into my life. I am humbled and in awe of the magic and the miracles that came through them.

Introduction

This is a story of love, life, and the messages of light that guide us to miracles. I am an empath, and so are you. All people are born with the ability to sense and perceive energy. There is a knowing that all children possess, an innate understanding of the divine. There are a mystery and a wonder in childhood that are meant to stay with us as we grow and design our lives, but life's struggles and challenges can make it difficult to believe in the magic of creation.

In the old days, when we struggled, we were able to turn down the volume on our emotions or even mute our empathic gifts. This resulted in a society of stressed-out and unhappy people who became increasingly unkind to one another. God, in his infinite wisdom, has issued a course correction. The gift of the empath is being awakened and amplified in everyone. The energy of the world is shifting. You know you can feel it. We are no longer able to ignore our feelings and emotions. It's time to recognize those emotions for what they are: divine guidance. Now is the time to understand the gift of empathy and to learn how to use it to heal your world. We are here to create lives filled with happiness, peace, and love. Let's get to it!

If you are drawn to this book, there is a reason. Know that in these inspiring true stories, you will find some valuable tools to help you and navigate the swiftly changing energy of our times. This life is full of fear, pain, trauma, and drama, but we are always guided, loved, and supported by a power that is greater than we know. This book is intended to remind you of the magic of childlike faith and reignite a sense of awe in you, just as the messages of light did for me. This world can be a wondrous place when we learn to tap into the divine flows of love and light.

This is the story of how I learned to connect with that greater power many call God. Through that connection, a two-way flow of communication formed, and I learned to find the miracles in the madness of this life. The experiences in these pages not only highlight the presence of an infinite, all-knowing energy in our lives but also show that this energy is constantly interacting with us in remarkable ways. Miracles are real, and they happen all the time.

I trust that as you read this book, you will be inspired to look for the messages of light in your own life. I know you will find them and the miracles that come with them too. You are here in this world, in this body, in this remarkable time on earth, on purpose. Make no mistake: you are reading this because you are being called to amplify your own natural gifts and talents and to express your own authentic and divine nature fully. You are a living, breathing extension of God, and you add more value to the world and the lives of the people around you than you will ever know. As you read my story, I hope you will rediscover your own relationship with the divine and learn how to create a life filled with magic and wonder for yourself. Miracles happen all the time. Wouldn't it be fun to see them? Wouldn't it be more fun to be part of them?

PART 1
Concept: Understanding the Gift of the Empath

Chapter 1

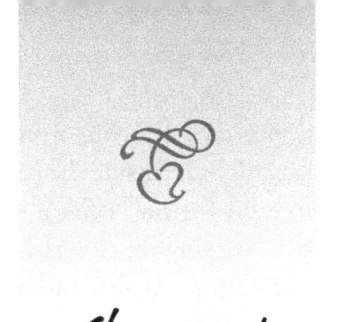

The Whisper

The Vision

On the evening of my thirty-second birthday, I was gifted with a rare moment of solitude. The festivities were over, our family and friends had gone home, and the loud buzz of our usually busy household had settled into a quiet hum. Jumping at the opportunity to read in peace, I blissfully sat down with my favorite book. After rereading the same paragraph three times, I realized I was having difficulty concentrating. Instead of indulging in the story on the pages before me, my mind insisted on cataloging the mental snapshots I had taken that day. Every smile, hug, and laugh was carefully placed into my mind's book of treasured memories, along with my sincerest appreciation for having had the happy experiences. Recounting the day's special moments spent with my loved ones filled me with a sense of serenity and deep appreciation for the many blessings in my life.

I was basking in tranquility and a sense of awe, when the sound of laughter brought me out of my reverie. My focus instantly shifted, and I began listening to my beautiful daughters playing happily together nearby. The fact that they were playing happily together made me feel particularly blessed. If you have children, you know exactly what I mean.

I was in that dreamy state of appreciation and gratitude, when I had a flash of something in my mind's eye. What was it?

As I searched my thoughts, I suddenly found myself filled with the exhilaration of anticipation. You know that feeling—it's what you feel when you receive an unexpected gift. Your mind races through all the exciting possibilities of what might be inside the package when you open it.

As I explored the sensation further, I felt a sort of glee. I was like a child riding a bicycle. I was coasting on the pathways of possibility, over the rolling hills of my imagination. At that moment, I felt the joy of the wind in my hair, the warmth of the sun on my face, and the fearlessness of daring to take my hands from the handlebars. I moved effortlessly from one blissful thought to another, floating in the feelings of freedom, contentment, and courage. In that instant, I saw the flash. I caught another glimpse of a scene in my mind's eye. It was a vision. It was cast within the fiery backdrop of a brilliant and colorful sunrise, with many of the details obscured by the blinding rays of the sun. Somehow, I knew what I saw was important.

As I snapped back into reality, I found my curiosity was ignited. I was embarking on a journey leading me to something new and beautiful. The feelings brewing inside me told me that it would be an exhilarating adventure. I had to know more. I'd had similar experiences before, so I knew what to do for further clarification on my vision. I began quieting my mind and opening myself to the energy. I started to breathe deeply and consciously, all the time focusing on the sensation, the exhilaration. Moments later, I found myself in a deeper state of tranquility. My thoughts and questions drifted out of my focus. My consciousness began to float upward and away from the weighty world of physical reality, and in the silence, I heard the whisper.

About Communicating

Before I tell you what I heard that day, I should probably give you a little background information about the whisper and where it comes from. It all starts with the gift of being an empath. Every human is empathic, but some have stronger spiritual muscles than others. The spiritual muscle of empathy allows the conscious mind to access divine guidance and intuition through vibration and emotion. The more it is used, the stronger the ability becomes. I must have exercised my spiritual muscle a lot growing up, because I have learned to understand and utilize my empathic gifts pretty well by now. Read on, and you'll see how and what I learned.

When I talk to God, my angels, and guides, I receive their energetic response to my questions in several ways. Their answers can come to me as a whisper, a picture of a scene in my mind's eye, or an emotional sensation. On occasion, the guidance comes to me in all those ways at once.

There are times when hearing the whisper or vibrationally receiving a vision can be challenging for me. You see, I can only hear the whisper or see the vision when I am quiet, centered, and feeling peaceful. In other words, when I'm not talking. Anyone who knows me will most likely agree it's unusual to find me not talking, hence my challenge. When I am too busy talking over my guidance, the communication will come in the form of an emotion.

I have found that these are all effective methods of communication from divine energy, but the whisper and the visions tend to be more fun. When the communication comes as emotion, well, that can go either way because I don't need to be peaceful and quiet to receive it. That's the gift of being an empath. Whether we realize it or not, we always receive divine guidance through our emotions, no matter how challenging a situation or circumstance is. Unfortunately, sometimes that guidance feels like anxiety, especially when it comes from emotion. To me, it feels as if God is screaming at me from inside, trying to get my attention. You can see how that might not be fun. So the trick is to recognize God's guidance for what it is, trust it, and learn to follow it.

About the Whisper

The whisper I mentioned is guidance that comes from God, my angels, my ascended ancestors, and my guides, and it sounds almost like any ordinary thought in my mind. It's a voice in my head that sounds just like me. That's why it took me such a long time to distinguish between my own personal thoughts and the guidance I receive—they sound very much alike. It wasn't until I realized I could hear this guidance in my deaf ear that I began to make the distinction between the two. You see, I was born completely deaf in my right ear, but somehow, that is where I sense the whisper. I guess in that ear, the whisper doesn't have to compete with external stimuli to be heard. Who knew being deaf in one ear could be such a good thing?

Another helpful distinction between the whisper and my own thoughts is that the whisper always comes as an answer to something I have been questioning or contemplating. In other words, when I ask a question, I get an answer. Conversely, my normal thoughts don't occur in a question-and-answer format.

Through my gift of empathy, I have learned to tell that the communication is divine by the way I feel when it comes to me. My emotional reaction to hearing it is something to the effect of "What? Where did that come from?" or "Huh?" It's the reaction of hearing something for the first time or a powerful "Aha!" response. It feels like the excitement that comes with the surprise of a sudden realization. Sometimes it feels like a wave of relief. The sensation I feel when my guidance flows is now unmistakable to me, but it wasn't always that way. I had to learn to strengthen my empathic muscle first.

I find that the messages I hear from the whisper feel so profound in nature that I know I did not come up with them all on my own. I consider myself an intelligent person, but you must give credit where credit is due. I recognize that the information is coming to me and through me but not necessarily from me. The guidance of which I speak comes from the source of all knowledge and inspiration—God—and it's available to everyone.

Lastly and most importantly, experience has taught me the difference between my own thoughts and the whisper. I have learned that when I follow the guidance from the whisper, a sense of happiness and inner contentment is always a result. It becomes clear that a higher wisdom or intelligence directs the flow of the information coming to me in every circumstance. Also, the outcome of following this guidance is consistently in the highest interest of everyone concerned.

As I mentioned, I hear the whisper most easily when I am in a peaceful, happy state of being. Walking outdoors is my favorite form of exercise and the quickest way for me to reach a sense of tranquility. It is sort of my way of tuning into higher consciousness. I get my blood pumping, and I get those endorphins flowing. I appreciate the beauty around me, and I feel serene. I bask in the flow of gratitude, and I feel closer to God. That's where I talk to him, in the beauty of the world he created. When I am outside, my energy level rises; my mind clears; and in the quiet, I can hear the whisper. I ask a question, and an answer comes.

Now you probably have a picture in your head of a strange woman walking the streets and talking to thin air, right? Well, close. I have actually responded to this communication out loud, and the result was comical.

Let's just say I didn't like the guidance I was getting. I was being directed to do something far outside my comfort zone. I disliked the mission so much and had such a strong reaction to it that I responded aloud.

My response to the whisper that day was "No! Um, no!" as if I were arguing with a friend.

I was passing our neighborhood church at the time, and the groundskeeper happened to be working outside. He instantly stopped what he was doing when he heard me practically yelling, "No!" I could see the wheels turning in his mind. He was wondering whom I was talking to. He saw no one beside me. There was no phone to my ear, and this was well before Bluetooth technology and earbuds existed. In his apparent contemplation of my strange behavior, the rake he was carrying slipped out of his hand and hit the ground with a loud thud. I had stopped talking to invisible energy by then, but he still looked at me in a funny way with his head tilted to the side. Then he shook his head as I watched him stoop to pick up what he'd dropped.

I broke out into laughter when I realized what I had done. I'd surprised the man. Clearly, he was not accustomed to witnessing people talking out loud to an invisible force.

Looking back on it, I think my laughter probably made the situation more perplexing for him. As he stood from picking up the rake, his gaze remained on the ground. He moved his head from side to side, pausing periodically, as if he were sorting through the thoughts in his head.

I giggle to myself as I imagine what those thoughts might have been.

Live and learn. These days, I make every effort to keep my responses to my guidance silent, especially outdoors and around other people. I have to say, sometimes it's not easy!

I choose to believe that the whisper I hear is from God, because God is the highest power in my belief system, and I only hear the whisper when I have been praying to God or feeling really connected spiritually. It's important here to mention that for the sake of this subject matter, the reader should choose the higher power that fits his or her own belief system. To some, the whisperer could also be called the Holy Spirit, the Supreme Being, divine consciousness, love, light, vital life-force energy, universal life-force energy, or Source energy. They are all whole (holy) divine energy before the split to duality. They all have the same origin. They are all the same energetic vibration. To me, the name given to this energy is not nearly as important as the fact that I can feel that the messages delivered by the whisper originate from a Source of unconditional love and limitless light. I call the guidance I receive "messages of light."

Capturing the Messages

At first, I didn't know what I was supposed to do with the messages I was receiving, but I did know I wanted to remember them. So I began writing them down as they came to me. It wasn't long before I noticed a pattern. It seemed the more I wrote, the more often I received the messages. My ability was like a muscle, growing stronger with continued exercise. After a while, I found myself almost always in the flow of inspiration. If I wasn't prepared, I missed out on the opportunity to capture the message. This became an issue easily resolved when my flawless guidance led me to the perfect solution for me: spiral notebooks. I realize spiral notebooks seem archaic in this age of modern technology. Still, I have learned that following my guidance is always in my best interest, and it's been my experience that the simplest solution is almost always the best solution. Besides, spiral notebooks are portable, do not require batteries, and are not expensive to replace if lost or destroyed.

I became notorious for carrying around spiral notebooks. They were in my car. They were at my bedside. They were all over my house. If I was awake, there was most likely a spiral notebook within my reach. I carried the notebooks so often that my husband decided I needed a better way to efficiently cart them around with me. As a thoughtful gift, he presented me with a beautiful handbag. It was big enough to hold a three-subject notebook as well as my wallet, my keys, and everything else my children and I could ever possibly need. This large purse, equipped with a spiral notebook and a pen, became more than an accessory to complete any outfit. It became my office.

As I said, I didn't want to miss a beat. I wanted to spend as much time flowing in the positive energy of the messages as I could. So I made it my mission to go through each day looking for the things in my life that were beautiful and inspirational and then write about my observations.

Inspiration doesn't always strike at the most opportune moment, and odd timing can lead to some unusual situations. One day, while I was driving to pick up my youngest daughter from preschool, I had one such experience. I wasn't far from home yet. In fact, I was driving on the same road I had walked that morning while I meditated and prayed. I was drifting from happy thought to happier thought, when inspiration stepped in.

Luckily, I had my trusty notebook. I was excited about what I got from the inspiration; I knew I had to write it down right away before I forgot the information. I checked the time and saw that I was ahead of schedule for pickup, so I pulled over to write down the new message. I let the inspiration and information flow onto the paper. I was so engrossed in what I was writing that I became oblivious to my surroundings.

After a while, I got a weird feeling that I was being watched by some hidden force. When I looked up, I discovered I was, in fact, under observation. A police vehicle had pulled alongside me. The occupants were looking at me intently. I rolled down my window and spoke with the two caring and curious police officers. They explained that they had stopped to see if I was stranded or needed some help, because I had been sitting there for some time.

It's important to understand here that when I receive the messages and the inspiration to write, I become giddily excited. That day was no exception; at that moment, I was precisely that. You can imagine what I must have looked like as I waved the spiral notebook in the air while explaining that I had just pulled over to write. I wore a bright, shiny smile and was spewing the energy and excitement of someone on the verge of mania. The looks they gave me were priceless—a mixture of concern and humor. You would have thought they had never seen a thrilled person inspired to pull over and write in a spiral notebook before. It's good I refrained from mentioning the full detail of the inspiration. I didn't say anything about the voice in my head telling me what to write; otherwise, things might have gone a little differently. As it was, I must not have looked too out of hand, because after a sidelong glance at each other, they smiled and sent me on my way.

As I drove off with the patrol car in my rearview mirror, I contemplated the experience. There have been many times in my life when I have felt I was different and maybe even a little strange. That moment, as I recalled the priceless looks of discernment on the faces of the officers, coupled with the emotions I'd felt coming from them, I received confirmation. My self-assessment was accurate. People think I'm unusual, to say the least. The fact is, I am a little different, and that's just fine with me. I have since decided that normal is overrated, and I have grown to love and embrace the weirdness within. Now when I get wary looks of judgment or sense confusion coming from a stranger because of my unique yet authentic presentation of myself to the world, I tend to find it amusing. Just know it wasn't always that way.

The Birthday Message

Now that we're semiacquainted let's get back to my thirty-second birthday, when I heard the whisper that would change my life forever. As my consciousness drifted upward into a higher vibration, I felt a warm sensation around my head. The hair near my deaf ear felt as if it were standing on end, as if charged by an electrical current. My heart rate jumped; I felt the incoming vibration of love; and in the silence, I distinctly heard, "Write!"

Yep. That was it. That was what it said. I know I heard it correctly. The whisper said, "Write!"

Confused, I pressed on and contemplated the message behind the single word.

Write? I thought. *What do you mean? What do you think I have been doing all this time?*

At that moment, I looked up to the heavens. I grabbed the full spiral notebook from the table beside me and opened it up. As if I needed to show

God that I was already writing. As if I needed to say, "Hey! Look! See? I am writing! It's all right here in this spiral notebook."

I had been writing nearly every day for a while. However, apparently, I was still missing something in this particular message. I continued my contemplation. I knew there was a deeper meaning, and I just had to find it. This message was pivotal; I could feel it. The vision I had of the fiery sunrise told me that. I knew there was something more I needed to understand. So I asked. I have discovered the best way to get a helpful answer is to ask a good question.

"Write what?" I asked

"Write your story," I heard in response.

I couldn't help but think, *What? Write my story? Really? That's my answer? You've got to be kidding me! Why would anyone want to hear that?* I scoffed. *And what about the messages?* What was I supposed to do with those? I was confused. My contemplation continued. *Write my story, huh?*

At that moment, I thought about every aspect of the challenge, and I only managed to linger on the positive possibilities for about a split second. The more I thought about it, the more daunting the task became. I began to subscribe to the idea that I couldn't do it. I wasn't even sure I wanted to do it. I struggled and wrestled with the idea. I didn't understand what good could come of my recounting my life story. So why would I begin such a big undertaking? I mean, come on. I'd just started writing and collecting the messages I was given, and suddenly, without any direction for the messages, I had been given a new assignment.

My immediate insecurity about the task spiraled into profound self-doubt in a matter of seconds. I felt like a car in a drag race with a superpowered engine, taking off at the green light with no brakes and no control over the driver. Every excuse for mediocrity I'd ever heard popped into my head and played on a loop. I became so confused and distraught that I decided I was incapable of writing my own story. Sounds comical, right? I convinced myself this mission was more complicated than my previous task of just writing down the messages. Writing my story just seemed too big of a job. I could feel my confidence dwindling. The future was uncertain, and my role in it was unclear. Until then, I had been content in being a wife and a mother. I had everything I needed and even a lot of what I wanted. This detour of writing my story, this challenge, was not on my agenda!

As I sat there complaining in my mind, I heard the whisper again. I felt a flutter in my chest resembling a burst of anxiety. Again, I heard, "Write your story!"

The second time, it was stated in such a firm manner that it felt a bit louder than a whisper. The intensity caused me to take a slow, deep, centering breath. Breathing always helps. Suddenly, the vision became clear. My fearful thoughts fell away, and I was instantly infused with the answers to questions I had been contemplating for some time.

The first question was "What is my purpose in receiving the messages?"

I received the answer "To bring more love and light into the world."

Yeah, I know it sounds kind of generic, but it made sense.

The second question was "What am I supposed to do with the messages?"

"Share them."

Well, duh! I thought. Sounds easy enough, right? Sure!

The cool thing is, this experience, including the vision of the sunrise, was the answer to a question I hadn't even asked yet: "How? How do I share the messages?"

Yep, you know the answer: "Write your story!"

Well, OK then, I thought. At that point, I chose not to question. I was reminded that I can doubt, argue with, and even try to ignore my guidance if I wish, but nothing seems to go right when I do. When I do not follow my guidance, I find myself feeling lost and confused, empty and unfulfilled, as if something is missing. Conversely, when I do listen to the whisper and follow my guidance, something unusual and miraculous always occurs, and I'm left to wonder why I ever doubted in the first place. Fear should never have been part of the equation.

By focusing on this personal truth, I felt my inner struggle subside. There had to be a good reason I was getting this instruction. So that day, on my birthday, I resolved that this gift would not go unutilized. I would not let fear or uncertainty take over. I decided I would dare to write my story.

So here goes!

Chapter 2
The Early Experiences of an Empath

First Memories

I guess when you are telling a story, the best place to start is the beginning. Most people are surprised at the clarity of my early childhood memories. Sometimes I'm surprised too. I still remember a time before I knew words. I remember being a thinker and observer. I remember using my emotions and instincts to guide myself, and I remember reasoning to learn and what my thoughts were as I did.

I can clearly remember the moment I discovered how to sort yellow plastic shapes into a red-and-blue plastic ball. The ball had the corresponding forms cut into it in a puzzle design. I remember my thought process. I recall the accomplishment I felt when the shapes went into the ball and, ultimately, the boredom I experienced when the game ceased to be a challenge.

I remember potty training too. Strange, right? Yes, I know. I can vividly recall when I decided I no longer needed diapers. I was fifteen months old and on a road trip with my mom. Is that normal?

Most importantly, I still remember the wordless communication of spirit and what it felt like to receive the messages of light sent by God. I remember that sense of knowing I often felt as a child. It was an innate ability to understand my experience through my emotions and without a verbal explanation.

Now, as an adult, after a few stretches of amnesia on the subject, the sense of knowing I felt then has returned. I access it by focusing on the ease and comfort of the presence of God. I call on that feeling of being safe, secure, and loved. I ask a question, and the answers come.

The Tapestry

My family was not a religious family per se. We didn't go to any services on Sunday or attend prayer groups. We didn't really talk about God or heaven much when I was little, but my parents did offer me a spiritual foundation. They taught me right from wrong, of course. We said bedtime prayers every night, and I had my own book of children's Bible stories that I loved. I remember pulling out that cardboard-paged book to look at the pictures well before I could read, because I liked the way I felt when I looked at the illustrations. I also remember my crib and the two things that hung on the wall above it: a plaque and a tapestry.

There was something about that plaque. I couldn't read it when I was little, but I knew it was important. The plaque had the Lord's Prayer written on it. The prayer was handwritten in a delicate black script on a carved piece of white slate trimmed in gold lace and covered with tiny grains of translucent sand. I remember running my fingers over it to capture the texture in my mind. Situated beside the mysterious plaque was an elegant tapestry. I looked at it every night as I drifted off to sleep. It was beautiful and colorful. It had a velvety texture, and I loved to touch it, because the colors' hues changed depending on how the fibers were brushed. It was filled with deep shades of blue, red, orange, and gold. On it was a kind-looking man in a white robe with a crimson sash running from his shoulder to his hip. He was sitting on a large gray stone. He held a tiny baby sheep in one hand, and with the other hand, he gently stroked the head of what appeared to me to be the baby sheep's mommy. Above the man's head floated a ring that shone bright white, and it was backed by the indigo sky.

Looking at the tapestry was a religious experience for me, as in I looked at it religiously every night before bed because I felt peaceful when I did. I was connecting to divine consciousness. I was receiving messages of light, but they were coming to me through my emotions because I didn't think in words yet. By my viewing the beauty and the colors and sensing the love and serenity of the picture regularly, those nightly contemplations were way more than a way to ease into a dream world; they became a meditative practice strengthening my spiritual muscle. I was developing a relationship with the energy of the being in the picture, Jesus, the physical manifestation of the divine consciousness of God.

Tonsillectomy

For a time, I was terribly ill as a little one. I developed constant ear infections and frequent tonsillitis. Once, I became so feverish and dehydrated that my tongue cracked and bled. To this day, I have a six-pack of scars creased into my tongue from that event. I still remember the taste of the petroleum jelly that coated my tongue to help it heal. My mother must have been a nervous wreck. Nothing is more terrifying to a mother than a sick child, and I was often ill. When I was almost four years old, the decision was made that I should have my tonsils surgically removed to protect my health.

I remember the time leading up to my surgery well because of the confusion I experienced. For weeks, I got a cocktail of mixed messages about the surgery from every adult in my life. Too many opinions can be confusing for any child. Personally, I was confused on another level. I wasn't just confused because of multiple views and perspectives; I was confused because I could sense what the adults around me were feeling, and when what they said out loud didn't line up with those feelings, I found it upsetting. Now I equate that sensation to what I feel when I know someone is lying to me, but then I was so young and innocent I didn't know what a lie was yet. I just knew the feeling was awful.

For example, when my mom told one of her friends about the impending surgery, the woman's immediate reaction was supposed to reassure me that everything would be fine, but it didn't. She told me not to worry, as I would be fine because I was "such a big girl," but then in the same breath, she turned to my mom to ask if the surgery was safe for someone so small. It's funny how adults forget that children are always listening.

Another adult had a long talk with me about being brave and strong when I was with the doctors, while at the same time, I could sense her uncertainty and fear on the subject. I actually felt her fear. I hadn't been scared at all until that moment. Her fear triggered mine. Ah, the joys of being an empath!

Most importantly, I distinctly recall my mom gently assuring me that everything would be OK, when I not only knew but also felt that she was terrified even as the words left her mouth.

The fun things are there in my memory too. Promises of ice cream when the surgery was over and reassurances that I would be home soon were somewhat soothing. At the very least, the promises distracted me from the fear surrounding me.

I remember the surgery too. I recall the sharp smell of bleach stinging my nose. I remember the shivers I experienced from the icy chill of the air in the enormous, bare surgical suite. I even remember how the doctor took off his surgical mask as he instructed me to say my ABCs while I faded into the oblivion of anesthesia. I remember getting my tonsils out too, because I watched it. I guess you could call it an out-of-body experience, because I was definitely not in my body. I was in the air, looking down at my body. I didn't go wandering the hospital halls. I stayed right there in the room and watched as the surgery was performed. I knew that something unusual was happening. Still, I wasn't afraid, because the man from the tapestry was there with me.

Yep, Jesus was right there in the room, holding my hand, when I got to the letter *C* in my anesthesia countdown. I could tell it was him by how it felt to be near him. The peace and serenity were tangible.

When I looked at him, he radiated so much light it was hard to make out his features, but it didn't matter to me, because I was at ease in his presence. We watched the surgery together from a sort of ethereal surgical teaching amphitheater. Above us, there was a blue sky with fluffy white clouds. There were waves of rainbow light flowing in all directions, creating a canopy of shifting and swirling colors in place of what should have been ceiling tiles. We never spoke in words, but I still felt as though everything were being explained to me in a sort of telepathic communication. He was funneling in messages of comfort and peace. At the same time, I floated in the colorful translucent light, looking down at myself. His presence created a detached sense of calm and a powerful sense of serenity in me.

We watched together in reverence and appreciation as the doctors and nurses performed their duties in the artful flow of a graceful dance. I remember tiny details, such as the glint of the silver scalpel and how the metal tip disappeared into a stream of red liquid. I knew it should have hurt because I was on that table, but I could not feel the pain. I was mesmerized as the first blob of tissue was taken out and put into a shiny metal pan. It had a sickly yellowish-green aura, and it was dripping with red goo.

It was then that I looked back at my companion and noticed the glow of white light coming from him. It grew brighter and brighter, filling the room. Wherever he placed his attention, the white light would grow more intense. The light became particularly radiant around the surgeon and the nurses. Then I could barely see myself on the table, because the light he directed around me was so blinding.

Things got a little hazy after that, and I woke up to my mother's relieved and smiling face. This time, the emotions I felt from my mom matched the look on her face, and I felt peaceful too.

Looking back, I can see that Jesus, the divine energy of God in physical form, was with me well before the surgery. He was always guiding me. He was there inside me in that small and quiet voice, sending me messages, alerting me to the discrepancies between the words and actions of the people around me. His guidance came to me through the feeling of confusion I had when those inconsistencies occurred. That feeling, the discomfort I felt, was God encouraging me to look a little deeper and listen a little more intently to what was going on around me. God was at the heart of my every observation and contemplation, helping me to decode my life experiences. He also offered me solutions to my discomfort in the form of my instincts. When the emotion I felt coming from an adult didn't feel good, I cried. Naturally, this resulted in my removal from the person and the energy he or she was emitting. I believe this was God's way of protecting me from becoming part of the fear vibration of the world that surrounded me.

Again, the ability to feel what others are feeling just by being near them is not unique to me. All children are born empaths. We are all gifted with the ability to feel energy. This is guidance from God.

Think about when you were young. I bet you can recall a person from your childhood whom you felt uncomfortable around. That was God alerting you to a vibration that was not for your best good. Maybe that person was just in a bad mood, not necessarily a bad person, but either way, that negative feeling is contrary to God's peace and comfort, so you were naturally averse to it. This is evidence of God's guidance system in you too. It's there, it's always been there, and it will always be there. Now is the perfect time to learn about the gift of empathy and how to use it efficiently to create a happy and fulfilled life. Read on to accept the challenge.

Strange Sounds in the Night

After the tonsillectomy, my health improved significantly—so much so that my parents were able to go on a date every once in a while. On one of those evenings, I had a curious experience with the unknown. My parents left me overnight with my babysitter Ruby and her husband. The evening was routine. I got to play with all the day-care toys without any competition from the other kids, and I had fun. I wore myself out that night, because I didn't have any trouble going right to sleep, even though I wasn't at home in my own bed.

Ruby and her husband put me down to sleep in a crib next to their bed. All was well until I woke up to a strange sound and an unusual feeling in my chest. It began in my dream. I was in a dark place. I couldn't see much of anything, but the music I heard echoed through the space with an entrancing rhythm and cadence. I had never seen a place like it before. The closest comparison I had for reference in my young mind was a parking garage. It was large and open like an underground structure, but this place was different. It had less light, and there were no cars.

The sound from my dream grew louder and louder, thrumming in my mind, until I woke up. When I opened my eyes, I could still hear the sound. I sat up in the bed, trying to find the source of the mysterious, captivating rhythm. I could still hear it clearly, as if it were coming from somewhere in the room. At first, I thought it might have been one of my babysitters' snoring, but it wasn't. Snoring doesn't sound like a drum or chanting. When I discovered it wasn't coming from one of my babysitters, I was confused, especially because the sound kept getting louder and louder. I could feel the vibration of it moving through my body. Every part of my being was electrified and began pulsating and vibrating with the sound. It was an intense sensation, but something inside me told me to relax into it. When I got that message, I knew it was OK, so I settled back into the crib. When I did, I began to feel comfort, ease, and even a bit of elation. The thrumming I heard was in such a cadence, rhythm, and intensity that I felt as if I were inside the heartbeat of God. Perhaps that was why I didn't cry. I felt I was becoming one with the sound and vibration, and my confusion simply fell away. I settled back down into the comfort of the energy and listened to the sound until it lulled me back to sleep.

The sound was powerful yet soothing, and I found it strangely familiar, even though I hadn't had much life experience to draw from yet. I wondered what the rhythmic humming, chanting sound meant. Even as a child, I was curious why I could hear it so plainly, and no one else did. It was loud enough to wake me from my dreams, yet the other people in the room slept right through it. I stayed curious about the experience all of my young life. Eventually, I discovered what had happened that night, but I wondered about it for thirty years before I did. Stay tuned for that story.

The Piano

Another unusual thing happened when I was about four years old, give or take a few months. Let's just say I was pretty young. My mother, my father, and I lived in a small apartment complex. I remember it clearly. The complex had four two-story buildings laid out in the shape of a square. There was also a colorful courtyard with a large swimming pool adorning the center of the common space. To me, it was a wonderland.

While we lived there, my mom and I had a daily tradition: we sat together and watched cartoons for a few minutes every morning before she released me to go play with a friend who was not much older than I was. Each day, my friend and I would explore the area with glee. A small apartment complex seems like an immense palace to children that young. The seemingly large space had plenty to spark the imaginations of two bold and curious young girls. The apartment complex was so expansive, to us at least, that we had a new adventure every time we went outside. It was a magical land, and we were magical beings exploring it. With so much to investigate, the playtime narrative changed daily, depending on the person, corridor, or animal we encountered in our travels. Ah, the wonders of childhood! We were in a magical forest one moment, and the next, we were flying into outer space on a rocket ship. We were never bored.

One morning, before I ventured outside, I sat in my mother's lap, and a Bugs Bunny cartoon came on the air. As we watched, we swayed together to the tune playing on the show, and we cuddled. I was captivated by the classical music Bugs created by playing the piano. Bugs ran his fingers over the ivory so quickly that tiny sparks arose from the keys. The flames danced over the keys and then grew into a giant blaze in the background. Colossal orange and red flames rose and flickered to the tune of the music being played. I was mesmerized. It was the first time I had seen anything like that before, so I asked my mom what it was.

"That's a piano," she said.

I was excited. I'd learned something new. I knew what a piano was, and something inside me knew it was important.

Not long after that day, or maybe even the same day, my friend and I were on another playtime expedition. We had stolen up the stairs to the second-floor landing of the building adjacent to the building where I lived. Occasionally, as little kids do, we peeked into open windows. In fact, we made a game of it. That particular day, we were about halfway across the second-floor landing, when we discovered a new open window. Naturally, I walked right up to the window and peered into the room. Now, what do you think I saw on the other side of the glass? A real live piano!

Instantly, I knew something was wrong, even though I had no real basis for fear. The only other piano I had ever seen in my young life had been in a cartoon. Yet I knew I had to do something about this piano, because I felt afraid. Using my ability as an empath, God was guiding me through my emotions.

With that feeling of fear gnawing at me, I sprinted down the stairs as fast as my pudgy little legs could carry me. I found my mom and grabbed

The Messages of Light

her by the arm. As I tugged and pulled on her arm, interrupting her conversation, I told her about the piano. Of course, my mom had seen a keyboard before, so it was not nearly as exciting to her as it was to me. She said something all moms say: "That's nice, dear."

Well, something, or someone, told me not to let it go. I had an intense feeling nagging at me. There was a fear inside me, alerting me to a purpose and compelling me to follow through on it. I knew I had to make my mom come see. I knew it was important. I continued to screech relentlessly about the piano until she finally gave in and came to see it with me. You can imagine her surprise and horror when she arrived at the window to find that the word *piano* meant *fire* to me.

I don't remember exactly what happened immediately following my mom's realization. My guess is that my mom got me out of there and called the fire department. Later that day, I watched my dad, who was still in his law enforcement uniform, go bravely into the scorched apartment to make sure it was safe for the tenant to reenter. I recall trying to follow him into the room and being suddenly scooped up and told that it was too dangerous.

We later learned that the young woman living there planned to move out. Apparently, they had already cut off her electricity, so she used candles to light the room. She inadvertently had left one burning while she was on a trip to her new place, and well, we know what happened after that. The candle had caught something in the apartment on fire.

Miraculously, the fire had been limited to that one apartment. Although most of the girl's belongings were destroyed, it was a miracle that the other apartments in the building were saved. There was only minimal damage to the property from the water used to douse the flames, and most importantly, no one was hurt.

As I went to bed that night, I remember looking up at my tapestry and feeling love. It was as if Jesus reached his arms out of the fabric to hold me like the little lamb in the picture. I felt pleased and content, even though I had no concept of the significance of the event that had just occurred. This was the first message of light that I can remember involving someone else, and it began in the form of a cartoon. Go figure!

Now, as I look back on that experience, I see that the message originated with God. I know this because it inspired me to begin asking questions:

Who orchestrated the airing of that cartoon at the exact perfect time for me to see it? Who made my mom sit down and explain the cartoon? How did I know what to do or even know that the "piano" was dangerous? The answer to all of those questions is clearly God. Think about it. I saw the flame while watching a cartoon. Cartoons are not designed to instill fear, yet somehow, I knew to be afraid. The guidance I followed was a sense, a knowing from within myself. That *something* that made me take note of the dancing flame in the cartoon also made me take notice of the real live piano in the window. The feeling that compelled me to act and tell someone about it, the intense sense of purpose that made my usual means of communication turn into a screech, the knowing, and even the fear I experienced at the moment—all of it was direct communication from God. This was my guidance system in its full glory. The messages of light were sent by God and received by me without obstruction through my emotions. My path in that situation was all apparent to me. I could feel what I needed to do, and I did it without hesitation. Why? I hadn't yet learned to overthink or second-guess myself. I didn't yet care what people would think about me if I made a mistake. I just knew what to do. I followed my God-given instincts. I had the faith of a child, and the outcome was a positive one.

Imaginary Friend

As I grew, so did my powers of perception, and I began to sense beings and energies that the adults around me couldn't see or feel. Naturally, I was open to making friends with them. All children are open to the energy of love, however it appears to them.

When adults see children talking to angels or spirits, they don't know what to think. So to make themselves feel better, they refer to such instances as children communicating with an "imaginary friend." By those standards, of course, I had an imaginary friend. I was an only child, so I was often alone with my thoughts. I don't know if that was why I had an imaginary friend. I do know that with little social interaction outside of day care, I had a lot of quiet time. That meant I had little interference from real-world noise and distractions, which caused me to naturally focus inward.

The Messages of Light

I remember the day he showed up. I was playing in my room with my Bert and Ernie stacking puzzle. I was alone one moment, and I felt him there the next. I didn't see him at first. I just felt him next to me. We didn't talk out loud to each other. We communicated only with our minds, as I had with Jesus during my surgery. When my new friend appeared in my mind, I had a moment of doubt. For some reason, I thought to myself, *Imaginary friends aren't real.*

But he responded to my thought by saying, *Hi! My name is Tommy.*

As soon as I accepted his introduction as real, I could see him too. He materialized out of thin air. OK, maybe he was still thin air, but I could see him, not just hear him like before. He looked like a kid, but he was a little different from any other kid I knew. He was translucent and kind of looked like a hologram. In other words, he was see-through. He was taller than I was and lean and lanky. Like me, he had blue eyes and long blond hair. I thought it was strange for a boy to have long hair, because all the males in my world had short hair. My dad and all his friends were in law enforcement, so having hair over the collar was unacceptable in his line of work. Tommy's hair was almost as long as mine, which hung to the middle of my back, just below my shoulder blades. Tommy was just another kid, and the fact that he was different from everyone else I knew was of no real consequence to me. I was just happy I had a playmate.

So I went with it, and we played every day. I decided not to mention it to the adults. I find it strange that I chose not to tell people about Tommy. I think I had a feeling that an invisible friend might not be well received. I was too young to realize that imaginary friends weren't generally discussed in social circles. Still, a feeling of uneasiness washed over me when I thought of mentioning my new friend to an adult. I believe that sense guided me to stay quiet about it. Little did I know that emotional sensation was part of my empathic guidance system, the same guidance system, the knowing, that had enabled me to understand that a real live "piano" was not a good thing.

Maybe Tommy showed up when he did because all the grown-ups in my life were off in their own adult world of crisis, so to speak. If I had told anyone about my new friend, it would have been my mom. Unfortunately, I hadn't seen her in a while. I wasn't sure what was going on, because the adults were careful not to speak of it in front of me. All I knew was that I felt terribly sad and afraid when I was around them. I was surrounded by a fear vibration, so you can bet I was feeling it. You've got to love being an empath.

As all children do, I had a natural aversion to the feeling of fear, so I spent time with Tommy instead. He was my playtime companion for a long time, bringing with him both fun and wisdom. I often went to him for advice. We had entire conversations. There were many times when he played the role of my conscience. Tommy became the voice inside my head that warned me of the possible consequences of my actions. He was the angel in white sitting on my shoulder.

I have a few theories about the manifestation of Tommy in my life. Sometimes I think Tommy was God's way of giving me a physical reference for the guidance coming to me. It's possible that it was easier for my young mind to see God as another child instead of hearing him as an invisible whisper in my deaf ear. Then again, maybe Tommy was the spirit of my sibling who didn't make it to the earth plane. I believe that when a family loses a child, that child becomes a spiritual presence guiding and protecting the family, kind of like an angel. Or maybe Tommy was altogether something or someone else. Believe what you will, but given the timing of his arrival, the second theory makes as much sense as the first. All I know is that Tommy was a constant source of love. Our times together were filled with joy and lighthearted moments, and he was almost always by my side.

Tommy

As I said, Tommy was a little angel on my shoulder. I had my own personal messenger of light, and he kept me out of trouble more than once. I grew up in a time when parents let their children run free. I was up every day at dawn and out the door, exploring my world, the first chance I got. I was an inquisitive child who loved to be outside. There was something new to see at every moment, and I always found treasures to examine and keep. My mom wasn't keen on keeping my discoveries when they were alive, but I tried anyway. I was never squeamish. I loved the little critters, and Tommy did too.

There were many times when Tommy had my back, but there is a specific memory of Tommy playing the hero that stands out in my mind. My family was moving into a new apartment, and naturally, my parents were busy with the organizing of our belongings. There were boxes, tools, and hazards everywhere. Clearly, this was not a suitable environment for a small person. Like most at the time, my parents had a standard approach to a five-year-old underfoot: "Why don't you go outside and play for a while?"

They didn't have to tell me twice. I was out the door in a flash. There was so much new, unexplored ground to cover, and I was excited to investigate my new world. That day, Tommy was, as always, the voice of caution in my ear, because like most children, I was a fearless, free spirit. I didn't know any reason not to be curious and bold. So when Tommy told me I shouldn't go into the pool, I didn't listen. I mean, what did he know anyway, right? Tommy was just another kid like me, and he was see-through to boot! What could he possibly know that I didn't?

Well, I was about to find out.

When we moved into the apartment, it was late in the fall. The pool in the center of the apartment complex was drained in preparation for the winter. The fact that it was drained didn't make it any less of a hazard. You see, my interest was in the giant pile of leaves in the deep end of the pool. I loved to jump and play in leaves. What kid could resist the magnetic pull of a colorful pile of tree confetti?

So off I went. I climbed down the steps at the pool's shallow end in the blink of an eye. I headed straight toward the leaves, but I moved slowly because Tommy told me it wasn't a good idea. As I moved closer to the pile of leaves, envisioning my glorious romp through the colors, Tommy got upset at my refusal to listen to him, and he left. I didn't mind, because I could think only of that magical pile of leaves and the hidden treasures within it. If Tommy wasn't there, he couldn't ruin my fun!

That feeling of free rebellion didn't last long. Seconds later, I felt Tommy call out to me, and behind Tommy's soundless shouting, I heard another voice. This one was actually audible to the human ear; it wasn't just in my head. I looked up just then to see a young man calling out and waving at me. He was trying to get my attention. When I saw him, I instantly stopped where I stood. The person behind the voice was a handsome young man, probably in his late teens or early twenties. He was wearing bell-bottomed blue jeans and a white shirt unbuttoned just enough to reveal the top of a muscular copper-toned chest. I found it particularly interesting that this boy had long hair too, just like Tommy. He was the first non-see-through boy I had ever seen with long hair, and I found myself appreciating his luxurious brown locks. Then my attention shifted to the young man's dreamy deep brown eyes, and my focus remained there, as if I were entranced. There was something warm and comforting about his eyes.

The look of concern on the boy's face shifted to one of alarm as he approached my location and saw the condition of the pool. Just then, my attention shifted away from the boy's eyes to Tommy dancing around behind him. I was annoyed with Tommy because he was pleased with himself for getting me caught. I still didn't know what the big deal was. It was just a pile of leaves! Before I could argue the merits of jumping in the leaves, the boy with the beautiful eyes explained to me the dangers lurking in that spectacular mound of colors.

It seems I planned to jump into a thick pile of leaves floating on top of the rainwater that had accumulated in the pool over the weekend. The pool was eight feet deep at that end, so a few feet of water probably hid below those leaves. Apparently, I did not understand the hazards of a small person swimming in water weighted with leaves. Both Tommy and the boy knew that. So when I boastfully explained that I could swim, the boy asked me how I felt about snakes, spiders, and scorpions. With those thoughts entering my consciousness, I instantly stepped back and took a closer look at the leaves. That was when I saw the critters. Yep, there was movement there, and I couldn't see what was moving. Now, I liked to look at little critters. Sometimes I even liked to hold them and surprise my mom with them. However, I did not like the idea of having them crawling all over me or getting in my hair. So I quickly climbed back out of the pool, as I was guided to do. I was slightly disappointed that I wouldn't get to play in the leaves, but I was ready to accept the merits of the boy's logic.

After that, the boy saw me safely to my door and then went about his own business. When I was home safe again, Tommy was happy to be able to say, "Ha! I told ya so!" as he stuck his tongue out at me. I didn't mind. I knew how lucky I was. I'd had two heroes show up for me that day. Tommy was a hero because he'd found a way to get help to save me from my own

The Messages of Light

ignorance, and the boy with the long brown hair and dreamy caramel-colored eyes was my own personal superhero. Why? Because he had taken the time to talk to me like a human being. When he'd spoken to me, I'd felt security wash over me. The feeling had been empathic guidance telling me I should listen to him and could trust him, and it had been right. He'd explained the situation to me, ensuring I stayed safe. I never forgot him, the sensation of comfort he offered, or those eyes.

I can see that this was another example of God protecting me, even from myself. I had the free will to reject this guidance coming to me in the form of my imaginary friend, and I did. When I ignored the messages God sent through Tommy, God sent back up. God chose another route. He arranged an intervention. I mean, really, what are the chances of that boy walking past the pool at that exact time, immediately after Tommy said he was going for help? What made the boy notice me there in the pool? Think about it. What are the chances an average teenage boy would even go out of his way to protect a stranger's child? God is the answer to all those questions. It was all God planning for my safety despite my own stubborn will. I subjected myself to danger, and God corrected my course by sending another messenger of light.

Who Were You Just Talking To?

Fast-forward to when I was about seven years old. That was the first time anyone witnessed me using my empathic spiritual muscle to talk to someone who "wasn't there." My mother reminded me of this event, because she was there to witness it. I have a faint recollection of the day. It is vague because I often talked to spiritual beings that others couldn't see when I was a child, so it wasn't as unusual for me as it was for my mom. After all, Tommy was my best friend, and no one could see him. However, that day was the first time my mom noticed my unusual behavior. She said she was so fascinated by what I was doing that the details of the moment were etched clearly in her mind. I can only imagine what she must have been thinking at the time. It's one thing for a three-year-old to pretend to have an imaginary friend, but I was seven. In those days, most parents who saw their seven-year-old talking to an invisible person would have gone straight to the yellow pages to look for a psychiatrist, but my mom did not. She observed with an open mind as she watched me in our backyard, where I was sitting on a swing, singing, and talking to the empty seat next to me.

From the window, it appeared I was having a full conversation with the air, because I was the only person my mom could see. She said I was happy and smiling as I glided freely back and forth on the swing. My mom said she saw me nod a few times and then speak to the air some more. This went on for some time before I finally came inside.

When I entered the house, according to my mom, I was still singing, and I was beaming with joy. Her curiosity got the best of her, and she asked, "What were you just doing?"

I replied, "Talking."

"To whom?" my mother asked with one eyebrow raised in skepticism.

"To Jesus," I answered in a singsong, matter-of-fact way indicating to my mom that I did that often.

"Oh really?" she asked hesitantly. "What did he say?"

"Well," I replied, "he told me I should be good and listen to you." With that, I skipped off to my room to play.

My mom said something about my behavior that day convinced her I was indeed talking to Jesus. She also said the experience gave her a message of light. She said she was gifted with a sense of comfort in knowing I was being looked after. Her only child was loved and protected from beyond, and she knew it. I love that my mom got a new perspective from the experience instead of a rush of concern. Otherwise, my story might have gone in a different direction.

I genuinely believe that event occurred as a message of light, as my mom said, to alert her to the fact that I was protected. It also reminded her of the magic and wonder of youth. What my mom saw that day was an example of the free-spirited innocence of childhood, illustrating that there is much more to this world than can be seen with human eyes. All children are born with this innocence and faith, and this event reminded my mom of that truth. It may have even reignited her curiosity about the supernatural. At the very least, it pointed out to her that Jesus was not only real but also present in our lives, whether or not we went to church, which we didn't.

I think it's funny that my mother's skepticism about my noteworthy companion was wiped away by my confidence and behavior. She sensed the truth in what I said, but the demeanor I displayed was even more potent than the words I used. I radiated love and joy, reverence, and respect at that moment. I was, as they say, filled with the Holy Spirit. If you want to know what that looks like, look into the eyes of a smiling, happy child. That is the spirit of God.

Chapter 3

Shaped by Society

Ghosts

When I was about eight years old, I learned about ghosts. What I heard about ghosts was terrifying. I learned I was supposed to be afraid. Like any other child, I believed I should be scared of ghosts. So I was. I was told ghosts could hurt me, so that was what I believed to be true. Boy, was I gullible! I know now that ghosts don't hurt people; people hurt themselves in the moment of panic. But back then, I believed what I was told by the people around me, even though I'd had plenty of personal experiences with the supernatural before, and none of them had been scary to me. I was not scared until I adopted the ever-popular fear perspective from outside myself.

Suddenly, I was terrified to go to bed at night, because I was sure our house was haunted. My firsthand experiences proved it. When all the lights in the house were out, I could hear someone pacing the hallway in front of my bedroom door. We had plastic carpet runners on the more frequently traveled walkways in the house, and the sound of someone walking on them was easily audible. I often heard the distinct sound that came from bare feet on the plastic carpet runner, but I was never scared, until I was told I should be. The sounds were not new to me, but my fear about them was.

Not long after my fear of ghosts was ignited, I heard the sound again. I hoped my mom or dad was checking on me, but that wasn't the case. Both my parents were sound asleep. I knew because I could hear my father snoring. It was around three o'clock in the morning, and I woke up because my room was cold. I heard it as I sat up to pull my blankets over myself: the sticky sound of bare feet on plastic. I listened to each step get closer and closer to my room. Then the footsteps stopped right outside my open bedroom door. I hadn't gotten the covers over my head yet, so I had no choice but to look. I couldn't see anything there, but I was terrified because I could feel something there. My heart was pounding, and my body was shaking. I couldn't stand the fear I was experiencing, so I took a deep breath and said a prayer. I then bolted out of my bed and through the same bedroom door where I sensed the energy was hovering. I was in complete fear mode, and that doorway was the only way out. I ran blindly through the night. I sprinted through the dark hallways of our house until I found myself sobbing hysterically in my mother's arms.

My mother was a patient woman, but being awakened in the middle of the night by a frenzied eight-year-old was not her favorite thing. Still, she calmly took me by the hand and turned on the lights to show me that no one was there. She was so firm in her explanation of what was real and not real that it almost felt as if she were convincing herself.

That night, I chose to believe her. Ghosts were not real. I wished someone would tell the spirit that. The same ghost paced the house every night for a long while, but I guess either it got used to us and didn't feel the need to keep checking on us, or my new mantra of "It's not real! There's nothing there!" finally worked. The problem with that mantra was that no ghosts meant no Tommy either. Eventually, I stopped hearing the sounds of the footsteps in the hallway, but I also stopped seeing and hearing Tommy. The magic of my childhood faith was being washed away by the fear and the unknown given to me by society.

That was when my abilities began to fade, or maybe my fear caused me to mute an important part of myself. Because of free will, when I chose to believe that the supernatural wasn't real, I stopped seeing it. The muscle that allowed me to see and sense ghosts and Tommy was the same muscle I used to talk to Jesus and to hear God's whisper. When I stopped using it, the muscle atrophied. I stopped seeing ghosts, which was fine, but I also stopped seeing Tommy and Jesus as well.

None of the fear I experienced concerning those topics came from within myself. Fear is not a natural state of being for a child. It was all inspired by conversations with other people or from television. I experienced fear only because I was told I should be afraid. Because of that fear, I denied a part of myself that was real. I rejected my gift, a gift we are all born with, and in doing so, I denied myself access to the free-flowing love of God within me. I replaced that innate unconditional love with fear.

But I was not abandoned. Even though I stopped talking to Tommy, Jesus, and the ghost in the hallway, God never stopped talking to me. God continued to send me messages of light through the people and circumstances around me. Most importantly, God sent me guidance through my emotions.

Buying into Illusion

As the magic faded from my experience, I began to notice the real world and to buy into the strife that shaped it. I started seeing the problems around me. Things that were wrong in my life became increasingly apparent. My view on life became more pessimistic. I can recall the exact moment when I first began to feel sorry for myself because of it.

I was watching TV, when a public-service-announcement commercial started playing. It showed a kid sitting and crying. The kid in the commercial was distraught. His face was red and tear-streaked, and my heart broke for him when I looked into his eyes. That was when I realized I could have been doing the exact same thing at that moment. I could have been crying for the same reason. I decided the kid in the commercial was a lot like me. So from that example, I decided I should be upset just like the kid on TV.

I don't think the situation in question ever bothered me before I realized I was *supposed* to be upset. It's strange the emotions and thoughts we choose to cling to or relate to because of the influence of others. A TV commercial began to shape how I perceived my experience. Before then, I barely had noticed the discord in my life, but suddenly, it was all I could think about. That was when I began to worry and when I started feeling sorry for myself. That was when the "Poor me" vibration began shaping my identity.

I got lost in my fear and self-pity, and I forgot to pray. Instead, the empath in me began looking to others for energy and attention to fill the void. I started telling my sob story, and it got me the attention I wanted. It wasn't proper attention, but I began to mistake the energy of sympathy for the feeling and emotion of love. Many people do. Have you?

Looking for a Church

As I got older and more distracted by the outside world, my emotions became more intense and volatile. The fear was beginning to take hold, and I missed the feeling of the comfort of God's presence. I heard from a friend that I should go to church to fill that void. I figured the information must have been true, and it sounded like fun to me. It wasn't long before circumstances somehow lined up, and I was on a bus to Sunday school.

To this day, I am still uncertain how a third grader managed to get that arranged. There must have been a higher power at work, because a series of coincidences got me there. I couldn't have arranged that if I had tried. Thus began my exploration of faith through organized religion.

Through the years, I found many different churches to visit. I felt compelled to gather as much information about God, Jesus, and the Bible from as many sources as I could access. I was thirsty for knowledge and looking for a deeper connection with God. I went to church with anyone who invited me, and sometimes I even invited myself to go with my friends if they didn't offer to take me.

It's amazing how many churches there are, and I find it incredible that each of them teaches different interpretations of the same messages in the Bible. In my travels through the local church circuit, I discovered there are as many points of view as there are people in the world. Rather than being confused by the differences, I used my emotions as my guide, and I decided to cling to the main underlying message common to all of them: love.

Once, when I was between churches, I started a Jesus club with a friend who lived down the street. We got together and talked about God, miracles, and love. Sounds corny, I know, but I really loved to talk to and about God. I guess not much has changed.

Now, don't get me wrong: when I wasn't talking about God, I was getting into mischief. I was a strange kid but a kid nonetheless. Maybe that was why I prayed so hard every night. I wanted absolution for my sins. I knew right from wrong, but once I learned about sin through going to church, I became a bit compulsive. I prayed every prayer I knew every night, asking for forgiveness. However, the feeling of comfort I was looking for did not come when I prayed with a fear of being rejected by God as my motivation.

After a while of exploring different churches on my own or going to church with other families, I began to feel like an outsider. I started to feel lonely and a little bit lost. There was no church where I belonged, but still, I continued to search. I wanted to find my place. I hoped someday I would find a church that would stick.

In retrospect, I can see that God communicated with me through my emotions all along. The feelings of comfort and closeness I craved were God calling me to him, and the feelings of loneliness and confusion were sent by God to tell me I was misinterpreting the messages of light I was being taught from the Bible. I focused on my fear of rejection instead of God's unconditional love.

Little Bit

In the meantime, God knew I was about to deal with some real-life issues. My world was about to change, and God knew I would benefit from a physical, tangible source of unconditional love—a gift that would bring me serenity, peace, and joy by merely existing. What on earth could possibly do such miraculous things?

The answer: a dog. Take note that *dog* is *God* spelled backward. My Little Bit was a living, breathing message of love and light. She was a tiny little toy fox terrier, hence her name, Little Bit.

The way she came to me was a miracle. Little Bit lived out on my great-aunt and great-uncle's farm in the Midwest, where she was stepped on by a horse. The insult to her tiny body resulted in a broken hip, and she almost died. It was a miracle she survived, and I was reminded of that truth every time I looked at her. Her right side was healthy-looking, but the other side of her body, where her hip had been broken, had a weird concave shape. Her minor deformity didn't matter to me. I loved her from the first moment I saw her. My mamaw said she was an ugly little thing, but I thought she was the most adorable puppy in the world. This sweet little being was there for me to love, and it was clear she loved me right back.

I genuinely believe God saved Little Bit for me. That little black-and-white-spotted pup became everything to me. I loved her more than I had known it was possible to love anything, especially an animal. I thought she was the most beautiful creature in the world, and when I held her, everything was right in mine. She was my Little Bit, my little gift from God, and the timing couldn't have been more perfect.

When I was eight years old, not long after I got my puppy, my parents sat me down and told me they were getting a divorce. Was I surprised? No, because I am an empath, and I had felt it coming. Don't worry. There was no dramatic scene. To their credit, my parents did an excellent job of easing my fears and concerns about their split. They explained everything in a way I could understand, and they did a fantastic job of making their separation look like a good thing. Instead of feeling sad when they announced the divorce, I felt relief. Somehow, I was OK with it. Why? Probably because of a perfectly timed miracle on four legs.

I was floating in a bubble of unconditional love with my Little Bit. Having her to hold seemed to make everything right. Maybe my little messenger of light was there to remind me of what God's love really felt like after I'd spent so much time on my fear detour. Whatever it was, that day, when they made their announcement, I knew a divorce was a move in the right direction for all of us. My parents were making the decision to be happy. Happy but not together.

The Nanny

My mom and I moved into a small apartment with a nanny. My mom couldn't afford to keep the house on her income alone, so my dad stayed there. My room in our apartment was nice, but it was tight quarters because I shared it with one of my babysitters. My mom worked a full-time job and was trying to live a full life. That's hard to do while worrying about who is looking after your kid, so I had live-in babysitters.

As I mentioned before, I was not a timid child. In fact, I was pretty adventurous. That hadn't changed much from my early days with Tommy. On numerous occasions, I was known to have ventured off the campus of our apartment complex on my bike. Leaving the campus not only was forbidden by my mother but also was dangerous, as this was well before designated bike paths existed. I roller-skated through the busy apartment complex parking lot at all hours of the day. I was also known to climb trees, as any self-respecting adventurous child would have. Oh, and once or twice, I was seen jumping from the second-story apartment landing to the grassy earth below. So yeah, I probably still needed supervision while my mom was at work, and this arrangement worked well for everyone concerned.

Maggie was kind to me, so I didn't mind that we shared a room in the apartment. We often hung out together, each sitting on our respective bed, facing each other, listening to music and talking. We often listened to Olivia Newton-John, who was my favorite singer at the time. I loved to sing, and I was particularly drawn to her music because the words in her songs had meaning to me—that is, her solo albums, not necessarily the poetic artistry reflected in the songs of the movie *Grease*, although I sang "Hopelessly Devoted to You" all the time, and Maggie loved to sing it with me.

The environment, free of parental tension, was great for me. I had my puppy and a roommate I enjoyed spending time with, and as an added bonus, I was at a new school with the fresh opportunity to make more friends. And I got to participate in a miracle.

One night, when my newly divorced mother went out country-western dancing with some friends, I got a message of light. After my mother kissed me good night and headed out the door, Maggie and I began to watch TV together, as usual. A few hours later, about halfway through our favorite Friday night show, Maggie got up to go to the bathroom. I continued watching TV, but eventually, I noticed she had been gone for a long time. Something told me I should go check on her. It was an old feeling. It reminded me of times when Tommy had tried to warn me of danger, but this time, I didn't see or hear my imaginary friend. It was just a strong feeling, a message I couldn't ignore. God was using my emotions to get my attention again because this was important.

I got up to check on my babysitter. When I got to the bathroom, I called out to her. I listened and heard silence. There was no answer from the other side of the door. I called again and this time tried to open the door. It was locked. I jiggled the door handle and called out some more, but I heard no response. At that point, I should have begun to panic, but I felt a strange calm wash over me instead. The same energy that had given me the urge to check on her was now offering a feeling of peace. I began to think clearly and critically. I got down on my hands and knees and tried to peer underneath the door to assess the situation.

When I looked under the door, I saw the bottoms of her feet. From what I could determine, Maggie was lying faceup and lifeless on the floor. I couldn't tell if she was breathing, so I turned off the TV to listen. I could hear her breathing, but it sounded strange. I heard a gurgling noise, and I had the sense that something was terribly wrong.

Maggie was in trouble. I didn't know what to do at first. There were no cell phones back then, so I didn't know how to reach my mom. I was eight years old and alone. But not really.

Calmly, I figured out the next step. I called my dad, but there was no answer. It was Friday night, after all.

What next? I thought. The only thing I could think to do was pray.

"What do I do?" I asked, fully expecting an answer of some kind.

Suddenly, a phone number popped into my head in answer to my prayer. It was my friend Erika's number. I had her phone number newly memorized. We had only recently become friends because of the move. She went to my new school, and luckily, she happened to live nearby. I dialed the number, and she immediately gave the phone to her mom. Thank God she answered. They rushed right over. I was trying to remove the door handle when they got there; the screws were on the outside of the door, where we could reach them. Again, thank God!

Erika's mom was able to finish the job I had started, and she got the door open. We rushed over and tried to wake my babysitter, but to no avail. Her body was limp and noodle-like. It was as if she had no bones. Erika's mom called EMS. Luckily, there was a paramedic unit stationed across the street from my home, and they arrived in minutes.

Thanks to the first responders, doctors, nurses, and, of course, God, we got a miracle that night. I can't imagine what would have happened if I had ignored that feeling, that message of light, that direct communication from God, and gone to bed instead of checking on her. And what would have happened if Erika's mom hadn't answered the phone or if they hadn't lived nearby? What if the ambulance hadn't arrived when it did?

Many factors went into play in saving Maggie's life, and God was at the heart of all of them. Each of those circumstances was orchestrated by God on her behalf and mine. Although I didn't realize it at the time, it was a miracle, and I was blessed to be part of it. That experience gave me a new appreciation for life and the miraculous, but there was more to it than that. I learned to trust my guidance in a new way. It's one thing to pray and feel connected to God when all is well, and it's another to achieve that level of connection under duress. The fact that I even thought to pray was an indicator that I knew God would answer. The feeling that guided me throughout the experience was God sending me messages of light through my emotions, proving to me that being an empath is a blessing.

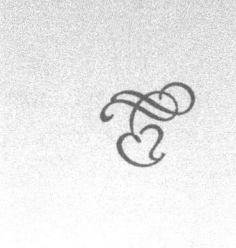

Chapter 4

The Wonder of a New World

New Beginnings

Every day is a new beginning, and at that point in my young life, each day was something different for me. By the time I started fourth grade, I had been the new kid in class at three different elementary schools. Twice, it was because we moved residences. The other time, it was because the school boundary lines changed. Either way, I attended an unfamiliar school every other year. That's a lot of adjustment. They say kids adapt quickly to change, and I think they may be right, whoever they are. I was doing well. My heart was lighter; I was having more fun and making new friends. My mother told me I was even doing better in school since the divorce and the move, and I knew it was true.

As I said, a lot was new and different in my life, but I did have some things stay the same in my new beginning. I still had my mama, who loved me, and it didn't matter where we lived. I had my Little Bit, and she traveled with me everywhere but to school. I still had my dad, my old room at his house, and my friends in that neighborhood.

My dad was a good father. He tried his best with me, and I wasn't easy. I was extremely sensitive, and I had trouble controlling my emotions. I was pretty intense, and admittedly, I was sometimes rather difficult to be around. I always knew he loved me, because he never stopped trying, no matter how hard I made it on him.

As I said, some things in my life were mostly the same—until they weren't. When my dad introduced me to his girlfriend, Mary, things changed again.

Let's backtrack.

When my parents were together, they got involved in stock car racing, and both of them worked on the pit crew of a racecar. Cool, huh?

After my parents got divorced, they both continued going to the races. My mom stayed on the pit crew of the car. She was the only woman on any pit crew at that time, and I liked to go watch her do her thing. My dad continued going to the races too. So it wasn't surprising that my dad chose to introduce Mary to me while we were there.

I remember that night well because my dad was behaving strangely. He seemed nervous and fidgety. On top of that, he wouldn't tell me where we were going when he cryptically said, "Follow me," and walked toward the other side of the spectator stands. We walked quite a distance, which amplified the feeling of anticipation inside me. We walked up several rows into the stands, and still, I wondered what we were doing. We finally stopped in front of two women—a petite blonde woman and her friend—and he introduced the women as his friends. I don't remember who was there with Mary that night, because my attention was fixated on her the whole time. Mary smiled kindly and shook my hand. The moment Mary took my hand, I knew she wasn't just a friend. I got a blast of information, a message, and I knew she and my dad were in love. That moment was forever ingrained in my memory as the day I met the love of my father's life.

Interestingly, I could feel all of that from a handshake. That was my ability as an empath, offering me valuable information. I could feel the love. See? This empath thing has its perks!

After some time, my dad and Mary were married, and I was genuinely happy for them both. It was good for me to see their affection for each other on display. They were a great example of a loving couple. They got along well, they were outwardly affectionate, and they rarely argued. Clearly, they were meant for each other. They complemented each other in every way. This was definitely a new perspective on relationships for me to explore.

In retrospect, I can see I knew that my dad and Mary were connected and that being together made them happy. The feeling I had when I met

Mary, the knowing that they had a future together, came simply from a touch of her hand. It allowed me to be more open and receptive to welcoming her into our lives. It allowed me to accept the change in my family unit as a gift. The knowing I experienced was a glimpse of the world from a higher perspective, from the perspective of pure love. The feeling I experienced was communication from God. It was a message of light.

Another New Beginning

My mom moved on from the divorce too. She fell in love with and married a man in the military. He was tall, handsome, and brave. He swept my mom right off her feet, and at one point, we landed in Europe. Just after my mom and Gerry were married, he was sent on tour to Europe, and we three lived there together as a new family unit.

From the moment I arrived at the Frankfurt airport, I felt an air of mystery. When we got on the autobahn and I took in my first sight of the new country, I was overcome by a sense of wonder. I wondered what I was looking at. Everything outside the car window was a blur—because we were moving so fast.

Just kidding—that was an autobahn joke.

You see, the freeway there didn't have a speed limit. Of all the novel things about my experience in another country, the high-speed freeway was probably the biggest culture shock to me. I am, after all, the daughter of a law enforcement officer.

Seriously, though, I recall my reaction to the countryside. I remember not only thinking it was different from home but also feeling it. I got a sense of mystery and exhilaration as the energy of that new world swept over me. The feeling was a message of light, letting me know I was meant to be there. God was using my emotions. He was telling me to embrace the new opportunity and to immerse myself fully in the experience. And I did.

I was captivated by the landscape. I had seen forests before, but these were straight out of a fairy tale. I had never seen so many unusual colors and shades of green. I was entranced by the energy. The trees took on an almost iridescent glow as the sun beat down upon them. Beneath the trees, there was an eerie darkness. Virtually no light permeated the canopy of leaves. Still, I could just make out the trunks of trees that were gnarled and twisted around one another like a wall protecting a magical world from being discovered. Everything seemed fantastical. I was excited and happy. I was ready for a new adventure, and it had already begun in a magical way.

Castles and Chaos

Many of my experiences in Germany were as magical as my arrival. One of my favorite moments was when I traveled to a real castle. I was obsessed at the time with unicorns, magic, princesses, and knights, so when I found myself standing with my mouth agape in front of a Disney castle in real life, I had a tough time believing it. I had never been to Disneyland, but I knew this was the same castle I had seen at the beginning and end of every Disney movie. The difference was that this wasn't a cartoon, and Tinker Bell was not flitting around. I was standing in front of the real Neuschwanstein Castle, one of the most beautiful castles in the world.

The place was amazing and awe-inspiring. It was more than 150 years old. To an eleven-year-old, that's ancient! Just looking at it, I could sense the history of the place. I easily visualized people in modest clothing moving about, performing daily chores to maintain the castle's beauty. I understood how a Disney movie could be inspired by that magical place. As I stood there, I felt as if I were in one. I was just waiting for the people and animals to break into song!

Inside the castle, the air was different. It was cold and damp. The towering, thick stone walls lined with colorful tapestries and the ornate ceilings trimmed in gold were beautiful. Still, they couldn't distract me from the eerie feeling that I was being watched and followed. I was fascinated by my surroundings. But still, I was glad to get out of there when we finished our tour. Besides being creeped out, I had begun to experience a headache and nausea like that associated with motion sickness. There was pressure in the center of my forehead, and the objects around me took on a fuzzy glow that made me have to squint to focus. It didn't feel good to me.

Luckily, the feeling of being watched and the feelings of physical discomfort dissipated once we drove away from the castle. I thought how funny it was that the feeling of motion sickness went away when we got

The Messages of Light

in the car and drove. Usually, driving in a car down winding mountain roads is bad for motion sickness, right?

All I knew then was that I felt better when we left.

Needless to say, I had a fabulous, unforgettable time. It was so unique that I still learned from it many years later. Even as I was revisiting this story in order to write it, I learned more. I got a message, an insight, that had to do with how I felt during the castle tour. The discomfort, the motion sickness, I felt back then was evidence of my ability to sense energy. I was perceiving vibrations from my environment and feeling them in my body. I sensed the people's energy around me, and I absorbed it. We moved through the castle in tour groups, cramming as many as twenty people into sometimes tight spaces. Every time I stood next to someone new, his or her energy mingled with a mine, causing my vibration to shift. In fact, the energy was shifting so frequently I felt as if my head were spinning. No wonder I felt dizzy and nauseated. Gotta love being an empath.

But the energy I was sensing was not only coming from the people bumping into me in the close quarters of the tour but also coming from people I couldn't see. Remember, I had decided that spirits and ghosts weren't real, so I couldn't see them anymore, but I guess I never lost the ability to sense them around me.

I know now that the discomfort I felt—dizziness, blurry vision, and third-eye pain—was intensified by the presence of earthbound spirits. The physical sensations were messages alerting me to their proximity. I didn't know it at the time, but there were spirits everywhere in that place. Maybe they were there just because the building was old. Perhaps it was because the six thousand tourists who visited daily had the spirits of loved ones with them. I don't know, but whatever the reason, I felt as if the spirits were tapping on my forehead, trying to get my attention. It was as if they were knocking on a hard wooden door with full force, trying to get in. The door was my third eye, and the discomfort came because I was unconsciously blocking their communications. I was ignoring their messages. Apparently, if you try to ignore the spirits, they get louder, and that is when the brain pain begins.

Christi Conde

Gymnastics Tryouts

The magic of the new world I was in continued. When I was in the seventh grade, I decided I wanted to be on the gymnastics team at the American high school I attended. The challenge: I would have to make the team first, and I had no prior training or experience. Anyone who knows athletics understands that seventh grade is a late time to start learning a new sport, but I was determined.

I really wanted to be on that team. I had dreamed of being a gymnast since I was little, when I had tiptoed, jumped, and cartwheeled barefoot on the brick landscaping in my neighbors' front yard, pretending it was a balance beam. I watched Olympic gymnastics and any other gymnastics event on television every chance I got. Nadia Comaneci was my idol, and Mary Lou Retton was a close second. Those girls were amazing! I wanted to be able to do what they did. They were powerful, graceful, and confident. That was what I wanted to be.

I went to practice and tryouts every day. It was only a couple of hours a day for a few weeks of training, but I learned the basics of all four events: floor, vault, balance beam, and uneven parallel bars. I practiced what I could morning, noon, and night. What I couldn't practice physically, I practiced in my mind repeatedly, until I was dreaming about gymnastics. I even woke up one night with a cramp in my foot because I had been pointing my toes in my sleep. Being a competitive gymnast was something I wanted badly.

After weeks of training, the day finally came when the coach would announce who'd made the team. We all lined up eagerly, anticipating the results. It felt as if the coach were taking forever to make the announcement. She spoke to everyone present, thanking us for our hard work. The coach went on to say that only so many girls could be on the team and that she wished she could keep us all.

I barely heard her voice as she began calling the names of the people who'd made it. Her voice was muffled and drowned out by the sound of my heart beating in my ears. The blood rushed to my head, my peripheral vision faded, and I felt as if I were alone in a noisy tunnel as she announced her team. One by one, my friends stepped forward, and when she was done speaking, my heart sank. I realized I hadn't made the team.

The Messages of Light

I was devastated. I was destroyed. As I stood there watching my dreams burn to ashes, the coach told those who had been cut that we could continue to practice, but we wouldn't compete with the team. Maybe next year.

Just as my heart was breaking, I caught a glimpse of hope. I had a thought; it was a message of light because it came to me in the second person: *Maybe you can make her change her mind.*

Filled with the feelings of hope and inspiration that came with that message of light, I said a prayer asking for help. Moments later, I found myself on the mat, preparing to practice my floor routine. The coach had said we could stay and practice, so I did. I wasn't ready to give up yet. I could see the coach was nearby, and mentally, I was screaming, *Hey, Coach, watch me!*

I decided I was going to show her she had made a mistake. When the music started, I felt exhilarated as my adrenaline began to flow. My mind was clear and calm, and I felt powerful. I never saw it, but I felt her gaze turn in my direction as if I had willed it. Then there was nothing but my routine. I gave those ninety seconds everything I had from start to finish. I was in a space that was beyond the physical. I found myself transitioning from one exercise to another in an effortless flow. I think I discovered the zone, as I have heard athletes talk about. It was like an out-of-body experience.

When I was done and came back to reality from that surreal place, I looked up to see the coach standing in front of me.

"What is your name again?" she asked.

"Christi," I answered breathlessly.

"Did I cut you from the team?" she asked.

"Yes, ma'am," I replied sadly, lowering my head.

"Well, I've changed my mind," she announced bluntly. "You're on the team." With that, she turned and walked away.

I couldn't believe it. It had worked! I had done it! My mom always had told me I could accomplish anything I set my mind to. She had been right. I'd made the team! I was so excited I bounced off walls for a week. I was in awe of the miracle I'd experienced. Maybe I still am. And believe me, it was a miracle. Not only did my dream come true, but I also found a way to connect. I found a new happy place. I was doing something I loved, and it brought balance to my life. (Ha! Get it? Balance! I know, corny pun! I couldn't resist!)

Looking back, I can see how my passionate focus on my dream helped me to manifest it. I spent every waking moment thinking about being part of that team. This constant focus on what I wanted aligned me with my wish. I do not recall even once considering the possibility that I wouldn't make the team. I wanted it so badly I never stopped to consider the possibility of failure. I was in faith mode the whole time.

That was my first great experience in manifesting a dream. It renewed my faith in myself and in the power of prayer, silent or outright. Believe me, I did both. I was a walking, talking prayer in human form. Every step of the way, I was rewarded with guidance pointing me in the right direction. I learned that hard work and a positive attitude are great and necessary. But listening to that little voice in my head, the whisper, made the achievement of my goal possible in a magical way.

The Gift of Travel

Through gymnastics, I received the gift of travel. Our gymnastics competitions took us all over the region. We went to Heidelberg and Wurzburg, Germany, and to Luxembourg, just to name a few of the more notable destinations. My mom always came with me, so the trips served both of us well, delivering some precious one-on-one time. I always loved a good road trip with my mom. The gymnastics trips were even better than some of our other trips, because she wasn't driving, so her undivided attention was on me. We had some deep and meaningful conversations as we traveled all over Europe. On those bus rides, I learned a lot about my mom. I began to see how she perceived and experienced her life.

While we traveled with my team, I noticed something special about my mom. I could feel with my empathic abilities that people were drawn to my mom. Whenever she was in a room, people gravitated toward her—not just the adults but the kids too. There were even times when I felt insecure enough to be jealous of her because she was getting all the energy I craved. I could feel that my friends liked her, and when I was having a difficult day, I felt as if they liked her more than me. Probably because they did at those times! Naturally, I complained about my insecurities to the only person who would listen, my mom, and she found a way to make me feel better. Just being around her could make a person feel better. With that, my attitude shifted from jealousy to pride. I realized I was the kid with the cool mom. She had a magical ability to comfort people.

Because of the gift of traveling with my mom, I got a message of light that led me to a deeper understanding of energy and human nature. I could finally see the difference between my approach to social interaction and my mother's. She went into conversations looking to *give* energy to the people she talked to by asking about their lives or by genuinely complimenting them. In contrast, I went looking to *get* energy from the people around me. I was a fisher of compliments, not a giver of them. I needed attention, especially when I felt sad or confused. I somehow got it with the "Poor me" attitude I learned from a TV commercial. I told whatever sob story I had at hand, and kindhearted people listened and shared their energy with me. I was happy to take it because I was an energy vampire. It's true. This is what happens when an empath goes looking for energy from other humans instead of from God.

I can see it clearly now. The differences were obvious. My mom didn't need attention. Half the time, she didn't want the attention she got. She was already overflowing with love. With remarkable grace, she gave attention to others. She had a way of making people she talked to feel unique and important. Instead of taking energy from the people around her, she supplied them with it. That was why people were drawn to my mother. I sure had a lot to learn if I wanted to be a giver instead of a taker of energy. In fact, I had a lot to learn about energy altogether.

Monastery Ettal

I was using my empathic ability to get energy in an unhealthy way from others. So God did his thing. He reminded me of divine energy and my ability to access it when we visited Monastery Ettal, or Ettal Abbey, as it is now known. I love that our travels while we lived overseas always took us to inspiring places where I learned more about myself and energy.

When we arrived, I was in awe of the place. The grounds of the monastery were meticulously kept. The landscape was splashed with so much color that it looked like a children's pop-up storybook. It was surreal. It had a maze of pathways lined with shrubs and rainbows of blooming flowers. It seemed that all the paths led to an open field of perfectly trimmed grass. The energy around me was light, happy, and peaceful. It gave me the urge to run through the maze of flowers and then cartwheel and spin in circles until I fell into a heap of laughter in the luxurious green grass. Of course, that might have been frowned upon, so I just let it play out in my imagination instead.

In that energetic space, I had a profound spiritual experience. As I entered the monastery's cathedral, I sensed a shift in the air. It was not only cooler but also lighter somehow. Just then, a sense of peace washed over me. The energy in the six-hundred-year-old domed building was tangible. We were on a tour, but I felt as if I were alone in the room. I felt a holy presence when I gazed up at the ornate hand-painted ceilings. My spirit moved out of my body for a moment, and I was in another time and place. I was floating weightlessly in the blue sky of the heavenly scene displayed on the ceiling above me. Entranced, I watched the picture unfold. The angels and cherubim were interacting blissfully while they bathed in the golden-white light of the heavens, and at that moment, I was with them. For a second, I even felt the warmth and serenity of that light.

A split second later, I was back in my body, back in the church, standing in the aisle. From the ornate dome, my eyes drifted to the tall windows high above the altar, where I noticed a beam of sunlight streaming in. My eyes followed the sunbeam of golden-white light to the ground before me. The light illuminated what seemed to be a direct path to the altar from where I stood. It was like a message from God literally lighting my way, guiding me back to my faith. Talk about a message of light!

The experience was breathtaking. I felt such a connection to God at that moment that I was overrun with emotion. God was still with me, and he used my empathic ability to prove it. In an ethereal cloud of bliss, I continued the tour of the grounds, noticing every detail of the beauty around me. I soaked up every element of the experience with the wide-eyed wonderment of a small child. I was in awe. My childlike faith was renewed with the blast of energy from that vision, from that message of light.

In retrospect, it is easy to see what my abilities as an empath taught me about energy. I could feel a difference in energy between Monastery Ettal and Neuschwanstein Castle. The castle was only 150 years old, more or less, and being there caused me to experience headaches and dizziness. On the other hand, the monastery was six hundred years old, and instead of driving me to discomfort, it brought me a feeling of connection to God.

I believe the difference between the energies of the castle and the monastery came from the differences in their purposes. The castle was most likely built to symbolize wealth and worldly energy. The monastery was created as a safe haven to help the inhabitants connect with God. The feelings I experienced in each place demonstrated the difference in the energy of the environments. How cool is that?

Chapter 5

Enter the Teenage Years

The Evolution of Concern

I enjoyed the renewed feeling of connection with God for a good while. I prayed often, and the empath in me was getting energy from the Source of all energy instead of from other people. Amazing, right? That lasted right up until I became a teenage girl. Ah! The horror! I got distracted by the world around me again, and I forgot how good it felt to commune with God in prayer. I began to fixate on what I looked like and what others might think of me. I made my choices based on popular opinion in every situation, and I was all about external validation. I thought I had to look, dress, and act a certain way to fit in. I wasn't authentically me, because at the time, I didn't know who that was. The more I tried to define myself through the perspectives and opinions of others, the more stressed I became.

I found myself stressing a little too often. OK, I was almost always freaking out about something at that time in my life. I was on high alert, ready for disaster all the time. I could turn any situation into a stressful situation, and most times, I did. I don't know how my family handled it. I was intense.

I was skilled at coming up with worst-case scenarios. I had a gift for playing out those illusions in my mind until it didn't matter that they weren't actually real. Every moment I focused on those fearful thoughts, I lived in the emotional reality created by them. Somehow, over time, the words of worry I used to express my fears became complaints about what was causing them. What was causing my worries? That is a relevant question. Back then, it was everything. Basically, I created my own hell on earth. Then I complained about it to the people around me, empathically siphoning their energy to fuel the flames.

I think that when I was younger and began to actively use my empathic power to absorb sympathy from other people to fill the energetic void created by fear, I must have forgotten to turn it off. By the time I was a teenager, the victim mentality was my go-to method of surviving my energetic deficit. The thing is, once an empath begins to absorb energy from others, there's no way to control what kind of energy he or she gets. Sympathy wasn't the only energy I absorbed. I was filling up all right, but it was with the heavy human type of energy instead of the divine energy of God, and now it was happening whether I wanted it to or not. So not only did I have my own emotions to deal with, but because of my empathic abilities, I had to deal with the energy of the fear and insecurity I absorbed from the people around me too. God tried to warn through my emotions, of course. The feeling of discontent from living this way was God trying to tell me there was a better way to get energy, and that wasn't it. Clearly, I missed the message that time, but God kept working on me and found another way.

About midway through my first year of high school, I was given a message of light that changed my life. I was informed by my boyfriend, Marc, as he was breaking up with me, that I was a complainer. His exact words were "Nobody wants to be around someone who complains all the time." I'll admit that at first, I didn't think it was true, but to test the theory, I began to pay attention to my words and comments around my friends. Eventually, I was forced to face the reality that I was indeed a major complainer. I complained to get attention, thinking it would fill the energetic void inside me. Well, it backfired. I learned that when you drain people emotionally, they take notice and eventually choose to keep their energy to themselves by avoiding you. Upon that realization, I was determined not to necessarily stay positive as much as to say only positive things. Would you believe that because of this personal challenge, for the first time in my young life, I couldn't find anything to say?

The problem was that something was always bothering me. Believe me, I wanted to change. But I couldn't just suddenly stop feeling all the negative things I felt simply because I decided not to talk about them. You see, the negativity was still screaming in my mind. My emotions were becoming increasingly volatile, and I knew I had to let them out, or they would consume me. I felt overwhelmed. The emotional void was filled but with the wrong kind of energy! I felt the chaos of energetic overload instead of the comfort I sought. I needed an outlet, or I would spontaneously combust.

Music was a good outlet for me. Singing sad songs at the top of my lungs triggered a release of tears. However, over time, the music lost its healing effect. Instead, it began to amplify the exact emotion I was trying to release.

I needed something more, some other way to process the emotional energy of being a teen. God must've heard my silent prayer, because I got a message of light, an idea that helped. While I was listening to a sad song, it occurred to me that the lyrics I loved so much were poetry set to music. I loved how poets could eloquently reveal the innermost workings of their hearts and minds through words. The emotions captured in words were raw, deep, and beautiful; and they were fused with rhythm, rhyme, and flow that touched me at the level of my spirit, not just my heart. I loved that each poem or song was as beautiful and unique as the person who wrote it. I was inspired by musical lyrics and poetry, and I imagined how good it would feel to express my own emotions constructively. It was as if the little girl in me who used to sing Olivia Newton-John songs was inspired to write songs of her own.

So I began to write my own poetry, and I found a strange sense of serenity mixed with excitement as the words started to flow. It felt good to get my feelings on paper, where I could see them clearly and sort them out. Even though most of what I wrote was sad, bordering on morbid, at least that energy was no longer in my body, growing and collecting intensity. Writing became a valuable tool, and I am sure it kept me mostly sane.

Not all of the poems were sad or dark; some of them flowed from divine inspiration. Below is one of the first poems I ever wrote that wasn't negative in energy and vibration. Remember, I was trying to say (stay) positive. It was written from the perspective of a confused teen, and watch what happens:

What do you do when confusion sets in?
When you're trying so hard, but you can't seem to win?
What do you do when your back is against the wall?
When you're feeling trapped, and you're starting to fall?
What do you do when you can no longer cry?
When you've lost all your strength and your last will to try?
When your life is in a chaotic state,
believe in yourself; it's never too late.
When you're feeling lost and out of control,
take time out, and find your soul.
When you find that inner love,
you can learn to cope.
You'll see the meaning in your life,
and then you'll see there's hope.

Did you notice? The poem started off with flowing emotion from my depressive, worried teenage state, but at some point, the energy shifted to the confidence inspired by God. Looking back, I can see that was when I first started to actually write messages of light. I kept those poems in a spiral notebook too! I'm awestruck as I see the patterns and circuitous flow of my life experiences. It's like playing connect-the-dots but with the grand cosmic plan for my life. It's so much fun!

First Love

Speaking of cosmic plans, my first love was in the plan for sure. Talk about a valuable learning experience! There is nothing like the rush of first love. It only happens once, and boy, did I feel it. I had that can't-eat, can't-sleep, one-track-mind kind of love. I put myself into my feelings for that boy 100 percent, and I genuinely believe he loved me back. The thing is, people are only capable of loving one another based on the love they know. Thus, self-love is imperative for any relationship to last. I'll be the first to admit that I was not honoring myself or loving myself the way I should have back then. Basically, every move I made at that age was still based on the need for external validation. I was looking for self-love, but I needed everyone else's approval before I could be willing to receive it. I was looking to others for their acceptance instead of looking inside and accepting myself. So basically, that relationship was doomed even before it began.

Remember, I needed external validation to feel good about myself. At that point in my life, I received that validation primarily through my relationship. My boyfriend Chris was a handsome guy and pretty popular because of it. He was also a successful athlete, which made him a good catch, and he had chosen me. For a while, the empath in me was satisfied with the external-validation energy of my first love. Yay me!

When we broke up, I was devastated. No, devastation doesn't begin to describe what I felt. By then, my identity was completely wrapped up in being his girlfriend, and I often wondered who I would be without him. I believed that if my boyfriend didn't love me, I must not have been lovable. I was so in love I thought I would stop breathing when it was over. How would my empathic energy-vampire self survive without that steady stream of validation? I desperately wanted him back. I could think of nothing else. Therefore, I would speak of nothing else. So much for saying (staying) positive! I was in a pitiful state, and that's an understatement.

I spent all my time wallowing in my grief and doing all the things that jilted girls do. I cried and watched romance movies on TV. I listened to sad songs, and I cried some more. It wasn't until I came across the song "Unanswered Prayers" by Garth Brooks that things began to change again for the better. The song totally hit home for me. It was a true message of light sent to help me through my grief. Garth Brooks captured the lovesick anguish I had been experiencing perfectly in his words and music. He was able to help the sad little empath in me to fill up with words and vibrations of hope and peace instead of pain. Thanks, Mr. Brooks!

It's incredible how something as simple as the words to a song could change the direction of my thoughts. The picture he painted through the lyrics proved that I wasn't alone in my experience. I wasn't the only person who prayed in desperation for the return of a love lost. Someone else had been there too and had come through it on the other side. It helped me to understand that maybe the fact that my ex-boyfriend didn't come back into my life was the gift. Had my prayer been answered in the way I requested, I wouldn't have been open to the wondrous and better future God had in mind for me. I listened to that song over and over until it became my mantra. It gave me hope that God was listening, only he had a different plan for my future. Maybe someday I would understand why things worked out the way they did.

Many things that happen in this world start off looking bad from our limited human perspective. If we could only see the bigger picture, we would understand the chain of events and all the miracles that come from it.

Chapter 6

Finding Myself

Searching for My Authentic Self

Once I decided to trust that God had better plans for me, it was time to figure out who the me in question really was. I had lost my sense of personal identity to the relationship, so I began the search for my authentic self.

Everyone needs a real, true friend, a messenger of light, especially after a breakup. You may already know that it can be hard to find the genuine article, especially in high school. In high school, the dynamics shift quickly, and people are so busy trying to fit in with the crowd they sometimes forget how to think for themselves. No one really knows who he or she is yet, and some develop chameleonlike personalities (author timidly raises hand in admission). They radically change their colors based on their environment. People who fall into that category tend to make dramatic shifts in their priorities and loyalties based on those with whom they associate. If a developing personality is surrounded by hateful people, he or she tends to morph into that kind of person him- or herself. Empaths are at exceptionally high risk because they often absorb energy from the people around them without realizing it is happening. That's why it's so important to surround yourself with good people, with messengers of light. Luckily, I did.

I was blessed to find many true friends over the years. In fact, I had a different group of friends every year to add to the great friends I'd found the year before. They were my family away from home. They comforted me, inspired me, and helped me find my compass the many times I was lost. Tina, Lina, Kelly, Angie, Corrina, Yvette, Michelle, Becky, Wendy, Chelsea, Pam, and Priscilla taught me so much about the person I wanted to be. They made the most challenging years of my young life pretty great. The energy of love and kindness they demonstrated and shared with me in their own unique ways was immeasurable. They allowed me to learn from them and grow through our friendships. I have to say that when I was an energy vampire, an empathic black hole, at least the energy I was absorbing was good! If you're going to be a chameleon, pick beautiful scenery to blend in with.

Of all my friends, Priscilla taught me the most by her example. She had a mind of her own. Prissy didn't care what anyone thought of her. She wasn't pretending she didn't care, as I was. She genuinely didn't. She was unapologetically her authentic self always. The typical societal pressures of high school didn't seem to affect her. She knew who she was, and she wasn't going to morph into someone else just to fit in. She was the kind of person who gladly put aside her personal stuff just to help someone she cared about, and she did so often with me.

Luckily, the energy-vampire thing didn't seem to affect Prissy. She appeared to be connected to an endless flow of energy. She was like my mom in that way. She was the kind of person who made you feel good about yourself just by your being around her.

Little by little, I started to get myself back together. The Beatles' "With a Little Help from My Friends" was my theme song. Prissy her and other friends welcomed me into their circle after my breakup, and they helped me find light in my world again. Joseph, Marla, Scott, and Claudia accepted me exactly as I was, heartbroken mess and all.

God knew exactly what to do to reach me when I forgot to reach for him. He sent me friends. Every one of the people mentioned here is a messenger of light. Each person made a positive difference in my life, and most of them continue to do so. I want to honor them all here for giving me the gift of friendship. Being surrounded by people who accepted me even at my worst helped me to find the confidence to be and accept my authentic self. Thank you! My life is better because of all of you.

Christi Conde

Still Searching

I lasted precisely one semester away at college. I was homesick. Let's just say I was not really living the college life of my dreams. When I returned, I expected I would slide right back into the life I'd had before I went away. I was in for a rude awakening. I'd been gone for only three months. Much to my surprise, time had not stood still in my absence. Can you imagine? Everyone had gone on with his or her life without me. I felt I had lost my place.

It was time to find my own way, so I decided to try out for a sorority at my new college. That was an experience and a half. The selection process is not for the faint of heart, especially if you have a deep need to be accepted. Oh yes, I was back to that again. If I wasn't constantly surrounded by people who adored me, without that validation, it was hard for me to adore myself. The empath in me was at an energetic deficit again. Did I remember to pray or write poetry to process the energy and fill the emotional and energetic void? Of course not! Don't be silly! That would have been too easy. Nope. Instead, God had to do his thing to reach me with his love. He had to send me more messengers of light.

Long story short, I got to be part of an incredible group of altruistic women who were determined to make this world a better place. They emanated light. I felt amazing when I was around them, because the empath in me absorbed that light. Through that incredible experience, we formed bonds that would flourish and last a lifetime. God knew what he was doing. It was a miracle!

The strongest bond I found was with my big sister, Alexis. She was the earth angel who brought a message of friendship and love that made me feel welcome as I got to know all my new sisters. Her contagious smile and great hugs drew me to her. Just being around her elevated my mood. Alexis is one of the sweetest and most loving, compassionate, generous, and genuine people I've ever met. I was blessed that she shared all those beautiful qualities with me. I loved her energy. There are few people like her in the world. She seemed to see only the good qualities in me and the people around her. She had an incredible ability to amplify those qualities and bring out the good in everyone she met. At that point in my life, I had almost forgotten I had good qualities to notice. I know for sure God lined up our friendship. Alexis amplified the light in me until it was bright enough for me to see it.

When I think of the messages of light sent by God that brought us all together from different communities and backgrounds at that particular time, I am amazed. I am mystified. Even the fact that I was inspired to transfer schools at that specific time was a message of light to guide me along my way. Who knew? There I was, judging myself harshly for being homesick and for not sticking it out, yet it was my decision to return home that led to the greatest miracles in my life. It was a truly pivotal time for me. Following that message of light pointed me toward a life filled with magic and miracles. Read on to see.

Finding My Way

As I mentioned before, the women in that group were nothing short of inspiring. Through my experience in that service organization, I discovered that service to others was fundamental if I wanted to be truly fulfilled. I realized why the empath in me was so content around those women. Their energy felt good because they were filling up with divine energy by being of service. They were intentionally flowing love out toward others, and they never seemed to run out of energy to share. The message of light here is "Service to others from a place of love will create fulfillment." Even the word *fulfillment* seems to reference "filling full" of something. In this case, that something is love.

I used this new experience to redefine myself. My sisters were examples of characteristics I wanted to emulate: strength, courage, ambition, altruism, kindness, joy, and love. I knew I already had each of those qualities in some way. I just needed to cultivate and fashion them within myself. My experiences with that group allowed me to do just that. Like clay on a pottery wheel, each attribute I defined and nurtured within myself brought dimension and beauty to my creation. Each characteristic added more substance and depth to the vision I had of myself. Soon I was on my way to becoming something more, something different and entirely new to me. I was becoming a better version of myself. Strengthened by my experiences and supported by my sisters, I went from an easily malleable substance—the chameleonlike personality previously mentioned—to something solid, formed, and balanced.

It was a pivotal time in my life. My sisterhood helped me reset and realign with love so that I could embrace the joys of life experience. In doing so, I became aware of my strength and compassion, my capacity to love, and my desire to be of service—all that just in time to choose a career path. I had to pick a major. So I looked at the qualities I was beginning to fortify within myself through my service organization. I combined that information with my love for science, solving puzzles, and helping people. Then I thought about my experience in helping to save Maggie's life, and in a flash, I got another message of light. By connecting the dots, all the way back to my tonsillectomy, I could tell I was being called to the profession of nursing.

Chapter 7

Life-Changing Choices

God's Sense of Humor

When I decided who I wanted to be and what I wanted to do with my future, finding a man became less critical. Did I mention I was a bit obsessed with the fact that I didn't have a boyfriend? When I came home from college, all my friends were coupled up. That was part of the reason I decided to find my own path. Third-wheeling is not fun. But the guys I had been dating were not in alignment with the future I wanted. Spending time with them left me feeling disappointed instead of uplifted. So I made a conscious choice to forget about men altogether. I decided to focus on myself. With my career and future as my main priorities, it was easy to swear off dating. I suddenly did not need to empathically leech onto someone else's energy to feel good. I was already happy and fulfilled.

God has a funny sense of humor. After I decided to write off men completely, decent men began coming out of the woodwork. When my attitude shifted and I decided I wasn't looking for anything, suddenly, everything started to appear. I went from chasing one heartbreak after another to being chased by suitors instead. That was a miracle in and of itself, or at least it would have been to the old lonely version of me. It was a refreshing change, but as I said, I just wanted to have fun with my life again. I wanted to focus on my own future. I didn't want to complicate things with a guy. I was not looking for a relationship.

And God laughed.

I was working as a server at Hudson's Grill, as I often did on Friday nights, when he and his buddies came in for some drinks after work. Their group had been coming in for quite some time. Because their office was in the building next door, it was a quick and easy stop for them to make. They liked to grab a beer together before heading to their respective homes.

I'd noticed him before. He seemed familiar. I don't know what it was specifically, but there was something about his eyes that always drew my attention to him. He usually smiled at me and made eye contact whenever he came into the restaurant, but that was it. He never had talked to me, but I felt an unspoken connection between us. I was intrigued by him, but remember, my focus had changed. I made no effort to pursue his attention. I was content with the occasional flutter I got when we locked eyes. OK, maybe I did volunteer for a few Friday-night shifts, hoping he would appear, but that was it!

Over time, we developed a consistent pattern of making eye contact and exchanging flirtatious smiles, but again, that was it. He never made a move. I couldn't figure out why he never asked me out. He seemed to be interested, but nothing happened.

One day I got a clue when a friend of his stopped me to ask how old I was. I had a sense I was too young. He looked more mature than the guys I had been dating. When I answered that I was nineteen, the friend said in an "Aha" sort of way, "Oh, OK, I was just curious." And that was that. The interaction ended there.

The man with the familiar eyes continued to come into the restaurant several Fridays a month with his friends. We continued on with our silent flirtation. He still didn't speak to me; he just smiled and made subtle eye contact. This little dance went on for almost a year. Then his friend got a message: the sudden inspiration to ask me about my age again. I know it was divine timing, because that day happened to be my twentieth birthday.

Excitedly, I said, "I'm twenty!"

Then nothing.

After that, I went about the business of serving tables while feeling somewhat disappointed. But I was about to get a glimmer of possibility. The attractive guy with those eyes waved to me as he left the building this time. As I waved back, I realized he'd never done that before. I was happy with the progress, but I wasn't about to get my hopes up.

The Messages of Light

Moments after he walked out the door, I got a phone call at the bar. It was a message of light. Keep in mind that I had eight full-to-capacity tables, and it was the middle of the dinner rush on a Friday night. So at the time, it didn't feel like a miracle was happening, but believe me, it was.

I hurriedly raced up to the bar, picked up the phone, and said, "Hello?" in an almost frantic manner.

The voice on the other end said in a sort of hesitant way, "Hi. I don't know if you know who I am, but I just left the restaurant. I waved to you on my way out?"

I responded with a hurried "Yes, yes, I remember. Hi!" while screaming, *Finally!* in my head.

He introduced himself as Ron and went on to say, "Well, I was wondering if maybe you'd like to go out sometime."

Internally, I was dancing my happy dance and shouting, *Yes!* I could feel in my heart that this was something big. What I actually said was "Sure! Hurry and take down this number. I have to go! I'm slammed!"

As I stood there waiting for him to repeat the number back to me, I could feel the impatient eyes of the patrons I was supposed to be serving, all focused on me. The empath in me could sense their frustration by the warmth of the energy centered on my back. Just then, my mind went straight to a vision. I saw my tips as a parade of dollar bills marching away from me and out the restaurant's front door. With every moment I lingered on the phone, the number of dollar bills leaving my tip count grew. Of course, the vision was an illusion brought on by my subconscious fear-focused mind, but it was funny to see. And it turned out it wasn't a prophetic vision. I was so happy when I got off the phone that my tips reflected it! My negative illusion never came to pass. Of course, in the moment of job stress, I couldn't tell, but all was in perfect order.

On our first date, Ron told me what had been happening on his end of the call. He had been calling me from inside his car, on his cell phone. I'm sure nothing is awe-inspiring about that to people in this day and age. Five-year-old kids carry cell phones now, but not many people had cell phones back then. And true to the times, his cell phone, which looked like a giant brick, did not have hands-free Bluetooth technology or Siri to help him record the information.

When he'd heard my voice, Ron said, he could tell I was in a hurry, but he hadn't had a pen when I told him to write down my home telephone number. Luckily, with divine timing, he'd arrived at a red traffic light, and his friend had been stopped in the car beside him. Ron told me he had offered up the universal hand signal for a writing device, indicating to his friend in the other vehicle that he needed a pen. Then he charmingly described the two of them frantically searching their cars for something that would write. Finally, as he'd memorized my number, his friend had found a pen.

The way Ron told the story, I imagined that pen illuminated in golden light as it flew through the air between the open car windows. Just as the traffic light had turned green, the pen had entered his vehicle and hit Ron smack in the face. Luckily, there had been no injuries in the making of this memory, and it all had turned out well, because Ron had gotten the number right.

By the end of our first date, we were already in love. Or at least I was. We hit it off right away. We had definite chemistry. It felt as if we had known each other all our lives. In fact, when we first got to the restaurant, we couldn't even get out of the car because we were so busy talking and laughing. I can honestly say it was the best first date ever. I realize now that the warm, fuzzy feeling I had when I was with Ron was communication. God was using my empathic gift to cheer me onward.

Strange Synchronicities

Now here's where things get a little trippy. About a month into our relationship, Ron picked me up for a date. On our way to the restaurant, we passed the apartment complex I'd lived in as a kid—the one with the pool full of leaves and critters I almost had jumped into. A wave of nostalgic energy came over me, and I felt compelled to comment on how I had lived there when I was small. Ron's surprised reaction was evident to me and clearly disproportionate to the random fact I had just shared. He then told me his uncle Jimmy once had owned the apartments to which I was referring. In fact, he had owned them at the time I was living there.

His grandparents had managed the property for his uncle, and Ron had gone there every Sunday to visit them for family dinner.

Suddenly, a message of light that I could feel hit me like a lightning bolt. I had goose bumps from head to toe when I made the connection. I felt the same comfort and security with Ron that I'd felt as a kid being guided safely away from the pool full of critters. Once I recognized the familiar sensation, I saw it in his eyes: Ron was the boy from the pool!

With goose-bump chills running down my spine, I began to tell Ron of the memory I had of meeting him for the first time, and he finished the details of the story for me. He remembered seeing the scraggly-haired little blonde girl about to jump into that dirty pool full of stagnant rainwater, leaves, and bugs. He had a slightly less romanticized memory of the event, but he remembered it as clearly as I did. He said he had been on his way to his grandparents' place for dinner that day, when he had seen me about to get into the pool. He specifically remembered the event because he'd told his grandparents about the crazy five-year-old in the pool when he got to dinner.

Talk about crazy coincidences! I couldn't believe it. I mean, just wow. Right? I couldn't help thinking it was a sign that we were meant to be together.

I was so in awe of the coincidence that I had to tell my big sis, Alexis, and another synchronicity revealed itself. I got another message of light when Alexis and I sat talking together at the sorority house before our weekly meeting. She listened to me excitedly go on and on about how I'd met him and how long it had taken him to ask me out. I told her all about our first date and how much fun we'd had. Then I watched her eyes widen and her jaw drop when I told her about the coincidence of my meeting him when I was so young. Alexis's excitement and awe at the story I told her made my experience of sharing it that much more thrilling.

When I was done telling the story, Alexis asked me expectantly, "Who is this mystery guy? When do I get to meet him?"

When I told her his name, I couldn't help but notice the look of shock apparent on her face, followed by the broadest grin I had ever seen, as she exclaimed, "Oh my gosh! That's my cousin!"

As if the synchronicities before then hadn't been surprising enough, the additional coincidence was mind-blowing to me. I was overcome with awe and wonder, and those emotions told me that God had his hand in everything. I mean, really, what are the chances?

Falling in Love

The beginning of our story was incredible, but my relationship with Ron was not without its challenges. The age difference between us was noticeable to our friends and family, with him being fourteen years older than I was. We were continually being cautioned and reminded that we came from different worlds. I was living college life; and he was divorced, had a four-year-old daughter, and lived in the adult world of responsibility.

The age difference didn't bother me, and Ron made it no secret that he had a child. I knew exactly what I was getting into. In fact, I thought it was adorable to hear how he boldly and openly talked about his little girl. I could tell she was the center of his universe by the way he spoke. I loved how his face would light up whenever he talked about his daughter.

I was initially introduced to Riane over the phone. I was talking to Ron, and she was there with him. He was trying to invite me over to meet her in person, but four-year-old Riane kept taking the phone out of his hand. Now that I think of it, she may have been trying to hang up on me! I definitely did not get the feeling that Riane wanted to meet me. Being an empath sometimes gave me clues about other people's emotions that I would rather have not known. It would have been easier to go into meeting someone if I couldn't already feel the other person's resistance.

Once Ron regained control of the phone, I shared my concern with him. The next thing I knew, there was a small, sweet voice on the other end of the phone line. I will never forget what she said in her sweet little singsong voice: "Why don't you want to come over? I won't be mean to you."

All I could think at the time was *No fair! Who could say no to that?*

Seeing Ron in his role as a father made me fall that much more in love with him. After meeting Riane for the first time, I was in love with her too. One visit with the two of them together, and I was a goner. My heart was no longer my own.

When I think of the series of events that led to that moment, I am floored. If I had done just one thing differently and ignored even one message of light leading up to that day, I would not have had such a beautiful moment of heaven on earth. The messages of light always seem to lead to miracles. Have you noticed?

Falling in love—now, that's a miracle.

Chapter 8

A New Trajectory

The Information

As if the way we felt about each other weren't enough, it seemed God had been pointing us toward each other all along. The discovery of such amazing synchronicities—our crossing paths so many years before and the fact that he was Alexis's cousin—added a hint of magic to our bond. When you notice such amazing coincidences, it really makes you think. I began to ponder the deeper meanings of everything: *Why are we here? How are we all connected? Is this all part of a plan? What does it all mean?*

> When the student is ready, the teacher appears.
> —Buddhist proverb

My mom was always my teacher. It seemed she'd been on a journey of spiritual self-discovery and expansion ever since she saw me talking to Jesus on a swing in my backyard. See? It was a message of light she got that day.

My mom had learned a lot about life through experience and exploration. Everything spiritual or metaphysical fascinated her, and I found myself interested in much of what she explored as well.

Whenever she learned anything new, she would share it with me. I was a sponge, eager to soak in all the wisdom from her experiences. In fact, the mystery and magic of all she taught me became obsession-worthy, especially given my recent personal experiences with the supernatural. Even though I wasn't consciously maintaining my relationship with God, he was still finding ways to interact with me through my emotions and by lining up synchronicities that could not be ignored. Wow!

One day early in the fall of 1992, my mom came across some information out of Boerne, Texas, that would become a teacher to us both. Talk about God lining things up in perfect flow and timing! My mom was ecstatic. Her enthusiasm was so contagious I found myself excited right along with her, even before I knew what we were so thrilled about. Being an empath can be fun when the energy offered is good.

It was some life-changing stuff: a box of cassette tapes by Abraham-Hicks. The set of cassette tapes, published back in the late 1980s and early 1990s, opened the door to a new world for me. When I listened to them for the first time in 1992, I got goose bumps. Goose bumps, to me, are always a message of light from God, saying, "You're onto something here!" When I heard the tapes, I stepped through a doorway to new possibilities, and because of what I learned from Abraham-Hicks, I knew I was the creator of what I would see on the other side of that door. I was inspired. I began to see the world as the unlimited place that it truly is.

I was in awe when I listened to the first cassette tape. Talk about a message of light! It was like being handed the solution manual to a test and being given permission to use it during the exam. The law of attraction and the other laws of the universe the tapes spoke of altered my approach to every goal I set for myself. I highly recommend listening to Abraham-Hicks for yourself.

Through Abraham-Hicks, I learned that my thoughts were responsible for the reality I was living. I was getting exactly what I was thinking about, because of the magnetic pull of my thoughts. When I focused on getting rid of a problem, I noticed I felt terrible because I was focused on the problem. I discovered that the vibrational pull of that emotion somehow always caused one of two things: my pain felt bigger, or I found more problems to think about. Why? Because I was looking at the struggle, thereby giving it more energy. Essentially, I was amplifying the creation of precisely what I was trying to eliminate. It was like trying to put out a fire with gasoline. On the other hand, when I focused on the scenario of a perfect chain of events resulting in my happiness and fulfillment, I got miracles leading to precisely the feelings of joy and fulfillment I was seeking. I learned how to energetically attract what I wanted by purposefully focusing my thoughts on the positive aspects of my life. By daydreaming and visualizing about what I wanted, the positive emotions became strong enough to magnetically draw my designs into my reality.

I began to see examples of the universal laws in my own life experience. I mean, the proof is on these pages. The times in my life when I was miserable, I was focused on nothing but my misery. The times when I was focused on the good stuff, I was mostly happy. And when I wasn't focused on anything in particular, what came to me then seemed to happen by accident, because of my habit of thought, or because of someone else's intention. I noticed that when I forgot to decide for myself how I wanted to feel, someone else would always choose for me.

Over time, I learned how to actively think the thoughts and choose the words that made me feel as if my dreams were already coming true. Everything I wanted was because I thought having it would make me feel good. When I spent my time intentionally thinking, writing, and speaking about my desires, I was actually drawing them to me. The bonus was that I already felt good in the process.

I quickly learned that being an empath was a gift that would benefit me in using the laws of the universe. When I used my emotions as my guide, I could feel the vibrations I was emanating, and I knew that whatever energy I was feeling would become the magnetic pull for my creations. When I didn't feel good about a thought, I tried to redirect it to something that felt better. I also noticed that when I visualized and focused on the good feelings, the empath in me wasn't in absorption mode. In fact, I hadn't been in absorption mode for a while. When I started focusing on myself and my happiness and service to others, I started accessing the divine flow of love. I didn't need external validation to fill up with energy.

I also noticed that contemplating and visualizing good things seemed to keep my default mechanisms set to the off position. When I was in a positive flow, I didn't revert to a victim mentality, and because I decided how I wanted to feel, other people had less influence over my happiness. I established a goal and then spent time every day thinking about how good it would feel to achieve it. I learned the trick of getting so enthralled in the vision that my body physically experienced emotions similar to what I wanted to feel when my desires came to pass. Again, the emotions became the force pulling what I focused on into my life. So basically, the mission is to daydream and focus on inspiring and joyful things. Sounds fun, right? Well, it is!

It's great to feel fabulous in a daydream, but it feels even better to actually have the dreams become reality. I learned that in order to manifest the abundance I was focused upon, I had to be open and willing to receive it however it came to me. It's all about faith. I have to believe that what I have envisioned, or something even better, is on its way. In other words, I have to ask for what I want and then trust it is coming in its highest form.

Looking back, I realize the law of magnetic attraction was the underlying force that helped me achieve my goals all along. The perfect example of how I naturally and instinctively applied these concepts to my advantage was when I tried out for the gymnastics team and made it without any prior experience or training. Remember, it never even occurred to me to be afraid that I might not make the team. I visualized what I wanted and believed I could have it so powerfully that I got it. According to the laws of the universe, because I experienced so much happiness and fulfillment in practicing and imagining myself on the team, I drew the joy and fulfillment of being on the team into my real-life experience. It's magic!

Dreaming and Designing with Intention

From that point on, every goal I set was an experiment in my ability to use the law of the attraction to achieve it. I was in my early twenties, I had my whole future ahead of me, and I was excited about that. Just knowing I had tools to help me achieve my goals created such a sense of optimism that my entire perspective changed. I began to think about what I wanted instead of what I didn't have yet. It sounds like the same thing, right? But it's not. It's all about the way you feel. When looking at what you want, you feel excited, motivated, and happy. Conversely, when you think about what you don't have yet, you feel anxious, sad, or disappointed. The different perspectives incite dissimilar emotional responses. What I *do* want feels good. What I *don't* have yet feels terrible. Being an empath makes it easier to tell where the focus lies, since empaths are so sensitive to energy. When you're an empath, you cannot ignore it when you feel bad. So I decided I would spend time every day focused on how I wanted my life to look and how I wanted to feel as my dreams manifested.

After I began to focus on what I wanted, I couldn't help but notice how quickly I came up with a plan for my future or how easy it was for me to take steps in that direction. I had already decided I wanted to be a nurse. But until then, I hadn't done anything about it besides go to my prerequisite classes. So I focused on how I wanted to feel. I imagined a sense of accomplishment washing over me after applying to nursing school. That inspiration led me to actually fill out applications to two different nursing schools in my area. It would be my first test at applying the concepts I'd learned. All I had to do was spend time every day getting into a peaceful, happy-feeling place; visualize what I wanted; and believe it was coming to me.

I enjoyed my time perfecting this exercise. I began to envision not just my future life and happiness, but I got even more specific. I started to focus on how elated I would feel when I got an acceptance letter for nursing school in the mail. I pictured myself jumping up and down and squealing with excitement as I read the "Congratulations" part of the correspondence. I imagined whom I would call and what their reactions would be when I shared the news. I did this visualization ritual every morning without fail. Then I went through the rest of my day looking for signs that what I wanted was coming to me. God loves to prove himself, so the signs appeared.

One day, while I was in my introductory computer skills class, the guy at the computer next to me struck up a conversation out of the blue. We had been in the same class all semester, but the first time we ever spoke to each other was right after I began my visualization ritual. He was pleasant, friendly, and easy to talk to. We were making small talk, when I discovered he was interested in nursing as well. We discussed the different programs in the area. Then he told me about a nursing program I didn't know about. I thought I had explored all my options, and suddenly, there was another one. I had to respect that this was more than just a coincidence; it was a message of light. It was guidance. So I applied to that school as well. I would seize any opportunity that revealed itself, because I had become fully invested in the visions and dreams. I saw the seeming coincidence as a definite sign that I was attracting my creation to me.

Remarkably, the timing of that conversation was perfect. I found out about the third program just in time to make the final deadline for applications. The guy in my class told me about the school on Monday, and the applications were due that Friday. What do you think? Coincidence or divine timing?

While I waited for a response from the schools I'd applied to, I spent as many hours dreaming and designing my future as studying for my classes. Both paid off, because I went to the mailbox one morning, and there it was: a letter had arrived from one of the nursing schools. I tore into the envelope without hesitation because I could feel in my heart that it was an acceptance letter. I mean, I had visualized this moment over and over for months, so of course it had to be an acceptance letter. Right?

Right! It was an acceptance letter! The correspondence was from the university I'd applied to because of the supposed coincidence of the perfectly timed conversation. My prompt acceptance to nursing school was a direct result of the message I'd received out of the blue from the stranger in my computer class. The coincidence became even more significant when I realized the classes for my program started a semester sooner than the other programs to which I had applied. I would start school the following semester instead of waiting nine more months for the other programs to begin in the fall. I couldn't believe it! It was even better than I'd dreamed. I could become a nurse almost a year sooner than I'd anticipated. Was it another coincidence, or had I created the opportunity using the method I'd learned from Abraham-Hicks? Whatever it was, it was a miracle. I was so overcome with joy that I broke out into singing, saying, "Thank you, Lord!" I knew however it had happened, God's hand had been in it.

I continued to use the concepts presented by Abraham-Hicks to create everything I wanted at the time. When I had to take a test, I studied, I visualized taking the test, and I saw myself confidently answering the questions. I even envisioned the excitement I would feel at making the grade I wanted. And it worked every time. I even graduated at the top of my class.

Once I graduated, I used the same Abraham-Hicks strategy for my licensure exam. The nursing boards were computerized even back then, and the way they were structured, you sometimes could tell if you passed or not just by the number of questions you were asked. If you took the test in fewer than a hundred items, you either passed remarkably or failed miserably.

I studied to get ready for the test, and I also took power walks while I practiced creating using the magnetic power of my thoughts. During my outdoor adventures with the universe, I visualized taking the test and how I would feel while I did. I imagined myself smiling because I knew the answers. I even imagined taking the test with as few questions as possible, and I saw myself happily skipping out of the testing room when the computer shut down.

When I took my licensure test, I was confident. As I sat there watching the questions appear on the screen, I realized I was living my creation. I was smiling. I felt I knew the answers. And when my computer shut down after what I am fairly sure was only seventy-eight questions, I knew I'd passed. I had been there for less than two hours, and I felt good about it.

I wasn't done yet, though. I spent the next month waiting for my board results, and while I did, I spent every day visualizing getting that letter telling me I was a registered nurse and how I would feel when I got the news.

Sure enough, I got the letter assigning me my license number. It was almost exactly as I'd imagined, only it gave me more joy than I'd thought possible.

I got my first job as a nurse in the same way. I filled out applications, and I visualized getting a call for an interview and the positive interactions I'd have during it. That worked too. I got one of the first jobs for which I interviewed. I started off as a Medicare nurse. I helped to establish the programs and protocols for two skilled nursing facilities so they would be able to begin accepting Medicare patients. The best part was that I got to do the hospital assessments for the new patients who were to be admitted. That meant I got to travel to all the hospitals in the city, meet new people, and experience the behind-the-scenes aspects of medical care. It was all new and exciting to me. I was having so much fun they promoted me to assistant director of nursing. In my first six months out of nursing school, I lived all of that. Talk about being in the flow of creation. I was having fun and feeling confident and fulfilled, just as I had envisioned in my daydreaming sessions.

Then another one of those synchronicities occurred: the guy I'd met in my computer class years before walked into my office with an application in his hand. This was the guy who had referred me to the nursing program from which I'd graduated. He had been part of my nursing school miracle, and he never even had known it. I think he was as shocked to see me as I was to see him. He was there to apply for a job because he knew one of the other nurses I'd hired to work on the floor. Coincidence? We were both so surprised that we talked about the likelihood of such synchronicities. I couldn't believe it. Not only had I gotten into my nursing school because of what he'd said, but I'd graduated in enough time to be in a position of hiring by the time he graduated. Crazy, right?

I was happy he walked into my office that day. I got to thank him and tell him how much that conversation had changed my life. Who knows what direction my path would have taken if it weren't for him? He was humble, and he gave all the credit to God. He was in awe of the miracle too.

It's funny the way things work. That coincidence had come full circle. His message of light years before had helped me get into nursing school and resulted in my ability to offer him his first job in nursing years later. I still find myself in awe of the way those events transpired. Yes, I believe in miracles!

Energy Work

I was getting good at designing and creating using my emotions as my guide. Meanwhile, my mom used her grasp of the knowledge of Abraham-Hicks's teachings to create some fantastic experiences in her life too. While I was in nursing school, my mom moved to the epicenter of the mainstream new-age movement at the time, Las Vegas, Nevada. While she was there, she obtained a vast amount of spiritual knowledge. She studied under a Lakota Sioux shaman, became an ordained Christian minister, and was trained as a Reiki master. She also studied Wicca and adopted those philosophies as her own. All these studies not only helped her to rediscover her innate spiritual abilities but also amplified her powers of intuition and manifestation exponentially.

My mom and I talked constantly, sometimes several times a day, and during our conversations, she shared basically everything she'd learned with me. I think teaching me helped her to solidify her grasp of the information in addition to widening my scope of knowledge as well. Talk about a win-win situation. When she came to visit for my graduation from nursing school, she taught me something that would alter my life course for the better. She taught me Reiki. In December 1995, I became a certified first-degree Reiki practitioner in the Usui system of Reiki. I must admit that when I took the Reiki certification class, I did so mostly to please my mom. The scientist in me was not willing to believe that divine energy could be accessed by humans, much less channeled for healing. I'm happy I kept an open mind.

Learning Reiki was a mess*age of* light about working with light! It involves accessing God's energy—also known as universal life-force energy, Source energy, light energy, or love—for healing and creating. Every culture has a name for this energy. You may recognize it in one of the following ways: Christians call it the Holy Spirit, the Chinese call it chi, Hindus call it prana, and the list continues. No matter what you call it, it is the energy of creation. It is the healing energy of God. Reiki is only one of an infinite number of ways to connect with and flow divine energy. Reiki energy flows through the practitioner to the recipient, amplifying the divine energy in him or her. The energy has its own consciousness, so it knows exactly where to go to facilitate healing. It clears and aligns the chakras and magnifies the light energy within the person already. I love it because the energy promotes healing on all levels of the human experience: physical, emotional, mental, social, and spiritual.

With me, the healing began with the spiritual aspect of myself. Each time I connected to and accessed the energy, I felt closer to God. The feeling of connection, the warmth, and the comfort of the presence of God came back to me as if I were a child again, and I could almost hear God's whisper. My sense of balance and wholeness (holiness), the feeling of unconditional love for myself and others, and the wonder of magic and miracles were amplified within me through my experience with Reiki. Flowing Reiki was another means of filling up with divine energy so that I could intentionally flow love energy out to others. It kept me flowing energy out so that I did not accidentally empathically allow other people's energy in. Reiki is a pretty cool tool for an empath.

Unusual Things

Living in a world where the miraculous was already seen regularly, I found that my experiences got more and more fascinating as my natural abilities were amplified by Reiki. It was as if the veil between the natural and the supernatural were lifting. I began to sense energy shifts in the air around me, and I noticed tiny details, such as changes in my surroundings, that others didn't see. This was my empathic muscle getting stronger. It was a bit disconcerting at first, but I had my mother to confer with on all things supernatural. By that time, my mother had the power of an Olympian when it came to her spiritual abilities. She had been focused on developing her spiritual muscle for years, and she was strong.

On the other hand, I felt like a toddler just learning to walk, because it had been so long since I'd used that muscle intentionally. Thank God for muscle memory. Luckily, muscle memory works for the spiritual muscle too.

When something strange happened in my life, I called my mom straightaway. As I said, I would notice unusual things, and I would ask her about them often.

For example, Christmas lights. Our house had three picture windows side by side, facing the backyard. Every year, we put Christmas lights up on those windows. We enjoyed the warmth and the serene glow they brought to our home. When we put the lights up one year, we had an unusual experience. When we first strung the lights, all three windows had a steady glow of multicolored brilliance. The next night, when I plugged in the lights, I noticed the Christmas lights we had strung over the middle window were flashing, while the lights on the other two windows were still shining in a steady glow. I pointed it out to Ron, and we laughed it off, declaring how weird it was. We didn't say anything else about it, but I had a feeling something supernatural was going on.

The next night, we were together when I plugged in the lights, and they were all in a steady glow again. Ron and I shrugged it off as a fluke until later that night, when I noticed the Christmas lights over the window on the right side were flashing, but the other two sets of lights were on in a steady glow. It was more interesting than alarming, but we really took notice. It happened the next night again, but this time, it was the third window with flashing lights, and the other two were on a steady glow.

At that point, I called my mom and asked her what she got from it. She checked in on it for me, and after a few seconds, she said it was Ron's grandfather saying hello. Something about that resonated with me. It just felt right to me. When I told Ron what my mother had said, I got a sudden thrill down my spine, and goose bumps emerged all over my arms and legs. It was as if his grandfather let me know he was happy or something, and I could feel it. Empath perks! Later, it struck me that the windows in question were situated above the serving bar and china cabinet from his grandparents' home. From then on, when the lights would change—and they did every year we lived in that house—we would just say hello.

His grandpa used the lights to deliver a message of light! Gotta love it!

Beyond Coincidence

Another mystifying experience happened shortly after that, centered on an oddly behaving black cat.

When the black cat appeared on our back porch one day, I wasn't sure what to think about it. It was strange. I was sitting on the couch, watching television. The blinds on the opposite side of the room were open to a view of our backyard. I was startled for a moment when I looked over and saw a beautiful, sleek raven-black cat staring at me with piercing green eyes. The cat stayed outside the window, watching me. Its tail fluidly swished from side to side, indicating great interest in what was inside the house at the time—me. My new companion made that spot his perch for the rest of the day. He sat there like a sentry, as if guarding me. It was strange.

When Ron got home, the cat followed Ron with its intense green eyes wherever he went in the room, as if trying to make eye contact. Now, Ron is not a huge fan of cats, but something about this cat got his attention. He didn't run it off, as he usually would have. It was as if the cat had a message for us, and Ron knew it. I was curious about the cat. I had a feeling there was more to the situation than just a random cat coming to visit us. So I asked my mom about the cat, and she checked into it for us on the spiritual plane.

My mom said she could see the cat, but she could also see someone there with the cat, and she went on to describe what she saw. She said there was a tall, blond, blue-eyed boy with long hair and a lean build standing next to the cat. As I listened to the description, a vision of my imaginary friend, Tommy, materialized in my mind. Now, keep in mind here I never told my mom about Tommy. So you can imagine my shock when my mom described him to us.

Now, get this: Ron was listening to the conversation because his curiosity was piqued by the oddly behaving feline too. Before I could say anything about my imaginary friend, Tommy, Ron said, "I know who that is. It's Tommy!"

Ron went on to tell me about his best friend, Tommy, who'd died when he was a young man. Ron said he and Tommy had been really close, like brothers. Then he took me on a nostalgic tour of some of their adventures together as young adults in the 1970s. It was a wonderful trip into Ron's past. The coincidence that Ron's friend Tommy was so similar to my imaginary friend struck a chord of curiosity in me. It made me wonder if his Tommy and my Tommy were the same being. Had Ron's best friend become my guardian when he crossed over? Had he shown up as my imaginary friend so he could watch over me for Ron? Or was this just a coincidence?

With the chord of curiosity still ringing loudly in my mind, I wondered why Tommy—his or mine—would decide to suddenly make an appearance. I was excited and fascinated by the experience. Still, I couldn't shake the feeling that there was a reason Tommy had picked that particular day to show up.

It turned out that feeling was right. The cat made its appearance as a show of support from Tommy on the other side, letting Ron know that he was loved and that his friend was still with him. The timing couldn't have been more perfect. The next day, while the cat continued to stand on our porch, we learned that Riane was moving away. Ron would need all the support he could get to help him navigate this colossal change in his life. The cat stayed on our porch for close to three days after that.

I loved Ron and Riane, and I wanted to be there with them and for them in any way I could. I think maybe I was uniquely suited to help in that situation. I guess you could say I understood what the world looked like from the view of the child of divorced parents. I'd had a similar experience to Riane's when my mom remarried and we moved to Europe.

Maybe what I'd learned from the experiences I'd had while growing up would be of value to someone other than myself. Perhaps I could help make it a tiny bit easier on them. Maybe this had been in God's plan all along, because while I thought I was helping Ron and Riane through the change, I was actually being helped. The crazy side effect of the experience was that I got a message of light. I got another perspective on my own childhood experience. I saw firsthand through Ron what my own father must have been feeling when my mom decided to relocate for love. I developed a new level of compassion for my dad. Until then, I never really had considered what my dad must have felt when I went halfway around the world from him. Something in me changed. Seeing my past in that new light, I felt closer to my father than ever before.

Connecting those dots gave me a new sense of confidence that I was exactly where I was meant to be. I could feel it. That sense of knowing from my childhood had returned. I had faith without a doubt that this was God's plan. The way Ron and I had met so many years before, the Tommy coincidence, Riane's and my similar childhood experiences—the synchronicities were too many to ignore.

We missed Riane terribly when she was away, but that only served to make the times when we were together more precious. We appreciated every moment. Even though the situation was complicated, it inspired a sense of awe in me. God had had it all mapped out all along, and he guided each of us every step of the way. I began to trust that whatever came next, God was in on it.

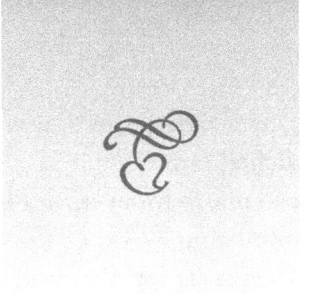

Chapter 9

Designing Dreams

Creating a Future

I began dreaming of my life with this man and his daughter, and I guess my dreams were contagious. Ron and I both began to look toward creating a future together. Energetically speaking, creating something with someone else is considerably more complex than creating something alone. Since the emotion is the magnet, both people must want to feel similar things for it to manifest. I knew what I wanted, and Ron knew what he wanted, but sometimes those wants were not necessarily the same thing. Since the universe responds equally to both people in a cocreation, you can see how it can get a little tricky.

I felt I was ready for the next step in our relationship. I had achieved every goal I'd set for myself so far. Graduation from nursing school? Check. Loving long-term relationship? Check. Successful, fulfilling career? Check. The next logical steps for me were marriage and more kids.

I was ready for what was next, but was he? I knew I could pretty much create anything I wanted in my experience. I had ample proof of that, but could I want something enough to create it for the both of us? I was about to try. I did precisely what I had done countless times before. I went outside and walked and meditated on my desires and the vision of my future. While I walked, I focused on marriage to Ron. What would it be like? How would I feel? It was easy to imagine being married to him, since we had been living together for almost three years by then. In and of itself, that was evidence that I was on the path to manifesting my wish.

The creation was actually already designed. It was just a matter of knowing whether Ron's desires matched mine.

Ron hadn't asked me to marry him yet, and I was beginning to doubt whether he would. Despite being aware of the messages, miracles, and coincidences that had brought us together and despite the evidence all around me that my dreams were coming true, I was still insecure. And I was getting impatient. I decided it was time I found out if we were headed on the same path.

We were at our favorite restaurant, Los Bandidos De Carlos & Mickey's, enjoying a lovely meal together, when I got on the subject of marriage again. It was not the first time we'd discussed it. Early on, we'd agreed that marriage wasn't even a consideration until I graduated from nursing school. Well, I'd graduated. I was ready, but as I said, I was starting to wonder if Ron was. I had no idea whether he intended to marry me or not. So, there at our favorite restaurant, in our usual romantically low-lit booth, I told him how I felt. I unloaded my insecurities on him, empathically trying to siphon his energy, but it didn't work. I was ranting. I admit I was getting myself pretty worked up. Especially because I could feel humor coming from Ron instead of the comfort I was empathically trying to draw from him.

Ron suddenly stopped me midsentence and said, "Will you shut up and marry me?"

I did shut up, but my mouth hung open despite that fact. I was so busy raving like a lunatic that I almost didn't hear what Ron said. After a moment, it registered. He had just asked me to marry him, and he was waiting for an answer.

And that, my friends, is how my engagement began.

I love that story because it just goes to show that I might have known and felt that Ron and I were already on the same page in our joint creation, but I was too busy spouting my own insecurities to notice.

Tying the Knot

I went through different phases of emotion throughout the engagement. I shifted from pure confidence and joy to periods when I experienced

The Messages of Light

fear and every feeling there is to feel except certainty. As far as Ron was concerned, I had no doubt I wanted to be with him for the rest of my life. However, I wasn't always sure that Ron really wanted to marry me. I know it's silly, especially when you look at the whole picture. That's why it was so funny that I was still freaking out about it in the limo on the way to the ship where we were about to be married.

We traveled across the country with his family, my family, and a group of our closest friends for our wedding and honeymoon on board the SS *Norway*. It was ridiculous for me to think he would skip out on our wedding with all of us on the verge of a seven-day Caribbean cruise together. But I freaked out anyway.

The night before the wedding, I was preoccupied with the old superstition that it is bad luck for the wedding couple to see each other before the wedding. Why was that a problem for us? Well, the cruise line insisted we board the ship together because we were ticketed that way. It was just another one of a string of complications that had me stressed beyond my limits. So my dear fiancé went out of his way to ease my distress. He made sure we wouldn't see each other before the wedding. The only thing was, he forgot to tell me.

So there I was in the limousine, on the first of two trips the limo would have to make to the ship. I was surrounded by my mom; my dad; my other mom, Mary; and my in-laws. Because Ron had sent Riane to the limo alone, I had a full-on panic attack. Just being in the same space with all the people previously mentioned was enough to cause anxiety, but I also was freaking out about a possible no-show groom. I was delving into my worst fears, and nothing could free me from the illusion. I continued to freak out even after Riane told me that Ron would be on the second limo headed for the ship. If I had been thinking logically, I would have realized Ron would never have sent his daughter with me to the cruise ship unless he intended to meet up with me again. But that thought process did not resonate with my fears, so I actually didn't believe her for a moment.

Oh yeah, the laws of the universe were at play there. My emotions were intense. I was so immersed in my fear illusion that I magnetically drew more anxiety-provoking situations to overcome. This is a true story; you can't make this stuff up! On our way to the ship, we encountered a terrible delay. The railway between our hotel and the boat was in full service for the first time in nearly ten years. It just happened to start up that day. Yes, a railroad line that had been shut down for ten years was causing delays on that day, my wedding day. Who could have anticipated that? The delay wasn't too bad for me. I would make it to the ship on time. The problem was that the limo had to drop us off and go back for the second group in our wedding party, and who knew how long that would take? At that point in my internal drama, I was sure that even if Ron intended to show up for the wedding, he would miss it because of the train. I mean, do you know how long it can take for a train to pass? Suddenly, it didn't matter anymore that my bouquet, the bridesmaids' gifts, the boutonnieres for the groomsmen, and the corsages for the mothers were lost in transit. The absent flowers and gifts would be insignificant compared to a missing groom.

Do you see how the magnetic power of my fear of a no-show groom actually manifested in my real life? Kind of crazy, huh?

It's funny to look back and see the snowball effect a little anxiety had on that day. Just as Abraham-Hicks said, "The better it gets, the better it gets, but the worse it gets, the worse it gets." The attractive magnetic power of thought is real! This is just one example of a lifetime of examples of that truth. I knew all that, but I forgot to apply those concepts to my experience. Given the intensity of the emotion behind my anxiety, the strong magnetic force creating chaos was gaining momentum. It was no surprise that the limo also dropped us off at the wrong entrance to the ship, and our names were not on the manifest. Nor was it a surprise that the best man and the matron of honor were still not on board the ship fifteen minutes before the ceremony. Thanks to the magnetic pull of my fearful focus, I was an expert at manifesting stress that day.

In hindsight, I can see how that whole experience could have gone better had I taken time to pay attention to my emotions and intentionally focus on what I wanted to experience that morning instead of what I feared.

Luckily, my deep desire to marry Ron was stronger than my fear's brief, attractive power. As it turned out, Ron and I were married that day, as I should have faithfully expected. But what can I say? I had to purge my panic first. As it happened, all the worries, fears, and physical stress I endured that day were for no reason. Ron and I were married and took our photographs just before the justice of the peace and his wife, the photographer, had to disembark from the ship.

My wedding was quite an experience. Many things went wrong, but quite a lot went right. I married the love of my life, my mama cried, and I danced the father-daughter dance with my dad just as I always had imagined. Riane, my friends, and family were all there, and I was happy. As crazy as it was, I wouldn't change a thing. The message of light I got from that experience was "It will work out however it works out, whether or not we stress. We can spend time fearing what might be, or we can enjoy what is in the moment."

The New Addition

Ron and I had been married for about eight months when we got the exciting news that we were pregnant. It was no surprise to me because I had been working on that creation for a while, even before we'd decided to get married. I spent plenty of time dreaming of our home, our family, and what that home would feel like with a baby in it. I wondered what it would feel like to be that close to another human being. I thought about how the body magically transforms to accommodate a whole other person being formed inside the womb. I spent time immersed in dreaming about holding that much love in my arms. I created images in my mind, imagining everything from what the nursery would look and smell like to bonding with the baby during late-night feedings. I got so deep into the visions they almost felt real. So once we were married and the time was right, I knew those visions would manifest.

I knew my dreams would come true, not only because I was confident in what I'd learned about the law of magnetic attraction but also because I prayed. I realized the peaceful, pleasant, or exhilarating emotions I felt in my visualizations were the same emotions I felt when I prayed. My visualizations felt like prayers in their own way. No wonder the empath in me didn't need external validation once I began focusing on myself and the good I wanted to do with my life. So the visualizations served a purpose similar to that of my prayers, but I also prayed outright. I asked God to bless us with a healthy baby. And he did!

I remember the moment my baby sent her first message of light to me. I am talking about the moment she first made me aware of her presence. Before I even took a pregnancy test, I knew she was there. I was driving to work, listening to the radio, and I felt something. It wasn't a physical sensation. It was more of a stirring of my spirit. It was a sudden rush of love, and I felt as if I were getting a hug from the inside. Suddenly, I knew I wasn't alone in my body anymore. As I was driving alone in my car, I had the irresistible urge to say, "Hi there, little one! I'm so excited you're here!" I didn't take a pregnancy test for another week, but I knew what the result would be. To me, the test was just a formality.

My pregnancy was a beautiful yet terrifying experience. I continued working for the first six months of my pregnancy. During that time, I pretty much lost all sense of emotional balance. I chalked it up to hormones, pregnancy health, and job stress, but all those factors combined were nowhere near as hard on me as the stress I caused myself. Luckily, I had an incredibly insightful doctor who could point that out to me. I loved Dr. Mendoza. He decided early on that I knew way too much about medicine for my own good. And he was right.

Over time, my nursing knowledge led me down a path of fear. The miracle of life is a delicate and intricate creation. I knew about way too much that could upset the natural balance, and it was driving me crazy—or, more accurately said, I was driving myself crazy with my choice to indulge in fearful thoughts.

I loved my baby so much already that the thought of anything going wrong was terrifying to me. For some reason, it seemed I could think of nothing else. It didn't help that one of the nurses who worked with me was also pregnant and had just attended a prenatal seminar. As a mother, she was a pro. She was pregnant with her fourth child, so she didn't think about the fact that I was a first-time mother when she shared the class materials with me. Let's just say the materials she shared with me were created for a nurse, not a new mommy. They pretty much covered everything and anything that could go wrong in pregnancy and delivery. I was reminded of all the possible pregnancy complications I had forgotten about since nursing school.

When I started showing up to my weekly checkups in near hysterics, Dr. Mendoza decided that something had to give. My stress level was too high, and by then, my medical condition had worsened from my being on my feet all day. Dr. Mendoza wanted to keep me calm and healthy for the baby's sake, so he put me on medical leave. He said to me, "I can't get you out of your own head, but I can get you out of that office." Ha! See why I love the man?

Clearly, I was spending more time in fear than in prayer. The empath in me was yet again set to absorption mode. Because I was working in a medical facility, I was absorbing all kinds of unwanted energy. Yet again, God knew what he was doing when he sent me to Dr. Mendoza. This messenger of light not only took care of my baby but also took care of me. My fears subsided when I got the chance to focus 100 percent on the miracle that was happening inside me. Those last months of my pregnancy were so beautiful and peaceful that I got a chance to intentionally focus on the good stuff again. I went out walking and meditating, doing my thing every day but with a baby inside me. It was then I realized just how off-balance I had become. I guess you can say I saw the light!

I had gotten so wrapped up in my life and all that was happening so quickly that I had forgotten I had a say in the direction of my focus. There is so much fear in the world. When you don't intentionally visualize your dreams, what is created by default tends to be fear-based and more like a nightmare. That's not a fun way to live, and I was living it. But thanks to God, Dr. Mendoza, and my training in the universal law of magnetic attraction, I was able to get back on track to the joyful pregnancy I envisioned. For the first time in a long time, I was able to go walking, meditating, and dreaming again. It felt good to reset my focus and thereby my energy. Over time, I realized that the more I connected to spirit on my walks through prayer and meditation, the easier it was to feel the energy of the baby inside. I was strengthening my energetic muscle. I practiced every day, and I could feel her. It was a magical time.

Special Delivery

I'll never forget the day I went into labor. Does any woman forget that day? It was the day before the baby was due, and I had a burst of energy like no other. With the excess energy, I did my usual walk and meditation.

Christi Conde

I cleaned the house and pulled the grass out of the rocks in our front yard for hours. Then I started having contractions. I actually loved the way they felt. My stomach contracted, getting harder than a bowling ball. When the baby reacted to the contraction by stretching out, resisting the force of my abdominal wall, I felt a rush of joy. It was awesome, as in creating a true sense of awe.

With my contractions still sporadic, I decided it would be a perfect time to go to the mall and get a watch fixed. Now, I know what you're thinking. Don't worry. There is no messy water-breaking-in-public scene to include here, because I had plenty of time to get to the hospital.

I had so much time.

It's strange the things I remember from that night. I was more frustrated than uncomfortable at first. Time wore on, and the empath in me went berserk. I went from flowing in the bliss of the miracle of birth and staying in vibrational alignment to being frustrated and soaking in the chaotic energy of the nurses and other mommies delivering that day, basically pulling myself out of alignment.

What caused the shift? It was not the discomfort of delivery as much as the fact that people kept standing in front of my focal point. The beautiful pewter fairy given to me by my mom had indigo wings, reminding me of my connection to the divine. She had one arm wrapped around the side of the crescent moon she was sitting on. The other arm was raised toward her face, and she extended a single finger upward by her pursed lips, as if to say, "Sh." That little fairy was a great reminder to stay peaceful and tranquil—when I could see it!

When it came time for the delivery, the little fairy was of no consequence because they left her in the room when they took me to the delivery suite (operating room). I think they forgot half the epidural in that room too. I was having contractions, pushing, and doing the work of labor. Although I was completely numb on the right half of my body, I could feel everything on the left side of my body. It seemed like some kind of cosmic joke to reflect my out-of-balance pregnancy.

At 3:10 p.m., I was still pushing with little result, so Dr. Mendoza opted for drastic measures. He went over to a supply cart and pulled out an instrument that looked like a metal medieval torture device. Then he threatened to use it on my baby! He said it was to grab onto my baby's head to help ease the baby out. At first sight of that, I pushed like never before. I wouldn't let him get that thing anywhere near my baby. That did the trick. I was finally infused with enough focused energy to deliver my little message of light, Kira Christell. She was a healthy 21.5-inch-long baby girl who weighed eight pounds and one ounce. We named her Kira because our book of baby names said *Kira* was a variation of a word meaning "Sun." I felt that was appropriate because she brought the light of a thousand suns into my life.

Chapter 10

Domestic Bliss

Beauty and Blessings Abound

Having a baby changes you. The world becomes new again. Every moment is a precious milestone that is celebrated with glee. You see things with a new sense of wonderment. You begin to look at the world through the eyes of a child—through the eyes of your child.

The world became a magical place for me from this glorious perspective. I was in love with my beautiful, healthy baby, and I was living my dream. I was married to an incredible man, and I was developing a good relationship with Riane. Riane loved her baby sister. We had a beautiful home and a stable income.

I was flowing in divine energy. I took the time to look around at my experience daily, and I was astounded by the beauty and blessings everywhere. I was so happy! Everything I ever had dreamed of, and even more, was right there in my life. Everywhere I looked, I saw God's artistry. It was almost surreal. At moments, I felt like an observer outside myself looking at my life, appreciating everything about it. I thought, *Wow! This is so cool! I can't believe this is my life. This is what it feels like to be blessed.*

I spent so much time calling upon the feelings of gratitude and appreciation that I reached a new level of awareness. I found my rose-colored glasses, so to speak. No matter what I looked at, I could see the magic in it. Everywhere I turned, I felt love, and in every experience, there was light. In fact, I got an incredible message of light one day when I was at a college football game. That day I was feeling particularly happy and blessed because I was there with my husband and our beautiful daughter Kira. As we approached the stadium together, we ran into Chris and some of his friends. Chris was the boy I was heartbroken over when the song "Unanswered Prayers" rescued me from the lovesick despair of my youth. When I first saw him that day, my heart felt like it had stopped, and I suddenly felt paralyzing anxiety strike me in the center of my chest. But then, I looked back at my husband and my daughter, and I felt nothing but pure love. Talk about a contrast of energy. At that moment, a familiar song began to play in my mind, and I heard Garth Brooks singing, "Some of God's greatest gifts are unanswered prayers." My heart was overflowing with love. I could tell because my eyes had sprung leaks. And yet again, I was in awe of the miraculous nature of God.

In retrospect, I can't help but think that the entire football game experience was a direct law of attraction manifestation that originated with the song that was once my mantra. For those who haven't heard the song, it is important to note that the events described in the song, that mirrored my experience, also took place at a football game! Crazy right? I believe that all prayers are answered in divine and perfect timing, but not always in the ways we expect.

Riding the Wave

I understand surfing a bit now. I've never been on a board, but I can understand the spiritual connection surfers most likely feel in their consistent communion with the sea. The ocean is powerful and unpredictable, but when they get in the flow with it, there is an obvious unity among the surfer, the surfboard, and the sea. Imagine feeling at one with a force as powerful as the ocean. Well, that was how I felt but better. I felt I was one with the energy that creates worlds, and I was designing my own world with it.

Communing with God in prayer, flowing in divine energy with Reiki, navigating my life with the principles of magnetic attraction, and seeing the miracles that come from the messages are all ways I learned to surf in my life. When I am in the flow with the magic of the miraculous, there is no feeling like it. It's exhilarating, exciting, and awe-inspiring. This is why even though I might get knocked down by life experiences and sometimes hurt, I always get back up and try again to connect with the flow. It is pure joy to feel at one with something so infinitely powerful. I understand now what it feels like to surf, even with my feet still on the ground.

During that time in my life, I was surfing. I was riding the wave of life, enjoying the flow of divine energy, which meant my emotions stayed mostly peaceful and balanced. I didn't empathically absorb the energy of people around me, because I was so busy flowing the happiness through me. I spent practically every waking moment in gratitude. I continued to walk every day, and I took my baby girl with me, as well as Riane when she was in town. I resolved to bask in and enjoy every precious moment of that amazingly beautiful time in my life, and I did. I told my baby girl how much I loved her. I played with her and kissed her cute little chubby cheeks every chance I got. I watched her sleep, and I took countless pictures. I treasured every priceless, miraculous moment. That whole time in my life felt as if I were living in light. I wanted to ride that wave forever.

The Process

Time passes quickly when you're living in bliss. It wasn't long before I decided I wanted more joy. I wanted more beauty, love, and memorable moments of bliss only a baby can bring. I was ready to try for another precious miracle from heaven.

So I did my thing. I walked, prayed, and meditated. I spent time every day thinking of carrying another child. I imagined another pregnancy and what that would be like. I daydreamed about another adorable little bundle of love. I visualized what our home would feel like with another person in it, with another someone special to cherish. I imagined the elation and joy I was already experiencing expanded by the presence of another resplendent soul.

I did everything right. So I couldn't believe it when I took a pregnancy test and saw that it was negative. I thought, *That's not possible!* I was so upset I went back to bed, essentially throwing a temper tantrum in my mind. Even in my frustration, I began to pray, wondering what had gone wrong. I was in the midst of fully and openly expressing my disappointment to

God, when I felt it for the first time: with my empathic muscle, I felt a stirring in my spirit and a sense of connection to someone else inside my body, a message of light. Then the words "I'm here!" came to me with a rush of warmth.

I said to myself, *That's what I thought!*

I got out of bed, marched back to the trash can, pulled out the test (I know—gross), and rechecked it. This time, it said the result was positive. I took another test the next day to confirm, and that one came back positive right away. There was no need to double-check after that; I knew it had worked. My process of praying and dreaming about what I wanted in life had worked again. We were going to have another baby.

The wonderment and fascination of the miracle of life took me over again. I got to really enjoy it that time. Never underestimate the power of experience in assuaging fear. It was not my first time around the pregnancy block, and I felt confident. Also, I had no job stress to regularly pull me into fight-or-flight situations. Did I mention that circumstances lined up by my using prayer and the attractive magnetic pull of my thoughts so that I could stay home with my children? Yep, that miracle happened!

Being highly sensitive to energy and emotions has helped me learn to feel my way through certain situations and access divine inspiration for guidance. My feelings told me when I was right on track or if I was misdirecting my energy. Thanks to my empathic gift, I stayed focused on the miracle inside me and the miracles beside me too. Because of the magnetic power of thought, the more I appreciated the good, the better everything got in my life. I wanted to keep that energy flowing, so I continued my routine of taking time every day to walk, meditate, and pray while I was out in the energy of nature. It was when and where I put on my rose-colored glasses. I felt incredibly connected and peaceful outside. It was where I felt closer to God.

Finding My Church

I loved the feeling of communing with God so much that I decided to take new steps toward that relationship. I decided to take classes to become part of my husband's church. Ron was religious, and as you know, I had been without a church of my own, so I decided to convert to his faith. I felt it was important to know firsthand the religion and values we agreed we would teach our children. So I enrolled in the necessary formation classes—and I experienced God's presence in a way that changed my life forever.

It was a time of wonder and magic. Because I started my classes at that exact time at that particular church, I witnessed and participated in a series of miracles that solidified my faith in God and in the power of prayer.

In the formation classes, I met a beautiful soul who would prove to be not only a dear friend but also an inspiration to me and many others. When I met Michelle, she was going through a rough time. The empath in me felt her pain, and although it wasn't my pain, I cared so much about her I suffered right along with her. That's what happens when an empath replaces empathy with sympathy. The difference is important. Sympathy is a vibration that amplifies grief, whereas empathy helps to dissipate the energy. When we are sympathetic, we amplify the negativity to the point where we also begin absorbing it. When we are empathetic, divine love takes over, and the weight of the burden is lighter for all concerned. Sympathy is flowing from sadness or fear, while empathy is flowing from love. I was about to learn how to flow from pure love and faith by my new friend's example.

In observing Michelle's situation, I felt a sense of awe. She found guidance and support in that community of kind and loving people who were coming together to form a deeper relationship with God. The experience renewed my faith. I was a witness as the impossible was made possible. I saw that God answers all prayers for our highest and best good.

Michelle experienced miracles through her faith, vigilant prayer, and the love of the people around her. She and I talked a lot about God and miracles. It was our way of keeping the faith. It felt good to take note of all the tiny instances in our days in which God chose to reveal his presence and love. We noticed more of them the more we talked about them, and soon we saw miracles everywhere we looked.

One day she told me about her small miracles. There were many more, but I just want to share one to show that even a minor miracle makes an enormous difference.

Michelle had been having a horrible day. She focused too long on her situation, and her fears rose up and overwhelmed her. She found herself in total despair. The spiral of fearful thinking took over. She told me of her

The Messages of Light

distress. She described how she sobbed as she prayed that day for a sign of hope from God that things might actually work out for her.

Miracles happen fast. Moments later, as she got in her car to go pick up her younger brother from school, she got her sign, a message of light. The perfect song came on the radio at the ideal time.

The song "When You Believe," performed by Whitney Houston and Mariah Carey and written by Stephen A. Schwartz, came on the radio. My friend knew she was loved and supported when she heard the words to this beautiful, hopeful song.

I know you may be wondering how a song could be a miracle. To see the miracle, just look at the lyrics, "There can be miracles, when you believe." Those words were a sign that God heard her prayer. Then look at the timing and think about how many things had to line up so that the first thing she heard after her prayer for a sign of hope was the song "When You Believe." The true miracle, though, was in the feelings of relief, love, connection, and support that Michelle experienced when she heard the perfect song at the perfect time.

It was as if God were speaking directly to her, answering her prayer for a sign of hope. What better way to feel hope than to know God has heard your prayer? The way I see it, God didn't stop there. He wasn't just letting her know he was with her in her time of struggle. He was giving her instructions that would ensure a positive outcome. Through the song's words, God was telling her that she had to believe the situation would turn out in her favor. Faith is critical to the manifestation of miracles.

So Michelle continued going to her classes, where we, her classmates, prayed with her and for her. She prayed her novena to Saint Jude religiously and played "When You Believe" anytime she started to doubt. And do you know what? It worked!

God not only heard our prayers; he answered them. Obviously, the result can only be called a miracle! The young woman we prayed for so vigilantly was blessed with a better experience than we'd thought possible, and it came in a way that no one could have predicted. Michelle received a miracle beyond any of our wildest imaginations. Because of it, her entire life trajectory changed for the better. This amazing woman continues to live her best life to this day, and she still serves as a source of inspiration for many. I hope someday she will share the whole story with the world.

Yep, I believe in miracles! I know the power of prayer is real! I have seen it move mountains. Talk about a message of light! To this day, this is one of my most treasured stories of a miracle. That experience changed everything for me. Besides witnessing miracles and the power of prayer, I found the thing I'd wanted since childhood: I finally found a church that would stick. I was baptized, and I received my first Holy Communion and my confirmation as well. I finally felt I belonged.

In that time of study, introspection, and service to others, I learned what it meant to receive the sacraments, so when I finally did, it was a truly holy experience. It was worth the wait to find my church. I can see clearly why it was supposed to happen the way it did. Any other way, I would have missed out on my new friend and her miraculous story.

Continuing Bliss

I went about my life for a time after that with an entirely new view of the world. I was still seeing my life through rose-colored glasses, but my insight expanded way beyond that. At times, I felt as if I were viewing the world from a higher perspective. At the core of my being, I began to understand that nothing is outside the expanse of God's love and power. I had just started to scratch the surface of the experience of inner peace, and it was terrific.

During my second pregnancy, I was calmer, and from a spiritual perspective, the pregnancy was lovely. That inner peace I felt added to the awe of the miracle of life. I treasured every moment. Every flutter I felt, every movement, and even the kicks to the bladder were constant confirmation of the miracle living inside me. The greatest joy I have ever experienced is being a mother. During my second pregnancy, I was in a continual state of gratitude pretty much all the time.

The much-anticipated time finally came we were about to meet our new addition. The birthing process was slow, and eventually, it got to be quite uncomfortable. For a while, I was handling it like a champ. I even considered not having the epidural—and then the real pressure hit. I used the same fairy I'd used for the first delivery as a focal point, and just like

The Messages of Light

the first time, people kept blocking it from my view. I find it funny now, but it was less than comical at the time. I'll just leave it at that.

Eventually, I opted for the epidural. This time, it worked on both sides of my body. It was lovely. My labor progressed well, and honestly, it felt like a party environment in a good way. Everyone was happy and jovial, but things changed when it came down to the real business of the final pushes. The energy in the room shifted. I could feel that something wasn't right. I instinctively took a deep breath and prayed for my baby, my doctors, and, of course, myself. I prayed for the highest and best good for everyone concerned.

Suddenly, I felt as if I were in a cloud, watching events happen from a distance. I was comfortable and peaceful, although everyone else became severely intense. I could feel no sense of panic on the part of my hero Dr. Mendoza, but the energy was different. He calmly got my attention and insisted I stop pushing that instant. Something in his tone offered up the strength for me to do just that. It took everything I had to resist what my body insisted on doing. Still, somehow, I managed to hold off on pushing long enough for Dr. Mendoza to unwrap and cut the umbilical cord from around my baby's neck. She was blue. There was no cry, only the sound of a busy hospital room. I should have been terrified, but I wasn't. I was still floating in the peace and security of the cloud. I didn't see Ron in the room or my mom, just the baby. Everything else was a blur.

After what seemed a lifetime, I finally heard her cry. I watched as they took her and suctioned her nose and mouth, and then they brought her to me and let me kiss her. Unfortunately, I only got to hold her for a moment before they whisked her off to the NICU with my husband close on their heels. There they put her on oxygen to keep her blood-oxygen saturation up, and they monitored her closely as a precaution.

My mom, who was in the room the whole time, stayed with me while Ron went with our baby girl. Did I mention my mother never has been good at hiding her concern? I could read her face and feel her emotions. She was worried. I should have been, but I wasn't because I could still feel my baby. They had cut the umbilical cord between us, but our connection was still there. I knew she was fine, and I was still floating in my cloud at that point, so I was fine too. I was filled with such peaceful and serene energy that I felt as though the baby and I were surrounded by angels. I was sure that all was well, and eventually, the doctor came in to confirm that fact. That message of light was received as the miracle it apparently was. I was overjoyed at the confirmation of my intuition, and my mother was relieved as well. Of course, Ron was the first to officially know, because he never left his daughter's side.

After I came back down from my cloud, I began to worry for a second. My mom had been exuding so much fear that some of it must have gotten to my empathic self. I chose to be concerned that our brief time apart would hurt our mother-daughter connection right at the time of her birth. Well, it didn't. Instead, it just affirmed the strength of our bond. I learned I could sense her even from a distance. It was an amazingly intuitive, almost telepathic connection I wouldn't have realized otherwise.

When they finally brought her to me, I was in a state of pure bliss. She was beautiful and angelic-looking. She was the exact same weight and length her older sister Kira had been, even though I'd gained twenty pounds less this time around. When the two girls met each other, they bonded instantly. We named our little light Aja Koren—yes, like the song "Aja" by Steely Dan. I chose that name because the baby name books said *Aja* means "Life." That name seemed appropriate to me. She might have been soundless for the first few seconds after she was born, but that little girl showed us all that she was full of vitality and life. She had some lungs on her, and I was happy about that. Whenever I heard her cry, I was reminded of how miraculous it was that I could listen to her voice at all.

That event changed the way I prayed forever. My instinct to pray for myself, my daughter, and my doctor and nurses gave me a new insight into prayer. Praying for all concerned helped to bring my daughter Aja, my little message of light, into the world without my fear affecting the experience.

Aja's birth gave me an in-depth understanding of a new way to pray. Now whenever I pray, I add the following to my request: "Lord, I give this to you and ask that you orchestrate the highest and best good for everyone concerned."

When I prayed, I relinquished my need to control the details and freely gave them to God instead. I started to feel his presence more profoundly and see evidence of his intervention everywhere. By praying for the highest and best good, I began to experience a whole new level of freedom. From that moment on, I no longer felt the weight of responsibility for my creations. I was able to rid myself of my old fear-based programming. You've surely heard the saying "Be careful what you ask for, because you just might get it."

This way, there is no negative karma, because the prayer is for everyone. I found a different level of understanding, trust, and faith. When I give a situation to God and pray for everyone involved, what I receive as a result is always better than anything I could have achieved on my own. It's always better than I imagined. This way of praying became more than a concept to understand and master. It was my truth.

Never Cease to Be Amazed

Abraham-Hicks is right in saying, "The better it gets, the better it gets." I like this statement because it changes the negative connotation of "When it rains, it pours" to a positive one.

By that time in my life, my daily routine of walking with prayer and creative meditation had become a habit. It was the best habit I ever formed. And adding the tagline "for the highest and best good of everyone concerned" to my prayers changed the game completely. Deliberately creating my experience was not only effortless but also incredibly exciting.

It was like getting an upgrade on a new computer system, and God was the programmer. Once I learned to operate the technology, the system did all the work for me. I put in a request, and the universe would grant it. The system ran on my thoughts. Basically, anything I thought about long enough would trigger the system to create more experiences similar to the ones I imagined. Once I learned that fundamental concept, I made a concerted effort to keep my thoughts positive. The best way I could do that was to spend time appreciating what I already had. The cool thing about appreciating what we already have is that when we forget to create intentionally, the vibration of appreciation continues to draw more things to appreciate into our experiences.

I was so involved in cherishing every amazingly blissful moment with my children and embracing every joyous moment of my life that I could barely keep up. The miracles just kept coming. Every day marked a new milestone for my girls, which made me genuinely appreciate all my mother had done for me. I finally had an idea of the depth of her love for me, because I had it for my girls. No words can honestly describe my connection with my mother, and now my daughters. It is love beyond the grasp of the human imagination, because the love is divine. There is no way to describe the depth of divine love. It is something that can only be felt firsthand.

Every time my mom visited us, I soaked up every minute I could get with her. She came to town every few months to work the psychic fair, where she used her abilities to offer invaluable guidance to help put others on a positive life-path trajectory. Her talents earned her the love and respect of her clients and colleagues alike. She was even featured in the newspaper for her contributions at the fair. The money she earned by helping people find direction in their lives paid for her visits to us and then some.

Some of the best memories with my girls are of going with Nana to the fair. From the time the girls were little, we went with Nana early on Saturday mornings to set up her table before the doors opened. We met all the cool psychic readers and the vendors of magical objects. My daughters were always the youngest people at the fair before the doors opened to the public. I think their presence in the early hours offered a message of light, reminding the older mystics of the magic of childhood.

My girls loved looking at all the goodies from the many different shops represented there. They loved having the first look at the merchandise. Usually, by the time the doors opened, Nana had already bought them each a fabulous little gift to keep and treasure. Sometimes the vendors would give the girls gifts too. They were so cute and fascinated by everything around them—who could have resisted? They never left a fair without some sort of crystal or magical item. They now have an extensive collection of mystical objects from those times at the fair with Nana. Each item carries with it a cherished memory of childhood magic and of Nana, who brought the magic to us. We always enjoyed our time together. It was unique and special. I mean, how many kids are raised around psychics, mystics, and shamans? Back then, there weren't many, which made that part of the experience more incredible.

Having my mom in proximity was the best feeling for me. There's nothing like a mother's hug. I missed her so much when she was gone that I often secretly wished she lived closer to us. I never said anything to her

The Messages of Light

about it, but I used my happy magic. Instead of looking at the fact that she lived so far away, I focused on the joy of seeing her several times a year and the fun we had when we did. And wouldn't you know it?? The power of magnetic attraction kicked in.

One day, during our regular morning telephone call, my mom had a special request. She'd decided she would move closer to her granddaughters and me, and she asked for my help in finding an apartment. I couldn't believe it. I was so elated and thrilled that I did a crazily spastic "Thank you, God" dance and went straight to work. My mom wasn't in a hurry, but I was.

I looked for a long while. I emailed her pictures and listings, but she was taking her time.

Looking at apartments all over the city helped me to appreciate where we lived. Ron, the girls, and I lived in a beautiful home in a quiet neighborhood with a stunning view of the city. I loved our house, which was probably why the next creation manifested so quickly. After a while of studying the Abraham-Hicks teachings, I was inspired to dream again, just for the fun of it. What do you do when all your dreams are coming true? Dream another dream! You stunt your spiritual growth when you don't dream and flow in divine energy. So dream!

I decided to put my skills to the test again. On my walks, I daydreamed. It couldn't hurt, right? I pictured every detail of our new home, and I mentally designed how I would feel to live there. I never had a clue how it would happen, but I thought it was worth a try. The energetic pull of my thoughts worked for everything else, right? Why not this?

As I was perfecting my technique, I noticed that while I was visualizing, I would get caught up in worrying about how this dream home would manifest. What a silly thing to worry about when your current home is already great! That thinking pattern always caused me to have anxiety, and I knew that feeling was God telling me that my focus was off target. So I practiced creating the new home in my mind without worrying about how it would come about. I just envisioned our little family in a place of our own. I didn't talk about it. I just spent time daily daydreaming about it. I imagined building a house from the ground up. I visualized lofty ceilings and big picture windows streaming with light.

The vision was so clear I could smell the sawdust. I envisioned being so close to nature that I could see wildlife running through the yard. I also saw myself standing on a balcony at night, looking at the sparkling sea of lights coming from the homes below. I was sitting there with Ron, enjoying the fantastic view. The vision was so real that I could feel the cool night air on my skin. I imagined this home would be away from the main roads and have a private entrance with trees lining the path to my door. It was far-fetched, but I dreamed anyway because it was fun. Of course, at the end of every daydream, I added the prayer asking for the highest and best good for myself and all concerned.

The next thing I knew, out of the blue, my father-in-law and mother-in-law invited us to lunch, and the magic began to manifest. They gave us a message of light, a miracle opportunity. At that lunch, my in-laws gave us a chance to build our own house from the ground up at cost. Can you believe it? I was shocked.

How did that transpire? Long story short, after working with NASA to put a man on the moon, Mr. Conde started his own civil engineering firm back in 1971, and it is still around today. When he retired from Conde Inc., his kids took over the company. His daughter, Yvonne, followed in her father's footsteps and became a civil engineer, so she took over the engineering department. My husband, Ron, being a registered professional land surveyor, took over the land-surveying department. Conrad, the youngest son, took over the business and financial aspects of the company. Tony, the oldest son, was the company's legal representative. I found it remarkable that each of them fit so perfectly together in their roles to maintain the legacy of the successful business when Mr. C. retired.

When I say Mr. Conde retired, I mean he retired from one company and started another, designing and building homes. That was where the offer came in. He already lived in the subdivision he was developing, but Mr. C. wanted his family close. What parent doesn't? So he found a lot in the subdivision and designed a building plan he thought we would love. Then he offered them to us. This was a chance to build a brand-new home. Can you say *miracle*? I wished for a new place of my own, and boom—it was on the way!

The opportunity was nothing if not divine, because right before that life-changing lunch date with my in-laws, my mom found a place she liked.

Can you believe it was right around the corner from the location of the home we were about to build?

Before I knew it, I was living in a beautiful home in a peaceful neighborhood with a breathtaking view of the city. It had a private entrance and trees lining the path to our house. It was everything I'd imagined, only assembled differently. It was more magical than anything I'd dreamed, and as a bonus, it was within walking distance from my mother's new apartment. I was living everything I'd envisioned, and it was definitely for the highest and best good for everyone concerned.

You tell me: Was it a creation, coincidence, or miracle? My mind was telling me I'd created that with the magnetic pull of my thoughts, and my heart was saying it was the miracle of prayer. Either way, let's just say I don't believe in coincidence any longer.

Reconciling Beliefs

After having experienced so many miracles, I lived in a fluffy cloud of love and faith. I began to contemplate how the information I absorbed from Abraham-Hicks and my Reiki training would fit my God-centered belief system. How would I explain my beliefs to my girls? How could I share what I believed, when I was not yet clear on that myself? Where should I start?

As you know, I am a God girl, a major fan of the Big Guy. So that was where I started: with God at the center of my vision. When Abraham-Hicks talked about Source energy, I always assumed they were talking about God. God is the Creator of all things. He is the Source of the energy that creates life. Still, I wanted confirmation that they were actually talking about God when they referred to Source.

So what happened next? It should be no surprise that I instantly got precisely what I was looking for. I heard the message of light on the next Abraham-Hicks tape to which I listened. Coincidentally, someone in the audience of the recorded gathering asked why Abraham never talked about God. Abraham's response was "We speak of nothing else."

At that moment, my theory was confirmed: it was *all* about God. I began to connect the dots. I was overcome by a wave of emotion. A verse of scripture popped into my head, and I realized that the power of magnetic attraction is even in the Bible. The three main components to manifesting are asking, believing, and receiving.

> If you believe, you will receive whatever you ask for in prayer.
> —Matthew 21:22 NIV

With a new enthusiasm, I decided to continue my exploration of the information offered by Jerry and Esther Hicks and how it connected to all I believed about God.

There was much more I wanted to know. I began to read and listen to anything I could get my hands on that would offer more insight. I continued to listen to Abraham-Hicks, but I also began to read countless books on spirituality, ranging from books on kabbalah, alchemy, Wicca, and animal totems to books on dream interpretation, numerology, and tarot. When I say I began to read these books, that's exactly what I mean; I don't think I actually finished more than a chapter in each book. I was fascinated by the wisdom traditions and the medicine associated with the many diverse cultures and belief systems I was learning about. But there were so many areas to explore that I got overwhelmed. After careful consideration and prayer, I established in my heart that everything I studied was leading me to develop my own truth. It's all God! The energy that creates life, love, light, beauty, and miracles—it's God. It is all God. No matter what belief system I studied, the energy being described felt like God to me. See? This empath thing is pretty cool!

I decided to put the books down and focus on mastering the information I thought would be most useful to me in my work and my life. I chose the tools that would help me with healing and creating. I decided to practice flowing God's love and healing energy with the Reiki, and I chose to create the life of my dreams with the magnetic energy of my thoughts and emotions.

PART 2
Application: Using the Gifts of the Empath

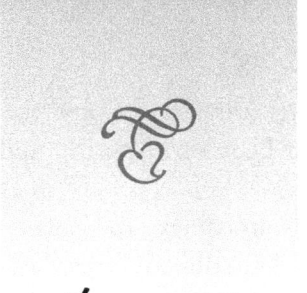

Chapter 11

The Messages of Light

Learning to Listen

I felt such a powerful connection to God and the energy I experienced when I was in communion with him that I wanted to savor it. I wanted to document all the miracles to recall them as new whenever I felt a need for inspiration. When you experience such a flow of miracles, the feeling is surreal. It's like living in a dream. I was in constant awe. Who wouldn't have been after all I had seen and experienced? I could feel God's divine presence within me and all around me.

I think it was the constant focus on God that caused the shift. The miracles and the awe I experienced from them made me feel a deep personal connection with God. We had a relationship, and I loved that, but I wanted more. I wanted to learn to hear God when he whispered the answers to my questions. I wanted to develop a two-way line of communication with God.

I continued to do what I had been doing, meditating and praying, but with a different intent this time. Before then, my meditations and prayers had focused on creating things in the physical world, sort of like an alchemist. I wanted to be a nurse. Poof! I was a nurse. I wanted to be married to a good man. Poof! I married Ron. I wanted a home for our family that hadn't been someone else's first. Poof! We built our own house. And so on. Now my focus or intent for my meditations and prayers was no longer only about creating things in the physical. I was creating something spiritual. I could feel God's presence with my empathic abilities, and I could easily see his miracles. I noted the coincidences that were orchestrated by God, but I couldn't hear his guidance directly. I couldn't hear the whisper.

I determined what I wanted next: to hear the whisper again. I wanted to receive the messages of light directly from the Source. So I did my usual thing. I went outside for my walks, and this time, when I prayed, I asked to receive communication from God.

It took time. I had to practice quieting my mind so that I could hear or perceive the communication when it did come to me. I had to learn to listen instead of talking over it.

When it happened, it was as if a switch flipped in my brain, and the information suddenly began to flow. Of course, that switch would flip while I was walking outside. I was doing my regular meditation. I was praying and feeling blessed. I was contemplating God, life, love, and anything and everything good all at once. Eventually, I calmed the internal chatter of my mind and focused on my breathing. It was just me and the sound of my breath moving in a rhythm like the waves of the ocean. I just listened to it, allowing myself to be lulled into a feeling of contentment. Then I felt a whoosh of serenity cushioning me as the energy began to flow. I recognized the sensation. I'd experienced it many times before, most recently as the cloud of comfort that had surrounded me during Aja's birth. That was when it happened: I heard the whisper clearly in my deaf ear. That was the moment when I actually began to hear the messages of light.

Direct Communication: The First Transcribed Messages of Light

This is where I shift gears. Until that point, the messages of light had come from feelings brought on by circumstances and events in my life or from messengers of light, angels in human form.

I was just becoming aware of being an empath. I was learning about my spiritual muscle and what it could do. I was getting pretty clear on the idea that God had made me sensitive to energy and emotion on purpose. I recognized my emotions for the communications they were. I began to use my focused thoughts to create powerful emotions that would magnetically draw to me the life I wanted to live.

Once I was living in the life of my choosing and flowing in faith, I began to use the gift differently. Suddenly, every thought and emotion, every empathic experience I lived, became the source of a powerful question I would ask. Once I learned to do what all of us have the natural capacity to do—hear God's whisper again—I rarely had to look for context clues from my emotions to receive guidance. I could ask a question and receive the answer in real time. People around me continued to be messengers of light, relaying messages of love and guidance from God when I was busy talking over the whisper. But for the most part, I was getting the messages straight from the Source, God. Once the switch on my two-way radio with God was flipped to the on position, I was blown away. The spiritual muscle I had been strengthening for so long, my empathic muscle, was finally strong enough to receive guidance clearly. I was excited to have access to this connection, because I had many questions I wanted to ask. It was as if I had my own internet search bar, with the Source of information being God. I suddenly had access to any information I was ready and willing to hear regarding my contemplations. That was so thrilling that I asked every question that came into my mind and wrote down every answer I received in my trusty spiral notebooks.

The answers came to me in a flash of information. It was like a download on a computer. The transfer of information took a fraction of a second, but the files were enormous, so when I translated the brief flash of information into writing, it took me quite some time to transcribe what I got into my spiral notebooks. It still blows my mind that so much information can be transferred to the human consciousness in such a brief time.

In these messages, it seemed as if God were speaking to me and sharing the wisdom of the ages. I asked a question, and the answer that fit my situation and belief system came through. When I started receiving the information, I thought of all the other people who might have questions similar to mine and might also benefit from reading the information, so I wrote the messages in the context of *we* because I felt God was talking to everyone willing to receive the information, not just me. Also, I wrote them in that context because it is the easiest way for me to stay in the flow of receiving and writing.

The stories will continue on from here, but the messages of light are more than quick minibursts of inspiration. Instead, they are an actual flow of information written in essay form. You will notice that the messages of light I transcribed begin with the concept or question I contemplated and are followed by my translation or interpretation of the information I was given. Also, the messages themselves are indented and set apart from here on out, so you can't miss them.

I was focused on God when I first heard the whisper, so naturally, my contemplations at that time in my life also centered on God and our relationship with him. The messages of light I received and transcribed were always direct answers to questions I asked or thoughts I reflected upon. Sometimes the messages led to miracles, and in other cases, the messages were the miracles. I never could guess which one it would be. You just never know how it will go. God is full of surprises!

Next, dear reader, I will share with you some of the messages of light I received and transcribed when I was first learning to sense and interpret them. They are answers to questions I developed throughout my life experiences as an empath. Maybe they are similar to questions you have been asking as well. Read on to see.

About God and Love

Who doesn't wonder about God and love? When I was growing up and exploring all the churches I could find, I was presented with various perspectives on God. The differing views ranged from the concept of a vengeful God who judges and punishes sinners to a God who loves his children no matter what. I often pondered the conflicting views, and one day, while I was walking and wondering about the true nature of God, I received the following message:

> God is love, and so are we. We become instruments of God
> when we surrender our conscious thoughts and beliefs.
> When we let go and just let ourselves be, when we allow

ourselves naturally to flow in our authentic vibration, we discover that we are love.

We can choose to subscribe to the illusion that there is an absence of love in our world, but there is not. We may delude ourselves into thinking we do not deserve love, but of course, we do. Love is our birthright. We can choose to look at all the fabricated illusions that elicit fear and anger if we want, but in doing so, we opt out of the experience of the beauty of love in our world.

The good news is that love always exists, even when we choose to prevent it from coming into our experience with our focus on fear. There is no absence of love, only the lack of attention to it. There is no opposite of love either. Light and dark are opposites. Sadness and happiness are opposites. Fear and faith are opposites. Hate is not the opposite of love; it is a variation of fear. Love is complete. Love does not need anything to make it whole. Therefore, when we choose to let ourselves just be (love), we are whole (holy).

And so, we know and rely on the love God has for us. God is love. Whoever lives in love lives in God, and God in them.
—1 John 4:16 NIV

Getting Close to God

As you know, my spiritual quest has always been about God. Now that I had the opportunity to learn answers straight from the Source, you bet I was ready to ask the question I'd contemplated my whole life: "How do we become closer to God?"

Have faith.
Ask a simple question, and get a simple answer.
The fact is that when we trust God, we feel closer to him. When we are fearful or doubtful, we pull ourselves away from the experience of his love. Have the faith of a

child! Children are connected to God. They remain close to God, and they are filled with divine energy. Children are trusting. They have a natural flowing affection. Small children are not afraid of rejection. They don't hold back in fear of getting hurt. They share love and hugs freely. Children are eager to do things to make themselves and others happy. They smile, they laugh, they sing, they dance, they explore, and they play. They don't worry about the opinions of others or about tomorrow. Children are naturally in a state of now-moment peaceful bliss. Joy is their default mode. Children experience the kind of happiness that comes directly from knowing God. Their world is not a cold, cruel place because God's world is not. Only when we choose to take our attention from God and place it in fear does the world become that place for us.

We will see beauty when we have faith like a child and put that faith in God. We will dance and sing. We will give love freely and be open and willing to receive love in return. We will experience miracles, and we will participate in them. We will be close to God, and we will be happy. When we trust God, we know that everything is exactly as it should be. Having faith like a child will bring us to the love, peace, and happiness that God is waiting to give us. We must let the child who dwells inside each of us be our guide to the joy that flows from faith.

> And a little child will lead them.
> —Isaiah 11:6 NIV

> And he said: "Truly I tell you, unless you change and become like little children, you will never enter the kingdom of heaven."
> —Matthew 18:3 NIV

Children and Faith

At that point in my life, I liked to hear what my guidance (God) had to say about children. I loved watching my daughters in carefree, imaginative play. I noticed they had a natural tendency to live in confidence and courage as they explored their world. I thought about how open and trusting children were and wondered, *How do children remain so close to God in faith?* The answer was the following:

> They have not yet been taught otherwise.
>
> Children believe what they are told, because they have no reason for disbelief. When we say to our children we love them, they trust that. When we tell them God loves them, they believe that as well. When we tell them they can do anything they set their minds to, they can. When we tell them that they are here to make the world a better place, they will because they believe it is true. Children already know this truth at the core of their being.
>
> We all learn through life experience. Through this life experience, children will learn to doubt and mistrust. When they hear, "You can't do that! It's impossible," the words put a cloud of doubt on their faith because they believe what they are told. Because of the adults around children and the beliefs those adults carry with them, children must learn to process the conflicting information between what they know through faith and what they are told. If the disturbing information comes from someone they love and trust, they become even more confused. This opens the door in their young, malleable minds to fear and doubt. The children who once believed that all things are possible don't know what to think. So they move forward in doubt.
>
> They say, "I can't."
>
> Why? Because someone told them they couldn't.
>
> They say, "I'm afraid."

Why? Because someone told them they should be afraid.

When children come into this life experience, they are eager to explore. They learn millions of things in a day, and their curiosity never tires. They go through life with a passion and a joy for all there is to see. They want to do everything. They look for what interests them and excites them, and they enjoy those things!

How many children say they want to be an astronaut, a firefighter, a movie star, a scientist, a ballet dancer, a singer, or even president of the United States? These dreams are real to them and are absolutely possible. Why do we squelch that desire? Because we, who have had our own wishes destroyed by doubt and fear, believe it is not possible. Why not encourage them? Don't give our children a realistic backup plan; give them a great start-up plan beginning with faith in God. Remind them of their inner strength and their abilities that are amplified by that connection with God.

Help our children create a world of love and peace where anything is possible. It all starts at home, and it's never too late.

On Trusting God in the Real World

As I continued to ask questions and transcribe the answers, I went deeper. I asked more complex questions. We all know that life is not always fun or easy. I specifically thought about all the disasters and tragedies in the world (this was not long after 9/11). I wanted to know where God was in all that. I wanted to know how to feel and experience faith when the world tells you to be afraid or distraught. What do we do then? I asked, "Where is God in a world filled with strife?"

> God is in all of creation. There is good in every experience on God's earth. This world is perfectly balanced, but

sometimes our human existence comes with a limited view. From our egocentric human perspective of the world, it is difficult to see the miracles in the madness. The pain and fear we experience become the forces distracting us from the good that occurs in challenging or traumatic situations. But make no mistake: the good is there! God is there! Even in tragedy, you will find God ever-present in those people helping the unfortunate. You will notice that there is always a massive outpouring of love when something devastating happens. We see God not in the devastation of the disaster but in the love that is amplified in the humans involved as a result. In fearful situations, God is in the person providing comfort to another. God is the person who knows the exact right thing to say to boost the morale of the downtrodden. For those in pain, God is the promise of relief. God is in the expansion resulting from every lesson learned by every one of his children. When we experience difficulties, God is the force creating the equal and opposite vibration of bliss to be had. We must simply trust God and look for the positive perspective, and it will be revealed.

> Ask and it will be given to you; seek and you will find;
> knock and the door will be opened to you.
> —Matthew 7:7 NIV

On God and the Universe

I spent a lot of time contemplating God and the universe. At first, I thought they were one and the same. I thought *universe* was another way to reference God, like calling him *Source energy*. The idea that God and the universe were the same caused me great confusion. I heard people refer to the universe as a personal assistant many times. That reference caused me to feel distressed. How can the Creator of all things be reduced to something as small as my own personal assistant? It didn't seem right.

Then I heard someone else refer to the universe as a personal benefactor. That felt a little better, but it still didn't fit my belief system entirely. I contemplated this concept one day on my walk, and this is what I got:

God and the Universe

> God and the universe are not the same. The universe is a system that God created to help us navigate free will. Think about it. God is big on systems. Everything he has created runs on highly efficient systems. Starting with humans. Everything in our bodies that keeps us alive runs on systems. We have a cardiovascular system, endocrine system, respiratory system, digestive system, etc. Our world has an ecosystem, and it is part of a more extensive solar system. Again, God is clearly big on systems, so it makes perfect sense that God would create a method by which we can navigate our free will. The universe is that system, and the law of magnetic attraction is the science behind it.

That made perfect sense to me. God gave us the gift of life and the gift of free will. He put us on this magical planet to create and add to all that is. We are here to experience the wonder that comes from exploring this world through our free will. Of course God would create a system to help us navigate it. The universe is that system. To activate it, we only have to ask, believe, and be openhearted and open-minded enough to receive what we've asked for, just as Jesus said. Once we know how the science behind the system works, free will can actually be fun. Now when I say the universe is my personal assistant, it feels good. I feel as if God assigned me a magical assistant. My assistant reads my thoughts, notes my words, and works efficiently behind the scenes to help me realize my own version of heaven on earth.

Practice

As the weeks and months passed, I continued practicing my process of walking outside and talking to God while I was there. The messages were flowing, and I wrote down every single one with a fervor I had never felt before. I was in awe of the words coming through me, and I felt humbled by the energy behind them. Don't worry, dear reader; I promise I will get back to our story soon. My adventures were just beginning, and there are many more miracles to speak of. But first, a few more messages from our Sponsor. Ha! Ha! I just had to say that! God is indeed the Sponsor of all that is good in the world, and the universe he created allows us access to that good.

On Energy

Over the years, learning about the power of magnetic attraction gave me a basic understanding of energy and how it works. Of course, I wanted to know more. Now that I could ask God, the Source of all energy, about it, I did. I wondered how we as humans experience energy in the physical world. I admit I wasn't super specific when I asked the question "What is energy?" so the answer that came was a surprise. I asked a big question that scientists have spent lifetimes trying to understand and explain. With such a broad and open-ended question, God narrowed it down for me and gave me what applied to my life and my level of understanding.

> Energy is the common thread that connects us all, one to another and to our Creator. It is the creative life force that flows to and through everything. An important thing to remember is that we are all made up of energy, and this energy originates from a source of love.
>
> Energy continually flows. It never stops. It is recognized as a vibration. It can vibrate at a high, fast level; a low, slow level; or anywhere in between.
>
> We perceive vibration as emotion. The emotions we experience are based on both where we are vibrating (high and fast or low and slow) and what we are focused

on while we are there. Some people experience the high, fast vibration as excitement or exhilaration. Others may experience that same high, fast vibration and become overwhelmed and call it anxiety. Let's just put it this way: some people like to fly, and others may be afraid of heights. It's all a matter of perspective.

The slower, lower vibration is often misconstrued as bad or negative. This is not necessarily the case. While some might experience a slower or lower feeling as if it is sadness or depression, another might view that same vibration as grounding and peaceful. Some kids like to play in the mud, while others feel they're stuck in it.

It's all a matter of perspective. It's not about high or low vibration as much as it is about whether the experience feels positive or negative, good or bad. Our focus determines our experience of reality. So whether we vibrate high and fast or low and slow, we can be happy if we choose our focus well.

Where attention goes, energy flows.

There is no benefit to the greater good in thinking about all the terrible things in the world. When we think about the world's problems, we add to the negative vibration with our own, essentially fueling the problems as they grow. Why amplify the world's negative energy by adding to it our own negativity? Why make it worse? We should be focusing our attention and, therefore, our energy on finding solutions to those problems and being of service in executing those solutions.

We create a positive energetic vibration when we think about our desires. We have access to new vision in the flow of that positive energy. We then amplify the vibration of the good we envision by our attention to it, bringing the idea to life.

When we believe that there is nothing we can do or that there is no good to be found, we must recognize that those thoughts are illusions pulling us into a current of negative energetic vibration.

There is always something we can do! We can always give it to God. We can always pray to raise our energetic vibrations. When we do, we can recognize the good that is found in the love that inspired that prayer in the first place.

On Prayer and Vibration

Oh boy, prayer and energy! What? Well, of course prayer would affect our energetic vibration. That makes sense. Right? I started thinking about the previous message. I began to wonder how prayer and our energetic vibration were linked. Until that moment, I'd assumed prayer would always raise our vibration, but the more I thought about it, the more confused I was. I knew many people who prayed a lot but were miserable anyway. The empath in me could feel it. So maybe I wasn't really clear on how prayer changes our energy. I went for a walk, and I asked another question: "How does prayer affect our energetic vibration?"

> Prayer is precious. When you ask and believe, you will receive! It is crucial, especially in contemplation with God, to place our attention on those thoughts that feel best. We can effectively raise our vibration to one of connection and peace through prayer, but we must pray in the positive. When we pray with love and trust, we feel good. The way we feel is direct communication from God. When a particular thought or contemplation makes us feel good, the elevated emotion we experience is God telling us that what we are focused upon is aligned with our desires. The emotion is God telling us that we are in a vibrational current that will bring us to more opportunities to love and trust. Conversely, our minds immediately conjure more things to fear when we pray in fear. It's the power of vibrational attraction. The good news is, God is there within us, warning us of the miscreation. We feel anxiety

when we are vibrationally flowing in opposition to our highest and best good. That anxiety is God telling us that what we are looking at or how we are looking at it is not aligned with our highest good.

Ignoring that guidance from God and continuing to think fearfully is like being at a fork in a river. Instead of choosing the direction that is easy-flowing and enjoyably free of obstacles, we choose the direction that is full of raging waters, sudden drops, rocks, pitfalls, and perils that can only lead to more things to fear. Both streams end in the ocean, but one is a more enjoyable way to get there. In other words, all prayer leads to miracles, but there is a more peaceful way to obtain them.

For example, it feels better to pray, "God, please help my day run smoothly," than to pray, "Please don't let anything bad happen today."

The first prayer raises the energetic vibration. God sends us the positive emotion to confirm that the prayer offered a vibration in alignment with the highest and best good of all concerned. The second thought process lowers the vibration, hence the negative emotion we experience as we pray in this manner.

The first prayer asks for what is wanted, not what is feared. The vibration of the prayer is one of love and harmony, and that is the energy it amplifies. In the second prayer, which asks that nothing bad will happen, the energy of the prayer is actually negative. Our attention is on the fear of the bad things that may occur. The universe created by God to help us navigate free will offers more thoughts about the possible bad things that may happen, because that is the vibration we chose with our prayer.

Luckily, most things we fear never happen, but in the meantime, we have, unfortunately, even in the moment of prayer, lived our fears internally. Because the person is praying that nothing bad will happen, it might not. But by praying this way, nothing good will happen internally either. The vibrational pull of that prayer will just bring in more thoughts and experiences at that lower vibration and evoke a sense of fear or exhaustion because that is what the prayer felt like. That is the vibration we chose with our free will.

On Prayer and Selfishness

When I was a kid, I prayed about everything and pretty much for everything I wanted. When I got older, I was taught the idea of selfishness. Someone told me that God had more important things to do than help me get good grades and that praying for myself was selfish. I was taught to think that if I somehow had my prayer answered, I would be taking a miracle away from someone else. I'd had no idea! Obviously, I wanted God to have time to deal with more important things, so I started leaving my wishes for myself out of the equation and began to pray only for other people.

Then, after years of my feeling selfish for praying for myself when I was younger, Abraham-Hicks sent out a message of light that made me feel a little better. They said that being selfish in our requests was not only OK but was a key component in manifestation. They said we should focus on what we want to create for ourselves, because we cannot manifest in someone else's reality. We cannot create for someone else, and others cannot create for us.

The Abraham-Hicks perspective felt better to me than the concept of selflessness that said I should ignore my own wishes. But I still didn't fully understand how it was OK to be selfish. So I pondered the concept of selfishness and prayer, and interestingly, the answer was about free will. I asked, "Should we pray for ourselves?"

> When we pray, we usually pray only for others. We can and should pray for others. To pray for someone else is a beautiful gift of support and love. Still, it is up to that individual to choose to accept God's intervention because of free will. When we surround someone with enough love-filled prayer, some of the love will eventually seep into his or her consciousness. Enough prayer can even

inspire the individual to welcome God's aid. So we should continue to pray for others and be joyous that we can.

How often do we pray for ourselves? Society taught many of us that praying for ourselves is wrong or selfish. To those who taught us, it was their truth. They believed God should spend his time and effort on those who really need it, and I agree.

But I ask you: Who doesn't need God?

God is omnipresent—he is everywhere at once. He can help all who ask for intervention at any time. He is unlimited. God is beyond time and space; therefore, time is not a relevant factor to God. Free will, however, is a factor to God. He created it. He gave us the gift of life, and he gave us the gift of choice. He created the universe, a perfectly designed system to help us navigate free will. God is efficient. The universe is set up so that all prayers get answered. This is how it works. The universe responds to our vibration and draws the focus of our attention to us. When we pray, the prayer is answered at the moment of the asking. Our vibration instantly shifts to a vibration equivalent to the focus of our prayer. The universe that God created lines up circumstances and events in the vibrational flow that will help the miracle we prayed for to happen. We can and should choose to ask for God's intervention on our behalf. We are free beings in the magical world of free will God created for us.

When we pray for ourselves, miracles happen because we are already accepting God's intervention with our free will. When we pray for ourselves, we choose to give God, who exists inside each of us, the power in our lives. When we pray for ourselves and trust that God's will is being done, we are open to receiving the magic of miracles. God's will is filled with more beauty and light than we can imagine.

Why not pray for ourselves? Why not ask for happiness? Each of us touches the lives of many others.

When we are happy, we can pass that on. We all know that anger and frustration are contagious. How many of us stop to realize that a smile or kindness can be too? A smile is like a single drop of rain on an undisturbed pond. The ripple effect spreads itself outward. Besides, we can do kind and loving things more easily when we are happy than when we are not. So why not spread love, kindness, and happiness? Why not start with praying for the people we spend the most time with—ourselves?

> Therefore, I tell you, whatever you ask for in prayer,
> believe that you have received it and it will be yours.
> —Mark 11:24 NIV

Thoughts and Prayer

With my attention focused on prayer, I began to contemplate the connection between the power of magnetic attraction and prayer. Abraham-Hicks talked about choosing our words mindfully and also about intentionally choosing the direction of our thoughts. I wondered why our thoughts were so crucial to our vibration and manifestations. Then I got a burst of intuition that fit my belief system. The information felt right to me, and this is what I transcribed:

> All thoughts are prayers! Every time we think a thought, who are we thinking it to? The answer is the silent observer inside us: God, who dwells within. So every thought we think is essentially a conversation with God. When we think in fear, we are praying in fear. Fear is the opposite of faith. So we must be mindful of our thoughts. God answers every prayer because of his promise to us of free will. When we pray in fear, the result is a feeling that matches the vibration of the prayer, alerting us to our potential miscreation. So we should not only learn to pray in the positive but also think positive thoughts because all thoughts are prayers. God doesn't select which

thoughts he hears or which prayers he answers. He hears and answers them all in response to the vibration of the prayer we offer. When we are mindful of the thoughts we choose to think, we access the magic of miracles. When we think happy thoughts, those thoughts are like prayers asking God for more happy thoughts to think, and we receive them. Our thoughts are the silent prayers that design our realities. Thoughts translate into vibration, and vibration manifests into physical reality through the power of vibrational attraction. The thoughts we think are the prayers we offer, and because of free will, this is how either magic or madness is born.

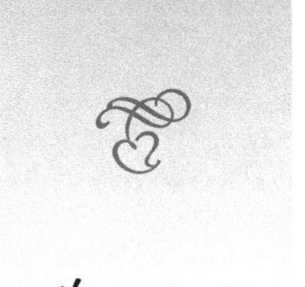

Chapter 12

Wait—Is This Real?

The Sign

As you can see, the messages were coming to me quickly and powerfully. I was on a roll. I was hearing God's whisper and beginning to actually channel information. Then I thought about it: *I am talking to God and hearing answers. That's not normal.*

What would people think? I know what I would have thought back then if someone had boldly said that he or she talked to God and that God talked back. I saw the movie *Dear God* starring George Burns when I was a little kid, and it taught me that people will think you're crazy, just as they did in that movie and in every other film of the kind.

I wasn't 100 percent sure I wasn't a little crazy myself. I didn't talk about what I was doing with anyone other than my mom. I was afraid of being judged. After a while, I began to wonder if it was all in my head. Knowing what so-called normal people might have said about me and my talking to God, I doubted. I started questioning whether it was really all just in my mind.

So what did I do? I asked a question. I went for a walk outside and asked, "Lord, is this really you?"

The answer that came with a feeling was a quick but peaceful *Yes*.

Keep in mind I'm a registered nurse and well educated on the symptoms of mental illness, so hearing the whisper, a voice inside my head, did not seem like the reassurance I needed at that moment. So I asked for a sign.

I remember it as clearly as if it were yesterday. I was on the downhill side of my walk, and I prayed, *OK, Lord, if these messages are really from you, please show me a sign. I would really like some sort of confirmation to help me keep the faith.*

God has an incredible sense of humor, because just then, at that moment, I heard a thunderous rumbling sound. I heard it even with my headphones blasting music. Naturally, I turned to see what was making the noise. I saw a big white truck. The fact that the truck causing the thunderous sound was white could have been my sign. White represents God energy. But that wasn't it.

God loves to prove himself, so when we ask for signs, we get them. Some signs are subtle, and some are loud and clear, like the sign I got next. The white truck that came rumbling down the hill at the exact moment I asked for a sign was carrying—get this—signs. The enormous white vehicle cradled a few of our local green street signs in the truck's bed. I asked for a sign, and God sent me a sign all right—a street sign! Gotta love it.

This could still be construed as a coincidence. I thought as much at the moment, even as I appreciated the comedy of the timing. The coincidence got to be too much to ignore because the name on the one street sign I could read was Burning Tree.

Didn't Moses talk to God through a burning tree?

At that moment, I thought, *Holy cow!* and the sentiment was correct. This was something holy all right! I'd asked God for a sign to prove he was sending the messages, and he'd sent me a street sign labeled Burning Tree. Of all the street names in the city, Burning Tree was the name on the sign I saw in the back of that truck?

Overcome with emotion, I began to do my strange laugh-cry thing I do when I am overwhelmed with awe. It was undeniable evidence that God was right there with me in that moment, showering me with grace and love. He gave me the definite proof I needed—and with a lovely, humorous flair—at the exact moment I asked for a sign. It was quite an experience. I'd lived on that side of town for many years, but I had never before seen a street named Burning Tree. Was that a coincidence? I think not. It was an unmistakable message of light.

As if that weren't enough to confirm that the sign I'd received was from God, years later, while I was revisiting this story in order to write it, one of my Reiki students and dear friends, Cindy, randomly sent me an inspirational message. In it was the following quote from the Bible: "As I was with Moses, so I will be with you. I will never leave you nor forsake you" (Joshua 1:5 NIV).

Holy moly! I choose to believe there is no such thing as a coincidence. I choose to believe the street sign was direct communication from God at the exact moment of my asking. I am still in awe. When I think about the number of circumstances and events that lined up to make that truck arrive on that hill carrying a street sign for Burning Tree on the exact day and moment when I asked for a sign from God that he was talking to me, I am blown away. Then, years later, I "randomly" got that confirmation again through a messenger of light at the precise time I was writing this story. To me, that's a miracle! It allowed me access to my faith, and I felt a more profound truth resonating within me. It prompted me to ask about the truth. I figured I might as well, right?

Finding Truth

How can we recognize what is true?

In our quest for spiritual growth, we will come in contact with new information, and sometimes this information is confusing. Just as we are equipped with a means of communication with God through our emotions, we are also provided with a method of deciding what is valid for our own individual belief system and what is not. Again, we only have to pay attention to how we feel. Those same emotions serve to guide us and keep us on track to our highest and best good. Also, they tell us if the information with which we come in contact resonates with our unique purpose and belief system or not.

We each have our own individual life experiences. Each experience is different from the experience of every other person on the planet. There are no two people on the planet who live the exact same life, just as there are no two people on earth who are here for the exact same purpose. We are as unique and individual as snowflakes. Even twins have different life experiences and are here for distinct reasons. Each of us intends to serve the greater good in our own way. Sometimes our purposes are similar, but they are never exactly the same. Therefore, what is true for you may not necessarily be true for another. This is as it should be.

> There is no "The" in front of Truth.
> —Robin Lynne

An effortless way to determine if the information is truth for you is this: measure it with your heart.

If it feels as if it is coming from a source of love and light, your energy rises, and you feel lighter. You feel comforted, and you know the information is from God and is right for you and your purpose. When you feel this, it's as if God is saying, "Yes! You are right on track to fulfilling your life's mission."

If it feels like fear, anger, or ugliness or if it's heavy or binding, your energy level will drop to discomfort. That is how you know it is not suitable for your highest purpose. When we feel bad during our contemplations, it's as if God is saying, "Either what you're looking at or the way you are looking at it is not for your highest and best good."

For example, if a child says that he or she gets a terrible feeling when thinking of going to school, in this instance, the guidance is not telling the child that school is not for his or her highest and best good. It is not saying to avoid school. Instead, the emotional guidance tells the child that the attitude he or she has chosen about school is not for his or her highest and best good. This guidance tells the child to find a new way to look at school and its experiences.

Our Purpose in Life

After reading the preceding message, I began to contemplate the deeper meaning of my existence. We all live our own truths, and I wondered if I was in touch with mine. It occurred to me that I never really asked what I was meant to do with my life, other than being a wife, mom, and nurse. I had no idea how to go about figuring that out. So I had to ask. I went on another of my walks, and I got the following information when I asked, "How do we discover our purpose in life?"

> Knowing and trusting that God's love is unconditional, we can go forward and fulfill our reason for being. Our purpose for this life was created in unity with God before we came here, when we were still one with God in universal consciousness. We designed our mission when we were still in full communication with God, well before we received our physical bodies. Therefore, God's purpose for us and our own intentions for this life are indeed one and the same. Because this purpose is formed in complete unity and alignment with God's energy, most would call this our "higher purpose," our reason for being. Simply put, it's what we came here to do with our lives.
>
> We knew our purpose before we came here to this life, but we forgot when we were born into our human bodies. It is part of the gift and extraordinary adventure of life to rediscover that purpose. Our life experiences will always guide us to that purpose, but we must learn to pay attention. Sometimes the illusions in life can be the reason we become distracted from our personal missions. Sometimes life experience can even be the reason we do not look for our purpose in the first place. We get caught in the trauma and drama of life. We allow fear, anxiety, and anger to cloud the light of God's love. That light is important because it illuminates the path to our purpose and fulfillment.

Because God's love is unconditional, we are free to do anything we choose. This is called free will. However, when we make choices that are not aligned with our higher purpose, we will find that a genuine sense of happiness somehow eludes us.

So we search.

We may look to others to fill our emotional gaps: "If I could only find the right relationship or friendship, I would be happy." When we reach out to others for completion, we will always find ourselves unsatisfied.

We may try reaching for material gain, thinking, *When I finally get that raise, car, or beautiful home, I will be happy.* This type of happiness is usually short-lived because the novelty of the new toy will eventually wear off. Then we find ourselves reaching and searching again.

To find our true happiness and peace, we should make choices that bring us closer to fulfilling our higher purpose.

How do we find that purpose? How do we remember?

Ask! To find our purpose in life, we need only to ask, be open, and listen through the silence. The answer will come.

When we ask God a question, he will respond. God will come to us with the answers we seek. We find the solutions in a whisper while sitting in silence. We hear them from a friend in a seemingly ordinary conversation. We feel them in the love and innocence of a child. He will send us our answers in any way we will receive them. No matter how he responds to us, the answer will come. It is up to us to be willing to accept it and to be observant enough to perceive it. We must connect the dots along the paths of our lives. Nothing is a coincidence. Everything is part of that design for the life we cocreated with God before we came here.

So we must take time to be still and receptive, have faith, and pay attention to life all around us. The answers to our prayers and our questions will come. They will continue to present themselves. They will be repeated over and over again if necessary until we understand. All we have to do is ask.

Chapter 13

Growth and Expansion

My Purpose

After receiving that message, I spent days contemplating it. There was so much to it. I even saw myself in it. I had been searching my whole life for something. I looked for it in other people, in churches, and in my work, but I never really knew what I was looking for. It wasn't until that message that I realized I wanted to know about my purpose in life. I wanted the sense of fulfillment of being on track.

So I got into my connected state by walking the hills of my neighborhood, and I asked, "What is my purpose in life? Why am I here?"

The response I got was so anticlimactic it was almost generic. I had to laugh out loud when I heard the whisper say, "You're here to bring more love and light into the world."

Well, duh, I thought, slightly annoyed, so I responded with another question: "Aren't we all here to do that?"

"Yes, each of you in your own way."

You can guess my next question: "Well, what's my way? How am I supposed to do that?"

"You're already doing it."

"Huh?" was my confused response.

That was where the conversation ended. I was getting frustrated, and because of that, I lost the connection. I couldn't hear the whisper anymore at that moment. All I could sense was humor, and it wasn't mine.

The Messages of Light

Later, after I relaxed a bit, I got another message of light that I found exceedingly helpful: "Regarding questions: The answers you receive are only as clear as the questions you ask."

That message left me plenty to contemplate and just in time for my birthday. This brings us back to my birthday all those years ago, to the beginning of this story.

It was the evening of my thirty-second birthday. I was sitting in my living room, reading and listening to my girls playing happily together, when I had a vision of a brilliant and beautiful sunrise. I knew it was calling me to a new beginning. The vision was calling me to my purpose. Just the day before, I had been contemplating my purpose, but my frustration had broken the connection, so I couldn't hear the answer. But that day, on my birthday, the energy of happiness overrode my frustration. I felt connected and peaceful. That was when the vision of the sunrise came to me. That was when I heard the whisper answering my still somewhat scattered and ill-defined questions. I had been asking how to share the messages of light I was collecting, and I wanted to know how to fulfill my purpose in life. That was when I heard, "Write! Write your story."

Once I got past questioning why anyone would want to read my story and got into the actual writing of it, the real adventures began. I use the term *adventure* instead of the term *struggle* because I'm trying to keep the narrative upbeat here.

Everything started off great. I was focused on my mission. I was excited and found myself eager to begin. After all, I had been writing the messages for some time, and I felt I was getting good at that. I thought, *It should be easy to write my story, especially considering I'm the one who lived it. Right?* Well, when I started to write my story, things got complicated.

I felt as if my life were going haywire because of my mission. As I wrote about my experiences, I noticed my mind went directly to the painful times of my youth. I found myself experiencing all the hurt and uncertainty associated with those times as I wrote about them. I agonized over that. I wanted this book, my story, to positively impact my life and the lives of others. What was coming out of me and onto the paper was not that! If I felt triggered and sad from reading what I wrote, what would the reader feel?

I didn't know what else to do, so I stuck to the mission. I kept writing. I chose to keep the faith and trust that God had known what he was doing when he told me to write my story. I was hoping for the best and following my guidance, but it began to stress me out. I started to question whether my mission was worth the discomfort I was feeling. Had I even gotten that message right? Was I really supposed to write my story? I couldn't figure out what writing about my history had to do with sharing the messages of light, and I had no idea how to go about completing the task. I felt I'd been given a destination without a map. I felt lost.

I felt so much discomfort in writing about my past that I fell into the illusion that my life was going off track. I didn't know that sometimes we have to move outside our comfort zones to grow. In the instances when I wrote about the struggles of my youth, the feelings of negativity I experienced were still communications from God. The emotion was God trying to tell me that the way I was looking at my past was not for my highest good. It wasn't what I was looking at that caused me pain; it was the way I was looking at it. God was trying to tell me to find a higher perspective. Of course, I was so busy living my struggle I missed that message altogether.

I thought I'd lost my way, but in reality, my life was on the trajectory necessary for healing. I was experiencing a spiritual transformation, only no one told me what was happening. I was freaking out! I wanted to know what was going on. I had to have clarification on the emotional chaos I was experiencing. I had been so happy for so long, and now, suddenly, I was moving through my days in a feeling of constant struggle.

So what did I do for answers?

I did my walking and praying thing to connect. Naturally, the next message I received explained what I was going through at the time: growth.

Growth Experience

We all have down days, some of us more than others. It is because we choose to focus on negativity in our lives that our days are filled with discomfort. Challenges can frequently evoke a sense of struggle. What if we looked at the challenges as growth experiences instead? This is our opportunity to learn something about ourselves and the world around us. If we run from the challenge or get caught up in the details of the struggle, we miss the opportunity to grow. These growth experiences are there not only to teach us the lessons of life but also to provide an opportunity to witness and enjoy the miracles that flow from them. We can always decide to focus on something other than discomfort. When we do, our energy level rises, and we can see out of the doom and gloom into the light. We can look at the struggle or look at the wisdom we obtained from the challenge. We can look at the discomfort or look for the blessing in the lesson.

How do we do this? We recognize that the experiences in our lives that are uncomfortable are there to help us grow. We could easily remain in our comfort zone, and some people choose to. But when we step outside that comfort zone, we can understand more and expand in universal consciousness.

We can choose to find the good in the person who has hurt us. We can look at any situation from a different perspective and see how that might be a good thing in the long run. When we get out of our negativity and look for the positive, we will find it. Then we will wonder why we spent so much time feeling bad in the first place. We can always find new ways to approach others to yield positive results. We can use our experiences to discover how to avoid repeating an adverse action if we are ever again in a similar situation. We can grow by forgiving ourselves and others. We can vow to rise to a higher perspective instead of being bothered by the events or circumstances around us.

Remember, any discomfort we experience is only temporary. Change is the only true constant in this world. We are the ones who choose to experience it peacefully or not. The good news is, when we decide that what we have gone through was not what we wanted, we are one step closer to figuring out what we do want. This is our opportunity to embrace the challenge and grow with it.

Oh, Goody! Growth and Expansion!

Boy, was I growing! I was going to learn firsthand how to handle growth experiences. I was about to have many of them as part of my mission. I spent a good long time writing my story, as instructed. I spent so much time and energy vividly describing my self-destructive behavior and the victim mentality of my youth that I began to move into vibrational alignment with the very emotions and behaviors I described.

In that effort, I struggled. As I wrote, I kept finding moments in my past to heal. But was I healing? I actually felt sick to my stomach when I read some of my stories. Even though I wrote about the good that came from those growth experiences, it didn't matter. I noticed that I fixated more on the details of my dramas than I did on the miracles that came from them. When I reflected on what I wrote, I noticed I could only think about the negative stuff. Our brains are wired that way. Trauma, real or perceived, is embedded deeper in the memory, so we will learn not to do that again. But there I was, doing it again. I revisited all my perceived childhood struggles. In essence, I made them part of my adulthood too. Apparently, I'd missed the part in the previous message, "Growth Experience," that talked about finding a higher perspective in order to grow. Because I was looking at my past from the same mindset I'd had when I lived it, I failed to learn anything from the experience. Instead, my vibration shifted with the flow of my focus. Over time, I went from feeling happy-go-lucky and loving the miracle of life to outright misery. One day I just woke up angry and in pain. The old thought processes of self-recrimination, shame, and blame had taken over because of my attention to them. Life can be tricky!

Of course, this thought process led me to contemplate life, the experiences we have in it, and how they relate to our life's purpose. There had to be a reason for every dramatic thing I went through in my life. Those experiences had to be leading me to my purpose. Right? I wanted to know where this adventure was taking me. I was still looking for clarification on what was happening to my joy. The mission to write my story was messing with me, but I was still asking questions. The thing is, I had to find the right question to ask so that the answer would unlock the mystery of my missing bliss. I hadn't done that yet.

Luckily, my detours into my inner darkness didn't keep me from using my spiritual muscle to connect to my inner guidance. No matter how upset I got, I was always able to tune in to my higher self when I went outside for a nice long walk. So I did that—I went for a walk. I contemplated life, our experiences in it, and what they mean to the greater good. This is the message of light I got from that contemplation:

Life Experience

We have come to this planet to experience life. Each of us has a path, chosen when we were one with the vibration of God. The path we choose is designed to add to the greater good and the expansion of all of existence. Many of us choose the path of love and peace. Many others choose one of fear and struggle. Most of us tend to wander around between the two paths. There is no wrong path. All lives and the experiences in them add to the expansion and evolution of humankind. Without the experience of what we do not like, we cannot know what we prefer. Without the feeling we consider bad, we cannot know the deliciousness of the good feelings.

People come into our lives to offer various experiences from which to learn. Some of the experiences, especially the more traumatic ones, seem thrust upon us. Even then, we have the opportunity to learn and grow from the situation. We can become an example of triumph by overcoming tragedy, ultimately inspiring others in similar situations. The other option is to succumb to pain and fear and become a cautionary tale for those around us. Both experiences are valuable for the greater good. Both perspectives can be inspiring. Motivation is motivation. However, one perspective feels much better than the other to experience. One source of motivation is healthier for the physical body. It efficiently yields results, while the other leads to struggle, chaos, and, eventually, illness.

The universe that God created is one of balance. So for every struggle, the universe is creating the equal and opposite vibration of fluid prosperity to be found. Still, we must choose prosperity in order to find it.

Choice is our birthright. We must choose the perspective that makes us feel whatever we want to feel. We can choose to focus our attention and, thereby, our vibration on our desires at any given moment.

We are guided to our highest and best good always. God prepares us for all of our life experiences. He sends clues. He sets up proverbial road signs on our paths, leading us toward the highest and best good for ourselves and all who are concerned. Some signs are evident, visible, and easy to follow, while others are obscured by our fear, like overgrown trees blocking signs in the roadway. The signs and clues to guide us are there nonetheless. All paths lead to God one way or another. Some trails are smooth and easy, while others are difficult and appear treacherous. The choice is an individual one based on that individual's life purpose and desires at the time. When we feel lost, we need only stop and ask for directions. God will answer every time and in perfect timing. When he does, he will illuminate the path, explain the lessons, and enable us to feel the love and the light in every experience.

Challenges

I realized that what I wanted was to grow as a person, but I was already experiencing some serious growing pains. I might go as far as to say I developed a phobia of facing myself in my past, because of my tendency toward self-recrimination. I was really mean to myself.

I was about to learn that in order to grow, we must heal, but we can't heal what we choose to ignore. But what was I ignoring? You would think

The Messages of Light

that at that point in my life, as happy as I had been before I was sent on my mission, I didn't have a lot of damage to heal anyway. I was leading a healthy and productive life, and I had good relationships with the people in it. I mean, I thought I was pretty healthy at the time. What was left to heal?

Well, friend, I was about to find out. As I wrote about certain situations in my past, I found plenty of things I apparently still needed to heal. Unfortunately, instead of learning about myself and finding a new perspective on old situations, I kept finding myself emotionally re-creating the pain of my past. And would you believe that the discomfort seemed to be way worse this time around than any pain I had experienced as a child?

It turned out I was amplifying the problems and the negative emotions of my youth with my focus on them, instead of finding the higher perspective I was supposed to be looking for. Where attention goes, the energy flows. It's magnetic attraction. Talk about misdirecting energy!

What I really needed to heal wasn't my past. My life was exactly what it was supposed to be. According to the previous message, "Life Experiences," it was my perception of myself in the past that caused me so much grief. That was what needed to change.

I realized I had been contributing to the greater good all along. I just repeatedly chose the paths of drama and struggle to do it. I decided to be a cautionary tale instead of one who flows through life with love, grace, and ease. I chose to judge myself harshly for every mistake I made instead of offering myself love and forgiveness for being what we all are: human. Even as an adult, I had no idea how to forgive myself for my mistakes, much less how to find a deep inner love for myself. Maybe that was because I always avoided thinking about my mistakes. Now I could think of nothing else because I was busy writing my story.

After a while of struggling with the mission to write my story, I questioned why God would do this to me. I wondered why he would want me to suffer. Why would he want me to write my story if it caused me such distress? What I couldn't understand only frustrated me more, but I just kept writing. I'd made the commitment, so I kept at it. I had to trust that God knew what he was doing. But, friend, it was getting hard for me to deal with my discomfort around this particular challenge. It seemed everything I'd learned about staying balanced went right out the window.

Especially when I looked at myself in the times, I was off-balance in the past.

My writing at that time became as dark and cynical as the emotion I was experiencing. I didn't like what I was feeling. But instead of exploring the emotion and looking to learn from it, it seemed I was assigning blame to everyone in my life except myself. I had fallen right back into being the "Poor me" complainer I had been so many years earlier. The more I looked at the old me, the more like the old me I became, thanks to the magnetic power of my thoughts.

I didn't like that version of myself, and I didn't want to feed into it. I didn't know how to heal it yet, so I just stopped writing about it. I freaked out and quit! I put the pages I had written away in my old briefcase and refused to think about my story anymore. I washed my hands of it, which would have been great except for the fact that it was always there in the back of my mind, reminding me that I was now, on top of everything else, a quitter. So maybe I wouldn't actually quit, I thought. Perhaps I was just taking a break. Regardless, I ran away from my mission, only to find that running away made my self-loathing and self-recrimination more overwhelming as time progressed.

Eventually, I learned that if you run long enough, your feelings catch up with you, and when they do, you tend to be too exhausted to productively process them. Ah, what I know now. But back then, I kept running from my emotions.

Over the following years, I continued to pray, meditate, and write whatever messages I received. Writing my story, however, was no longer a priority. The more I ignored my initiative, the less content I became. I knew something was off, and I knew exactly what it was: I wasn't following my guidance. I was acting like a five-year-old child who was told to clean her room and went off to make a bigger mess instead. I was putting off the necessary work, when I should have been using the opportunity to shift my perspective and vibration.

It weighs on you when you put off something you know you're supposed to do. It's simple and true, yet many of us procrastinate anyway. We all recognize that we'd have one less thing to worry about if we would just get the job done. I am and have always been clear on that. It is the application of the concept that caused me difficulty. Adding to

The Messages of Light

the emotional discontent I felt because I'd quit writing my story were my preexisting conditions of constant worry and self-judgment. The result was more added stress.

I was thinking about that, and it led me to ask, "Why do we stress?"

Fear

We stress because we subscribe to the illusion of fear. There stems a thought process from fear, a chain reaction of negativity that leaves us feeling vulnerable and helpless. In actuality, we need never become victims of fear. Danger is a real thing, but fear is an illusion that can be found only in the mind. Fear can only take over when we give it the power to do so. It is a choice whether or not to give our attention to fearful things and, therefore, give fear influence over us.

The more we focus on a fearful thought, the more we experience the physiological reaction to fear. Our body releases chemicals into the bloodstream that cause the heart rate to go up and the hands to shake, and we may even cry if we are in enough distress. None of these things are good for us to experience regularly. When we put ourselves through all that, we throw ourselves off-balance. And in most cases, it is only to find out there was nothing really to worry about in the first place. The relief, in the end, is delightful; but why go through the distress to begin with?

The fact is, most of us don't know any better. After years of practice, fear, worry, and stress become our natural reactions. We must learn to retrain our thought processes. We must redesign our natural responses.

We have a choice in where we place our attention, and we should choose mindfully. A good rule of thumb is this: if you begin to worry about something, take a deep breath, and try to think of something you can do to ease the stress. If there is something physical you can do, do it. If there is nothing you can do about it, you can still breathe, pray, and give it to God. The important thing is to take a proactive approach.

When we focus on our problems or fears, we experience them in the form of helplessness. When we focus on finding solutions to the questions or stressors in our lives, we experience empowerment.

Fear and Faith

The good news is that while I was busy having the life experiences that were producing growing pains and was busy looking at things to heal, I was actually living the stories I was supposed to write about. Who knew? Maybe it was OK that I wasn't writing my story anymore. At least I was learning the lessons I had to learn to transform my life so that I could eventually be of service to others. I was growing as I was going through life. I continued my meditation and prayer, and I walked to connect to my guidance. With the weight of the mission off my mind, I felt free to ask questions and contemplate so many concepts that I felt like a kid in school again, but the teachings were coming from a voice inside myself. The energy I felt behind the voice was always love, so I learned to trust it. After all, I already had gotten my sign that the information was coming from God.

With access to the wisdom of the ages, I decided to ask about the most significant limiting factor in my life. I wanted to know all that I could to understand my fear in order to get past it. I asked, "How can I overcome my fear?"

The answer came quickly through a message of light: "Have faith." This is what followed:

Faith and Free Will

Faith and fear cannot coexist. Faith and fear are like light and dark. They cannot occupy the same space at the same time. When a light is turned on, the darkness dissipates. The same is true with faith and fear. When we have faith, when we truly trust God, fear cannot continue to exist. Fear will be driven from the mind, and all that will remain is the love in our hearts.

When we are in fear, it is because we are focused on what we do not want to happen instead of trusting God to help us achieve our dreams. Technically, he won't help us until we ask for his intervention because of free will. God gave us free will. We have the freedom to choose. We can decide to ask God to take charge, or we can instead choose to go it alone. Our attention to fear and doubt amplifies the power they have over us. With this power, they grow, causing damage to our mental and physical health. Like weeds, fear and uncertainty spread to all areas in our lives and choke out our ability to experience all that is good.

When we are in doubt, we are choosing to give that fear power over us and our lives instead of intentionally giving that power back to God through our faith. This is how we exercise our free will, whether we realize it yet or not.

Believe that God loves us, and understand that his will is for us to experience our highest and best good in life. He wants us to grow and expand in love so that we may share it with others. Knowing that what God wants for us is better than anything we could ever imagine for ourselves inspires faith. We realize that he will support us when we ask. Faith elicits a vibration of peace. Having faith is choosing to ask for God's intervention and believing we will receive it. Having faith is using our free will to ask God to help us solve a problem and accepting that he will. When we have faith in God, we eliminate doubt and fear. When we pray, "Thy will be done on earth as it is in heaven," we have to trust that God's will for us is to experience love, happiness, and fulfillment in their highest forms. When we have faith, we are in alignment with God's energy, and we experience God in us and all around us. We experience pure love.

> We can choose faith over fear. We all have that option. Free will gives us that choice. Choose faith.

Believing

After receiving and reading the previous message, "Faith and Free Will," I began to examine my beliefs, including where they came from and whether or not they still were valid.

Times change, and we are here to change with them. Reevaluating belief systems is not a thing that usually happens overnight, but it should be done. Developing new patterns of thought is a process. Mine started when I received the following spiritual download. This message of light was perfectly timed to help put me on my path, and it seemed to flow in perfect alignment with the message on faith and free will I had gotten days before.

> On Believing
>
> Why is it so hard to believe that God loves us and is always with us?
>
> When we do not see or feel the evidence of God with us, it is because we are not asking to see it. He is there always, but we must choose to focus on love and light in order to experience it.
>
> When life happens, we allow our focus to drift away from God. We easily give our full and undivided attention to the drama in our lives. We spend countless hours focused on anger, frustration, fear, and anything else that comes our way. Unfortunately, the things that come to us in times like that will only fit in perfectly with the feeling of disconnection from God because of the attractive power of our thoughts.
>
> At times, we get so wrapped up in our lives that we forget to look toward the Giver of that life for comfort and reassurance. We spend so much time and energy on the illusion of darkness and chaos that we create a veil

that obscures the light in our lives. This veil made with our thoughts becomes thick and heavy with the weight of our negative energy. By choosing to be afraid and by not trusting that everything is as it's meant to be, we direct our attention and creative energy to fearful things. It's as if we are saying to God, "I think I believe that you love me, but I'm not sure I can trust you to help me. So I'll just create chaos instead."

We can always trust God to answer our prayers, but because we have free will, our focus determines what those answered prayers look and feel like. Thoughts determine the way we experience our reality. So if we believe in what we fear, it is real, if only in the mind.

The good news is, God is love, and love is the primary component of our universe. Love is unfaltering, constant, never-ending, and always present, whether you believe it is or not. If you do not have faith in love, it's because you have chosen not to. You have instead subscribed to illusion. The thick and heavy veil of fear begins to obscure your view of all the good in the world.

To drop the veil and release the illusion of disconnection to clearly see God's love and light, we must change our focus. We must remember that along with the gift of life, we were also given the gift of free will. We acknowledge that we are as free to choose happiness as we are to choose misery. We are solely responsible for covering the beauty in our lives with the veil of fear. Our choice determines our experience.

Choose love, or choose fear. The more we choose love and the more we look for the beauty and miracles in this world, the more we will see. The more miracles and magic we experience in life, the more we believe they exist. To realign with our faith and repattern our beliefs, we must continue to ask for miracles and then be willing to observe them and even take part in them when the opportunities arise. The more we ask, the more we experience, and the more we believe. The more we believe, the more we will receive and in the most miraculous ways.

Looking at Life from the Fear Perspective

After the bombardment of information and messages of light pointing to the vibration of fear as the leading cause of my emotional discontent, I realized I was living in constant fear. My beliefs were tied to old illusions, and my thoughts became toxic. I lived with the fear of rejection daily, and I was afraid of failure again. Apparently, just because I'd stopped writing about my past didn't mean the vibrations I'd activated when I wrote about it went away. I became a fearmonger. Again. I worried about serious things, and I stressed about ridiculous things. When I didn't have a real reason to be concerned, my mind would conjure one up. It was as if there were a dial in my mind. It started on one end at the baseline value of concern, and the dial could be turned all the way up to the terror setting. Somehow, my thoughts kept that dial consistently set somewhere in between the two negative emotions.

I knew I was accessing the information that would help me change all that. So I continued to ask questions about the concept of fear to help myself redefine my beliefs around it.

The Lens of Fear

When you look at life through the lens of fear, the grass is never greener when you get to the other side. Fear makes you color blind. When we try to escape a feeling, we end up running right to it. Feelings are vibrations. The vibrations that create our life experiences emanate from within. Negative energy is like a dust bunny. If you don't clear it out, the uncomfortable energy begins to take on a life of its own. Because the energy comes from within, it follows us wherever we go, tainting our views and perceptions. In other words, we can run, but we cannot hide from that which resides within us. All we can do is be conscious of the vibrations we are emanating and then clear that energy often through play, dance, artistic endeavors, exercise, breath work, meditation, music, or whatever inspires us to a feeling of freedom and ease. In this effort, the lens of fear is broken, revealing the rose-colored world of God's love.

After getting all that information, I thought about fear a little more. It's a big subject! I was thinking about our thoughts and how the vibrations translate into emotion. I got a quick jolt of energy and, with it, more information. That message of light said the following:

> Fear is from focusing on the future. Pain comes from looking at the past. For peace, be in the present moment. Life is a gift! Open your present, and make it last!

Changing Focus

Changing my focus from the fear of facing my past to looking instead at the beauty and wonder of the present opened the door to my future all in one big swoop. It made all the difference in the world. I chose the lens of faith. My focus shifted away from the perceived wounds of my past back to thoughts of appreciation for the now. I moved out of the vibration of fear of future failure and into a flow of faith. My meditations and prayers felt more positive and, therefore, more potent in their ability to affect a beneficial change in my life. I began to experience miracles more profoundly as I learned from and applied the messages of light I was receiving.

As I moved forward from my happy place, the illusion of the unhappy and damaged me that I'd bought into as I relived the stories from my past faded. My life was becoming magical again. I shouldn't say *again*, because my little girls made everything magical. It was just that I was so caught up in my emotions about the past I had forgotten to notice the magic, mystery, and wonder all around me in the present.

Watching my little ones make new discoveries and develop their unique personalities was the most beautiful and incredibly precious time of my life. Seeing the wonder and awe of every new experience reflected in their happy, shining faces helped me see life through their eyes, and everything became miraculous to me as well. Because I chose to focus my attention on the present and live in faith instead of fear and because I was praying for the highest and best good for all concerned, I lived in a bubble of unconditional love, complete with cuddles and spontaneous hugs. If heaven were a moment in time, this would be my heaven.

Talk about an about-face maneuver. Once I began to assimilate and apply the wisdom I received from the messages of light, it seemed all areas of my life got better.

Chapter 14

Discovering New Opportunities and Abilities

The Miracle of Motherhood

I was receiving messages of light regularly, using the spiritual muscle that began as empathy, and my consciousness was in the process of shifting from fear to faith. It still required effort on my part because happiness wasn't yet my natural flow. Reprogramming the brain takes time, but at least I was accessing the vibration of happiness on purpose.

Kira was at her fabulous preschool for three hours a day. Just the fact that we got into that particular preschool when we did was a miracle in and of itself because the waiting list was long. It was one of those schools where you basically had to put your kid on the list before your child even had a name to have any chance of admission. I was not that prepared as a pregnant mom, so either I got lucky, or maybe magnetic attraction really is as powerful as they say. I really wanted Kira to have the opportunity to learn there, and she did.

I loved that time in my life; every morning, I took my girls to school early, and we played together in a childhood wonderland. The school had a fantastic playground. Our favorite part was a tire swing that hung so that the kids could sit on the tire and spin in a circular motion with a good push from an adult or another kid. The girls loved the "spinny swing," as they called it.

The spinny swing became an honored daily tradition. When we got to the school in the morning, the girls ran as fast as their chubby little legs would let them. They wanted to see who would climb onto the swing first. Kira and Aja would sit together on one side because Kira wished to ensure her baby sister, who was still so small, was secured. Other kids there climbed on to take the other two spaces. When everyone was loaded up, I would spin the swing for them. I treasured the expressions of joy on their pink faces as they clung to the ropes in opposition to the centrifugal force. I also enjoyed the squeals of joyful laughter I heard as they spun. My favorite feeling, though, came from the hugs of gratitude when they were done. My girls were pure love, and I was in love with them and my life.

Focusing on the good in my life and the miracle of motherhood made being present in the moments of beauty possible. Joy overrode the negative vibrations I amplified by focusing on the pain from the past. I began to flow from love again instead of fear. How awesome is that?

How Could I Refuse?

After a year of watching her big sister go off to preschool and after the novelty of having her mom all to herself wore off, Aja began to ask about going to school. So we put her on the waiting list for the preschool and went about our business, thinking it would be some time before she got into a class there. I wasn't in a hurry, because Aja and I had fun together, and the time Kira was at preschool went quickly. Aja and I spent plenty of time at the park near the preschool, went on play dates, and sometimes ran errands together. It was a full morning for us, and I loved every minute.

One day over Christmas break, the girls and I were making our traditional Christmas cookies, and we decided to give a batch to the surgeon and staff who had recently taken care of my varicose veins, the one negative physical consequence of my pregnancies. It just took one surgery, and all my pain was gone. I was happy and wanted to thank them.

We took the cookies into the office to drop them off, and I walked out with a part-time job offer. The doctor remembered that I was a registered nurse from our interactions before my surgery, and when I popped in to drop off the cookies, he got the idea to hire me. The doctor needed someone to work with his patients in the office, and that was where I came in.

When the doctor offered me the job, I was amazed and shocked, and I pulled out every reason that would prove I was not a good fit for his practice. I had been blessed to be home with my daughters so far, and I wasn't willing to give up any of those special moments for work. It was important to me to be with my girls as much as possible, especially while they were little. They were growing fast, and I wanted to savor every moment of those years. That was no deterrent to the doctor. In fact, he seemed to appreciate my attitude toward motherhood. The next thing he said was "Bring her with you," referring to Aja. I continued to resist, saying I was incredibly involved in preschool activities and intended to stay actively involved. Still, that was not a problem for the doctor. I had the job if I wanted it.

After much debate and contemplation on the synchronicity of the events that had led to what seemed to be a perfect opportunity, I decided to give it a shot. I accepted the job. How could I refuse? You never know unless you try, right?

When January rolled around, the medical office had a day-care center set up in the break room, complete with toys, a TV, and music. I was with Aja between patients, and the office staff, who loved her, kept my little Aja occupied while I was busy working in patient rooms. Don't worry, folks. We treated vascular patients. None of them had communicable diseases. While I was busy with patients, Aja would entertain the office by singing Avril Lavigne's "Sk8tr Boi" or another of the many songs we listened to together. Aja loved to sing and dance around the office. She was great at brightening everyone's day.

The setup at the doctor's office was a pretty sweet deal for me. I would even venture to say that it was a miracle. I was happy. I was paid to take care of people using my nursing license, and I had my baby girl right there with me while I did it. Meanwhile, Kira was right around the corner in school, only a ninety-second drive away. Talk about a win-win situation! All was indeed well.

I also discovered something new. I got a message of light that taught me about how my Reiki was helping the people I was working with. I discovered that the Reiki energy I had flowing through me was actually helping my patients. I never did Reiki treatments on them, but the Reiki energy is always flowing once you've been attuned to it.

I was never very graceful or gentle in my actions before Reiki. In fact, I was often referred to as a "bull in a china shop" when I was growing up. But when I worked in peripheral vascular care, I was able to perform the most delicate wound care procedures without causing my patients pain. More than once, I was told I had the hands of an angel. I knew it wasn't me. It was the divine energy flowing through me that minimized their discomfort. I'm sure the Reiki helped. I guess my mama was right when she said, "If you're going to be putting your hands on people, it's better for them and you if you are flowing Reiki."

More Amazing Coincidences

Blessings abounded! The shift I made, moving into the vibration of faith by praying for the highest and best good for all concerned and focusing my attention on the gift of life in the present moment, worked. There were many unbelievable coincidences in my life. I knew they were messages from God, pointing me in a positive direction, guiding me through my life. Right around that time, my family got another miracle that made life even better: our beautiful Riane came home. Talk about a message of light! Riane is a light.

With Riane home, our family unit was complete. We were all in the flow of pure positive energy. I had everything I'd ever wanted in life and more. I was happily married. I spent lots of time with my beautiful daughters, and I had a rewarding job helping people. We lived in a home more beautiful than I ever had imagined, and Ron's business was doing well. We had good friends, and I was still doing my thing, walking, praying, and writing down the messages. When people look back on life, I believe these times are what they refer to as "the good old days."

I was at a point in my life when I felt I only had to intentionally dream and visualize, and it would happen. I moved out of the vibration of healing and back into the vibration of creating. When I added asking for the highest and best good for all concerned to my prayers, the synchronicities were almost magical. For example, the only thing I could think to wish for at the time was a bigger backyard. Talk about feeling blessed! I wasn't attached to the dream. I figured it would be fun to practice creating by using magnetic attraction. The cool thing about my wish was that the lot next door was still empty and unsold, so I believed it might be possible.

I decided to practice using the magnetic power of my thoughts to get a bigger backyard, but at the same time, someone else was deciding she wanted to build a home on the lot next door. That seemed to be the end of that creation. I was surprised to find I was OK with that. I wasn't attached to the outcome of my vision. I was just dreaming and having fun. In fact, whatever disappointment I initially felt faded when I found out who was going to buy the lot. In fact, I was excited about the person who intended to buy it: Sonia was a friend of mine, and she had children my girl's ages who went to the same preschool. She even worked in the medical field and came on business calls to the doctor's office where I worked. Cool synchronicities! I could see how we might be vibrationally aligned enough to live next door to each other.

Just as I was about to accept that my vision of a larger yard would not happen, even as I was getting excited about our new neighbors, circumstances changed again. Sonia decided to buy a home that was already built, and the lot next door was available again. The situation worked out great with Sonia, because the house she bought was just around the corner from us and was still within walking distance. We were still close enough for play dates, and I was pleased about that. I was also getting a little excited that the empty lot was still up for sale. So I prayed again for the highest and best good for all and waited to see what would happen.

A week later, my father-in-law came to us with a message of light. He had another incredible offer for us. He was still involved with the development of the subdivision. He told us that prospective buyers wanted to purchase the lot two houses down from our own. However, the floor plan they wanted wouldn't fit on that single lot. So my brilliant father-in-law had an idea: he proposed we split the middle lot with our new neighbor, which we did. Can you believe those circumstances and events lined up so perfectly? Ron and I bought half the central lot, and the neighbor man and his wife bought the other half. Everyone was happy.

I still look back on this in awe. Not only did I get what I had been dreaming about for my girls—a bigger yard—but Ron got to add an entertainment room to the house. To top it all off, somehow, we miraculously had the financial means to accomplish it all. Sonia got her new home, and the man next door got to build his home to the specifications he wanted too. It worked out perfectly. This was an example of how vibrational attraction and praying for the highest and best good for everyone concerned really works.

I find it funny that people who don't understand the science behind magnetic attraction often go into fear mode when they see the magic of manifestation. I told this story to a friend once, and her response was not what I expected: she told me I should be careful whom I shared the story with, because she was worried people would think I was a witch. Thinking she was joking, I laughed and shared the message of light that popped into my head at that moment, something my mom used to say all the time: "What others think of me is none of my business." She looked at me a little funny, and it was then I realized *she* may have been the one concerned I was a witch. So I decided to change the subject.

I am still amazed at how the addition to our home manifested. I am so in awe that I will say it again: combining the universal laws of magnetic attraction and prayer for the highest and best good for all concerned is so powerful that it's almost magical. The scientific or magic formula for manifesting miracles is the following:

> power of vibrational/magnetic attraction + prayers for the highest and best good for all = magic

The Joys of Being an Empath

I was extra busy in the unfolding of the new addition to the home. I was so busy that I didn't notice what was happening, because it was a happy kind of busy: I got so involved in what was going on in my life that I forgot to prioritize self-care. Talk about a recipe for disaster! I didn't walk and meditate as much anymore, I stopped writing, and I stopped dreaming new dreams. I felt I was too busy. Before I knew it, I was feeling drained of all positivity. It seemed that whenever I was around people, whatever positive energy I was able to muster up would be gone in a split second.

I wasn't sharing my overflow of positive energy; I was dipping into my reserves and giving it away. Every interaction with another person left me feeling exhausted, but whoever I talked to seemed to happily skip off into the sunset. It appeared I was helping the people around me to lighten their emotional and vibrational load, but I was the one to pick up that load and carry it away. That wasn't a big deal when I only interacted with people outside my household a few times a week, as I had when my daughters were younger. However, now I had to interact with my girls' schoolteachers and the other parents at the school. I had a job working with people who were scared and feeling unwell, and they could carry some heavy energy. I also had the chaotic energy of the contractors coming in and out of my home for months. They were infringing on the energy of my sanctuary space. The number of people I met daily had grown significantly in a brief time. That was a lot of people and a lot of energy. Needless to say, I found myself feeling engulfed with the energy. I felt I should have been ecstatically happy, but instead, I felt heavy and emotionally exhausted.

At that time in my life, I realized that I was and always had been an empath. It wasn't a sudden epiphany or anything. I always had known I was emotional, and sometimes I got feelings about things, but I never had realized it was the empathic muscle until then.

Remarkably, the writing of my story allowed me to see that I had been an empath since birth. The same spiritual muscle that allowed me to sense energy and feel emotions so profoundly was the reason I could feel God's presence and now hear his whisper again. Oh yeah, did I mention I'd started writing my story again? Once I got back to my happy place, looking at my past wasn't as difficult. I was actually learning about myself as I wrote this time. I was finding different perspectives on my past experiences, and the discovery of my empathic gift was one of them. I'd had no idea that the cause of much of my childhood stress had been my gift. When I started writing about my youth, I realized I had the same profound experiences with energy as an adult that I'd had when I was a child. It was all the same muscle, and I was the same person using it all along.

I was starting to see that there was something more to the mission of writing my story that I hadn't expected, a higher perspective. I find it funny that so many of the messages of light included guidance telling me to look for the higher perspective, but I simply failed to look. So of course, I never found it. When I went back to writing from a happier place, I discovered the higher perspective the guidance had been leading me to all along. There is always magic behind the mission when God is involved. So I decided to go with it.

Now, remember, an empath is someone who is extremely sensitive to energy. Empaths' senses are so acute that they not only can sense other people's emotions but also can sometimes experience others' feelings as their own. As you can imagine, that can be quite uncomfortable.

Empaths can also absorb energy from others, as you probably know from personal experiences. This is usually great for the people who spend time with empaths. They feel better and lighter through interaction, but it stinks to the unaware empath, who walks away feeling the weight of the other person's energy piling up on top of his or her own.

Most empaths don't realize they have this gift, and few know how to use it. It is the spiritual muscle that allows us to feel God's presence and hear God's whisper. So yes, it is a gift.

I admit sometimes being an empath made me feel crazy because I couldn't control my emotions like so-called normal people. From the time I was little, I could feel it in my heart when someone was off. All kids can, but it didn't stop there with me. I could feel it when someone's words conflicted with what I felt from him or her. Adults could not put on a happy face around me and get away with it. Not only could I sense what someone was feeling, but I felt it as if it were happening to me. Or I would think I was responsible for the negative emotions the people around me were feeling. This almost always made me cry. The biggest challenge for my parents was that I was often overwhelmed. I cried a lot, especially around adults, as they carry the most negative emotion. Basically, any of my parents' social interactions resulted in my being hauled away in tears, which could not have been fun for anyone involved. I did not understand the feelings I was experiencing, nor did I know where they were coming from. As a small child, I did not know what to do with the adult emotions I was experiencing, so I would cry. People would come up to my mom to say how cute I was, and I cried. If my mom or dad had a difficult day, I would start crying. And let's not forget the usual reasons kids cry, because I cried at those too. Remember, emotion is communication from God. When it's negative, it tells us that what we're thinking about or how we are thinking about it is not for our highest and best good. But as a kid, who had a choice? We had to be wherever our parents decided we should be. Unfortunately, that wasn't always ideal, so crying did the trick. Crying helped me release the adult energy I absorbed, and it usually got me away from the source of that energy.

Over the years, I was labeled as temperamental and overly emotional. Some would say I was challenging to manage. When I got stressed out, I got out of control. I would throw big temper tantrums—the embarrassing kind where the people around me wanted to pretend they didn't know me. That happened more than once with me.

As an adult, I got overwhelmed too. I began to notice it during my first pregnancy. I was excessively emotional, and I was easily overloaded with the deluge of emotions I didn't understand. I chalked it up to pregnancy hormones, and that was partly true, but I knew there was more.

At that point in my life, I was able to ask questions and receive the answers, so I asked about the reason for my emotional overload. The message I got said the following:

> When a pure energetic being of light is inside a human woman, that divine being resets the energetic flow of the mother. It amplifies her authentic nature, which is love. It enhances her spiritual gifts, such as intuition. Pregnancy, to an empath, is like being hooked up to a superpowered battery that adds a powerful charge to all spiritual energy. When the babies are born, the switch stays in superpower mode.

The amplified ability stuck with me even after giving birth. I was busy mothering, so I didn't notice. I was happily performing my walking self-care ritual consistently, which meant I was filling up to overflowing with divine energy. My empathic ability never really went into absorption mode. I wasn't around many people when the girls were small. The energy shifts weren't as evident until they got older, when we were around more people. But my empathic ability was there the whole time, and because of my pregnancies, it was on steroids.

It wasn't until I began going with my girls to school functions that I noticed just how superpowered that battery was. I was highly uncomfortable in crowds. This prompted me to start paying attention to energy and vibration while around those masses of people. That was when I saw the frequent energetic shifts happening in me. I was being affected by everyone. Every person I met had a different vibration, and my energy was shifting with each interaction. I felt like a Ping-Pong ball being batted around the room. Each wall (person) I hit caused my vibration to get heavier. By the end of any function, I felt heavy and energetically drained. It wasn't that I didn't enjoy the interactions, because I did. It was just that I carried the weight of other people's energy with me when the events were over. Sometimes it would take me weeks to regain my balance after a single on-campus event, such as a health fair or a festival. I began to dread all social gatherings because it took me so long to recover my vibrational balance afterward. I felt like something was wrong with me.

At the time, I didn't know that being an empath is a powerful gift, not the curse I was living. In every interaction from which I walked away feeling heavier, the other person got lighter. I was being of service. In some energetic way, I was helping the other person to unburden him- or herself. I didn't understand it, and I certainly didn't know how to deal with it yet. But my ability to sense energy was there, inspiring my spiritual growth and giving me all the insight I could have wished for about being an empath.

Just as my empathic gift was unfolding in my conscious understanding, unraveling my previous perceptions of my life experiences, I was confronted with death.

A New Perspective on Death

It was one of those strange times when several deaths happened simultaneously, and the people around me were grieving. There's a superstition that deaths come in threes in hospitals and nursing homes. In this case, it wasn't just a superstition; it happened.

It began with two people I knew and loved. Kathy, my sister-in-law, and my friend Julie were both suffering deeply at the hands of a sudden and unexpected loss of a close loved one. I grieved deeply for them and with them. The empath in me was overwhelmed. As a friend, I wished there was something—anything—I could do to help. So I prayed about it. What could I do other than make food or offer condolences? I had never really

The Messages of Light

tapped in and gotten a message of light about death before, but the empath in me needed to help. So I prayed and meditated, hoping to get some kind of message of light that might help ease the pain they were enduring.

I didn't think I would have much to offer in terms of consolation. My personal experience with death was limited because I had never really lost someone close to me. But as an empath, being around people in grief was a profoundly personal experience. As I reached out to console the people left behind, I somehow absorbed their grief. They seemed to feel better, if only for the moment, but I would walk away feeling as if the person who'd died had been my own family member or friend. I absorbed their grief and took it on as my own. Then I tried to find a way to process it.

Whenever I had something to work on emotionally, I went straight to the Source for understanding. That always brought me comfort. So I decided to use my gift of receiving messages of light to help them and myself through that pain.

As it turned out, I was inspired to undertake that mission at the exact perfect time for me. As I was reaching for the words and energy to try to help the family and friends suffering from their losses, I had a loss myself. Remember, they come in threes.

My papaw, my only biological grandpa in the picture, was the third person I knew who died. I adored him, and I felt his absence profoundly. There are no words. When I think of the happy, carefree moments of my childhood, my papaw is there in my memory banks, front and center. My papaw was always focused on me. He always had time to help me explore the world around me. He would sit with me till all hours of the night, watching cicadas come out of their shells in the screened wooden terrarium he'd made for me by hand. He took me often to feed the ducks at the park, and he always bought me Bazooka bubble gum whenever we were at the store together. He was also a carpenter, as Jesus was, and he made me many things I still have today. The most incredible thing Papaw did was talk to me often about prayer, Jesus, God, and love. He was a messenger of light.

I was blessed to have my first personal experience with death be guided by my papaw and filled with miraculous events. The blessings were profound.

The first miracle was that I got to talk to my papaw on the phone and say, "I love you," during the brief period of lucidity he had just before he died. That was good for me because I got to say everything I needed to say to him. I got to hear his voice and listen to him say, "I love you," one more time.

Another miracle was that he fulfilled my mamaw's request, or demand, as the case may be. Mamaw told him, "Don't you die on my anniversary!" Well, he didn't. He waited until the day after their wedding anniversary to let go. Papaw was always so thoughtful.

The most profound experience was when my papaw came to me in a vision after he died. It was my first time interacting with a spirit as an adult. Talk about perfect timing! I had been strengthening my spiritual muscle by writing the messages of light, so I was able to see and sense spirits again when it mattered most to me. Thank you, Lord!

We were at his house for the funeral, and I could feel his energy still strong. When I entered the family room, I could still see the familiar image of him in his armchair with his magnifying glass, reading his Bible. It wasn't just a memory; it was as if he were right there in front of me. He looked up at me, smiled, and said, "Hi, Chris. Why don't you come sit with me for a while?" He was so real. I almost forgot he was gone. As I headed toward him to sit down, someone else came into the room, speaking to me, and the image of him vanished.

That was the first time I sensed him from the other side. It was a vision and the first sign of his continued presence, letting me know he was still with us.

That night, I saw him again. I was sleeping on the pull-out mattress of the couch situated next to his favorite chair—the one in my vision—when he came to me in a dream. I knew it was him, even though he looked fifty years younger. He was in his late twenties or early thirties. He was tall, handsome, and strong. He was wearing a dark suit one moment and a military uniform the next. His dark hair was slicked back in waves, and his cheeks had a youthful pink glow. He was dapper! His pipe was in one hand, and he waved hello with the other. The beaming smile on his face was contagious. I could even smell his aftershave as it drifted in with the waves of tobacco smoke swirling from his pipe. At that moment, I had a flash, a sudden knowing, as if he relayed the information to me telepathically. It was a communication that would have resembled a conversation if we had offered actual words in the interaction.

The Messages of Light

He showed me that he still existed, even without his physical body. He wanted me to tell everyone that he was doing fine and that he would continue to love us and guide us from the other side. When I woke up, I could still smell him, and I knew it wasn't just a dream.

That event changed my outlook on death. I suddenly realized from firsthand experience that death is not the end. My papaw was still around, just in a different form. After that, I noticed energy the shifts. When I thought of him, he appeared in an energetic form right there with me, and we would sort of hang out. At least that was what it felt like to me.

Thanks to Papaw, I found a door to a new world that was propped open just enough to let me glimpse inside. Knowing it was there, I had to explore further. I wanted to connect to those on the other side. I already knew I could sense the energy around me more tangibly after I had exercised or meditated, so I kept doing that. I prayed, meditated, and wrote all about what I received.

Then, one day, I had just finished my walk and was in the bathroom, washing my face, when unfamiliar thoughts started popping into my head. I felt a rush of energy coupled with exhilaration as they came. I recognized the sensation, so I knew what to do: I grabbed my trusty spiral notebook and started writing. As I wrote, I noticed a pattern: the lines were rhyming. I hadn't written a poem in years.

I thought, *Where is this coming from?*

Then I heard the message "Never mind that; just keep writing." So I did.

When I was done, I looked at what I had written. The passages began to highlight in my mind, as if to indicate the order of placement in the flow of the piece. I followed the wordless guidance. I moved a couple of things around, and when I was done, I had a beautiful poem.

When I looked up in my mind, asking who had written the words, I got a picture of three people. Standing beside my papaw were M. E. and Grandma Honey. I recognized them as the people I had been praying about in the first place, just before Papaw died. This is what they wrote:

You May Think

> You may think you cannot see me,
> but you do.

The butterflies,
the flowers
are beautiful for you.

You may think you cannot feel me.
I am the caress of a gentle breeze.
I am the warmth of the sun on your face.

You may think you cannot hear me.
I am a whisper in the silence.
I am the sigh in an embrace.

You may think you cannot hold me.

I Am holding you.

I wish I could take credit for writing that. I mean, I did write it, but I feel it didn't come from me. It came through me. I was just the conduit, the channel through which it came. My prayer and connection allowed me to work through this crisis of faith to find inspiration. The gift of empathy forced me to a new level of connection, which could help ease the pain of loss.

I was thrilled with the experience, but realizing I was communicating with people on the other side caused me to think the following cascade of exclamations in my mind: *Wow, what a gift! Oh, what a responsibility! Yikes! Am I crazy? Is this really happening? Oh my God, now what?*

That was when my world shifted and opened up some more. That was the moment when I truly awoke. I have never looked at death the same since. But with that awakening came a whole new set of concerns. What was I supposed to do with my newly rediscovered ability? It was not as if I wanted others to know I talked to dead people. What would they have thought?

With that, suddenly, I cared what people thought. Not again! It's funny: I didn't care if they thought I was a witch, but I did care what they might think about my talking to dead people. Oh, the joys of expansion and growth.

The Messages of Light

But before I could sort any of that out, I had to deal with the task at hand: the poem. So I prayed and asked, "What am I supposed to do with this poem?"

At that moment, I received a clear instruction: "Give it to them."

I understood from that message that I was supposed to go find the two other people I knew who were suffering severe and tremendous losses and waltz right up to them to give them a poem dictated to me by their loved ones on the other side—and that was supposed to help. Really? The scenario was terror-evoking to me.

So I said to my guidance urging me to share the message of light, "Wait! What? No way! Are you kidding me? No! Um, no!"

And that was when the groundskeeper at the church across the street dropped his rake when he saw me talking aloud to air in the beginning of this story. Now, dear reader, you know why I was arguing with air in the first place. I had to laugh at the situation, but I also learned from it.

Note to self: Answer in your mind, not out loud!

My guidance was specific. I knew exactly whom I had to give the poem to, and I knew I had to tell her whom it had come from. Yeah right! I knew Julie, but we weren't close like that. I certainly did not know her well enough to intrude on her private grief.

I thought, *Nope. Not gonna do it.* I argued that it would cause more harm than good. But every day after that, I saw Julie, and the nagging feeling got worse. At one point, the spirit said, "I'll leave you alone if you just do what I ask."

Finally, I gave in. I said a prayer for the highest and best good, put the poem in an envelope, and carried it in my purse so I would be prepared for the right moment. The right moment happened almost instantaneously. Naturally, the day I put the poem in my purse was the day I ran into her alone. It was rare to find this beautiful woman apart from other people, because she is so loved. So I knew this was it. I had to follow through. My heart started racing, my face was flushing, and my hands were shaking, but I was pushed forward by the spirit who wanted me to talk to her. I timidly asked if she had a moment to speak, and of course, she did.

Our inner guidance is flawless! We sat down together, and I gave Julie the poem. Her reaction was not what I had feared: she was openhearted enough to receive the verses inspired by her loved one and the rest of the information I was receiving.

That was the first time I ever channeled information from someone on the other side, but it would not be the last. I still had to deliver the poem to Kathy.

Yes, I know I am omitting specifics, dear reader. You probably want to know more about the loved ones, what happened to them, and what the spirits said to them when I delivered the poem. The thing is, the details of the stories are not mine to tell. My purpose here is simply to honor the fact that these beautiful beings of light continue to exist. They live on, and they are constantly flowing love to those of us on this plane.

The three spirits who inspired that poem gave me a miracle. They opened my channel of communication. It was as if the three of them joined forces to amplify the broadcasting signal from the other side so that I would be able to tune in and hear them clearly. And it worked.

My Spiritual Path

That experience shaped who I was becoming more than I realized. It opened a door that would never be closed again. In fact, it seemed I couldn't have shut it if I'd wanted to, even for a brief time, much like my empathy. I felt bombarded continuously with spirits. I never had realized that pretty much everyone has someone on the other side wanting to communicate with him or her—that is, until I felt a spirit with just about everyone I met. What do you do with that? I would be sitting there minding my own business, having a coffee with a friend, when suddenly, there would be someone from the other side wanting to talk to whomever I was with at that moment.

Keep in mind I was just getting used to the idea that I could communicate with the consciousness I perceived as God. I guessed it made sense that I could communicate with spirits too. Still, even to my open mind, this seemed a bit too much sometimes. My challenge was overcoming my fear of talking about what I was experiencing. I was still concerned with what people would think, even though I tried not to be.

My little insecure self had a lot to overcome if I wanted to use this gift in any positive way.

So far, I'd found my path, and I knew it was a spiritual one. Whatever I was going to do with the rest of my life, I knew the messages of light were part of it. I'd found my purpose—to bring more love and light into the world—and I knew I was supposed to be writing my story. I felt as if I were collecting pieces of a jigsaw puzzle, and I had no idea what the picture looked like or how the pieces interlocked. So I just kept moving along my path, gathering the different pieces of the puzzle, hoping they would all someday fit together.

More Changes

About that time, my mom had a minor miracle of her own. She had been living near us for a while, when she started to remember the many reasons she'd left this town in the first place. Let's just say she was not in harmony with her environment.

So she put her request for a new environment out there to the universe in the same way I did, minus the walking part. And wouldn't you know it? The universal power of attraction combined with her excellent karma paid off. Someone she'd helped in the past, one of her distance Reiki clients, sent her a big check with no return address and told her to start over. There was no return address because he knew she would have returned the money otherwise. This was God's way of making sure she would accept the gift. My mom was a nurturer. She was not used to accepting help, even when it was a direct response to a prayer she had been offering. This was a message of light. The money was more than she needed to fulfill her desires and fund her free spirit. With that, she started another chapter of her life in Austin, Texas.

As much as I loved having my mama close, it was not worth watching her suffer. I suppose I could have begged her to stay, but to what avail? If she'd stayed here, she would have remained unhappy, and I would have felt guilty for my selfishness. And what if I had asked her to stay, and she'd left anyway? I don't know how well I would have handled that. So as sad as I was to see her go, I tried to focus on her happiness.

Before she could leave, though, she had to finish up my Reiki training. Up until then, I'd passed on attending all her Reiki II classes, because I didn't want to give up family time on the weekend. Her swiftly approaching relocation made it necessary that I complete my training then, or I would not become a Reiki master under her direction. I wanted to become a Reiki master for myself and my family. Still, I had no desire to practice Reiki professionally, much less the ambition to teach it. But there I was, taking the second-degree class. Then, when the proper amount of time and practice had taken place, I took the master-level class and was certified in the Usui system of Reiki in March 2004.

Before the ink had dried on my certificate, I already had two people in line to take my first-degree class—that I hadn't intended to te*a*ch. I even tried to get them to take the courses from my mom before she left, but they wanted to learn from me. So just like when I took first-degree Reiki after nursing school, I went kicking and screaming, when I should have been skipping and singing, as my grandmother would have said. My life was only enriched by the experiences that arose from my learning Reiki and becoming a Reiki master.

Spiritual Connection and Human Intervention

When my mom left town, I was sad. Because of that, some of my old thought patterns reemerged. I was falling out of my positive flow. I had to remind myself that I could still call her anytime, and she said she would be back every few months to visit. My mom intended to return to continue working at the psychic fair in town even after she moved to Austin, where she would be working the fairs as well. The girls and I missed her, but we wanted what was best for her, and this was it.

Around that time, I made the acquaintance of many beautiful people. In one case, I met a lovely woman, Rosa, and her mother. I knew we were meant to interact, because God kept making us cross paths. I became friends with both women, but ultimately, I was closer to Rosa, probably because we were closer in age. I adored my friend and her mother. Rosa's mother was a wonderful lady. She radiated love and kindness, and she always had a big smile on her beautiful face. The two of them were alike in that way. I am happy we met, because I learned so much from them.

By the time Rosa's mom made her transition into the light, I'd had plenty of time to get to know her and adore her, so when she died, her death affected me deeply. More importantly, Rosa was in serious pain. She was devastated over the loss of this loving and nurturing woman. I knew because I could feel it whenever I was around her. The energy of my friend's pain was so intense there were times when I felt it just by thinking of her. Being an empath is interesting, to say the least. I didn't know what to do with all of it, so I prayed about it. I prayed for Rosa and her family, her mother, and myself.

By that time, the word was out on the other side about my ability. The next thing I knew, I got what I affectionately call "incoming." It was Rosa's mom. She asked me to relay a message to her daughter.

Now, at that point, I basically lived in the closet about my abilities because I was always afraid of what people would think of me. Over time, I'd worked myself into a fear of being rejected or labeled as crazy because of my ability. So when I got the guidance to share the message with my friend, I did what I had done the first time I got a mission to convey a message of light—except this time, not out loud. I thought, *No! I'm not going to do it!* Then I began to list in my head every reason I was afraid to deliver the message.

As if interrupting the cascade of negative thoughts in my mind, the guidance I received at that point was "You know you're not going to be able to ignore this!"

I said, "Well, then help me get over my fear of being judged."

The response was "OK, then ask a useful question."

I figured if I understood judgment better, maybe I wouldn't be as afraid of it. So I asked, "Why do people judge others?"

> People judge because of fear. Some judge because it takes their attention away from their own perceived inadequacies and the parts of themselves they are afraid to face. Others judge because they think they know a better way of doing things than what they see happening with the people around them. Still others judge others

because it makes them feel better about themselves. If they put another person down, somehow, they feel uplifted. Judgment always originates in fear, and in any form, it is nonproductive. It pulls us away from our highest vibration.

The fact is, we are all individuals. God made us each perfect in our own way, the way he intended. Our perceived inadequacies and flaws are there for a reason. They help us learn and grow so we can be an influence on those around us, adding to the expansion of all that is. When we align with higher consciousness, the example we supply is positive. When we are out of alignment, we become the not-so-positive example of negative energy, so the people around us can see what not to do. We are not responsible for living anyone else's life, only our own. If we are looking for a better way to live, we have to make decisions for ourselves, and we should focus only on our own guidance when we make them.

We should not try to impose our own will on others by judging their actions or behaviors. That's not our job. They have their own life to live. We have ours. Even identical twins who carry the same DNA have different life experiences and different purposes for being.

We are all in constant motion. Some of us move forward, while others get stuck running in circles or even find themselves slipping backward. There is something to be learned in each example. When we look at each situation without fear, we can be inspired, even if we're only motivated to do things differently than the example before us.

The word *judgment* in and of itself holds a negative connotation. When we are judging others, what are we saying? The people we are looking at are not doing something the way we think it should be done. Remember, they have their own purpose, and how they fulfill that is between them and their Maker. It is not our business.

The actions of others only impact us when we give them our attention. In actuality, when individuals are focused long enough on others to feel the need to judge, they are being shown a mirror of themselves, and all they judge in another reflects their own fear or self-loathing. "Do not judge, or you too will be judged" (Matthew 7:1 NIV). When we judge another, we are actually just judging ourselves in the mirror he or she is showing us.

When met with apparent judgment, we must remember that we too are mirrors offering those who choose to judge us an opportunity for healing and expansion. When we feel judged by others, we must honor ourselves in our reflective role and move forward in love. They are not actually judging us but instead are criticizing that which they have in common with us.

We should also remember that there is a significant difference between judging and observing. The goal is to observe with the intent of learning from others and their experiences and then offer love and support instead of projecting and displacing our own (self) judgment onto them.

When we find ourselves in the destructive mode of self-judgment, we must shift our focus to observing here too. Observing allows us to learn what we came to learn from the experience. In observing instead of judging, we give ourselves a break for not already knowing the lesson we just learned.

Overcoming My Fear

Receiving that message of light was the boost of confidence I needed. I began to understand that it was more important for me to focus on myself and to do what I came here to do with my life than it was to worry about what people might think about it. I had to stop judging myself and my choices through the eyes of the people around me. I spent too much time determining my value based on my perception of what someone else may or may not think about me. I focused purely on my fear, which was the problem, not the solution. My default mentality was fear-based—so much so that one negative thought could quickly turn into hours of panic. Fear will always find a way to transform a small chore into an insurmountable task, and I had evidence of how that was unfolding in my life in several ways.

When I looked at the idea of relaying a message of love, regardless of the circumstances behind it, my fear began to fall away.

I realized the love in the message was more important to hold on to than my fear of delivering it. I started to conceptualize moving through my life without the weight of the fear of judgment. I decided that sharing the message from Rosa's mom was the solution to my problem of being afraid of judgment. It was an opportunity to practice faith. Maybe it would help Rosa too. I decided I would follow through with the current mission. I would talk to her. I shifted my focus away from my fear of judgment, and all I cared about was sharing the love.

Love conquers all, including fear!

When I relayed the message to Rosa from her mom, I was taken by surprise. I was overcome with a sense of relief mixed with serenity and joy. As before, I'd worried needlessly. She was incredibly open and accepting of the message I had to deliver. In fact, she seemed to be grateful for it. We sat for a while, hugged, and shed some tears as we spoke to her mother together. This time, the message I relayed wasn't on paper like before. It was as if I answered a telephone call intended for Rosa, and I put her mom, the caller, on hold until I got a chance to talk to my friend. Then, when we got together, I took the call off hold and put it on speaker mode as I relayed the message. It was an incredible flow of communication. As it was happening, I realized I was using the same spiritual muscle to talk to Rosa's mom that I used to speak to God. It seemed God was the telephone operator, or even better, God was the telephone itself. His presence was felt. Even the air around us was beautiful in a way that is impossible to describe.

I don't know what I expected to happen, but because of my earlier fearful vibration, I did not expect that miraculous experience. It was another example of how learning to trust God and let go of my fears brought more magic and wonder into my life.

To find beauty, all you have to do is open your eyes! Look for beauty in everyone and everything. In that effort, you will find your own, and the love and light within you will shine.

A Magical Manifestation

I felt God surrounding me. I saw love and beauty everywhere I looked. I enjoyed that time in my life. I was happy, healthy, and free, and I knew it. I was having fun. Music always has been one of my favorite things, and at that time, in my time of bliss, I was gifted with a mind-blowing musical experience.

It all started with Tim, Ron's best friend, who had been the best man at our wedding. One day, out of the blue, Tim gave Ron the Red Hot Chili Peppers' *Californication* CD and told him to get ready. "We're going!" he said.

Ron and I were both concert fanatics, and we'd attended more than our fair share of incredible shows, but this would be new for me. This would be my first major concert since I'd become a mom, and I knew I would have to leave my babies at home for this one. The show was in Las Vegas on New Year's Eve, which was neither the place nor the time for little ones. I knew the girls would be well cared for, because my mom would come to town to stay with them at our house; it was myself I was worried about. I was the one who got separation anxiety.

Once we got to that concert, I was over my anxiety, at least for the time being. Tim had us at the front of the line to get in, and we were some of the first people into the Joint, the venue in the Hard Rock Café where the Red Hot Chili Peppers would be playing on their *By the Way* tour. The whole venue was alive with anticipation and frenzy, including me. Watching them perform was nothing short of exhilarating. I saw the musicians connecting with the energy that streamed through them like magic while they flowed artfully in the ecstasy of divine connection. They played with such passion and joy that I was inspired in ways I never had expected.

After that, the Red Hot Chili Peppers' music was almost all I listened to when I went out walking. I called it my power music. I connected not only with the sound the band created but also with the message behind the music. Until I saw them in concert, my memory of their music was good, but it was their older stuff and only what I had heard on mainstream media. I clearly had not been adequately educated on all that was RHCP, so I decided to learn. OK, maybe I was becoming a fanatic. Like the kid in me who'd collected Olivia Newton-John albums, I collected and listened to the Red Hot Chili Peppers' music almost obsessively. I even joined the RHCP fan club. I played their music even with my little girls in the car. I was conscious of the expletives, so there were a couple of songs I skipped when the girls were with me—usually. (Insert oops expression here.)

One particular morning, while driving the girls to preschool, I was a little more lax than usual in my curse-word censorship. I was lost in thought on the way to the girls' dual-language Christian preschool, when I heard my beautiful three-year-old Aja enthusiastically singing along to a song on the RHCP CD, "Cabron." Imagine what went through my mind when I noticed how well she pronounced the word *cabron* in Spanish. It was impressive. At that moment, I got a message. I envisioned Aja skipping happily on the playground while singing "Cabron". For those who do not speak Spanish, let me explain: *cabron* is not a nice word or a kind thing to call someone. Although, the way I see it at least, the person in the song is being called that word in the context of being called out to be a better example as a leader. It didn't matter how well Aja could pronounce the Spanish or how inspiring the song's theme was; I felt those details might be lost to the administration of a Christian preschool, especially with a three-year-old singing it. But the image of my three-year-old singing that song at school made me laugh so hard I let her keep singing it till the end. Then I put on another song (with more age-appropriate language) and listened to her sing that song as well. My strategy worked, because she went into school that day singing the age-appropriate song, but from then on, I was a little more careful with my playlists.

I thought the story was so funny I sent it in to the Red Hot Chili Peppers fan club. This was back in the day when Blackie Dammett (Anthony Kiedis's dad) was the fan club president. He not only read the email I sent, but he responded to my email directly. He also posted my story about Aja on the fan club's page. I wish they still had that old fan club page available online in an archive so I could show Aja the response the other fans had to it. It was classic!

It wasn't long before Ron decided to take me to another RHCP concert. This time, they would be at the Journal Pavilion in Albuquerque, New Mexico. We invited Tim and his girlfriend to come as well, of course. Tim was the reason we'd gotten into the band in the first place.

When we got there, I was curious about the tour buses in front of the hotel. Ron and Tim even tried to find out who was traveling on the bus. Unfortunately, the hotel management was excellent about privacy and confidentiality. At that point, it was just a theory that the band was in the same hotel we were; there was no way to tell for sure.

Immediately, I began to imagine what I would say if I got to meet any of the musicians performing that night. I thought about how I'd started the New Year with them and the positive difference their music had made in my life already. Listening to it inspired me daily, and I wanted to express my gratitude for their art. The beauty their collaboration brought to the world was amazing for me to see and feel. Their spirituality was evident in their music, and I felt more spiritually connected by listening to it. I really wanted them to know that. I began creating the experience of meeting them in my mind, hoping the magnetic power of my intentional focus would come to my aid.

After checking in, Ron and I split up from Tim and his girlfriend; the couples went to our respective rooms to meet up later. Ron and I decided to go to the gym and then head to the pool to relax before the concert. We were lazily lying by the pool, when I heard Ron say, "No way!" He knew what I had been trying to create. I looked up and saw an attractive dark-haired man with familiar-looking tattoos walking in our direction. I must've looked ridiculous as I flew out of my chair as if I'd been stung by a scorpion, but I didn't care. Before I knew it, I had introduced myself to Anthony Kiedis, the lead singer of the Red Hot Chili Peppers and one of the most brilliant lyricists of all time (in my humble opinion). I actually got a chance to tell him what I'd practiced in my mind, but instead, I froze like a deer in the headlights of a Mack truck. I stuck my hand out to shake his, and all I could get out was "We're here for your concert!"

A giant smile spread across his face, and he said, "Thank you!" He nodded at my husband and went off to read a book and soak in the sun.

I was shocked. I couldn't believe I had manifested that meeting. I was also surprised at how cool Anthony Kiedis was. He didn't seem annoyed at being stopped by me. If anything, he seemed to honor the experience. He was a regular guy, like someone we'd hang out with. Stars—they're just like us! Ha! I had to say it! Seriously, he was humble and kind even to me, a perfect stranger interrupting his quiet time. How cool is that? I was so happy. I joked for the next half hour about never washing my hand again. Of course, that would have been gross.

Anyway, talk about crazy coincidences! That coincidence is one of my all-time favorites, and it is proof of the power of being in the flow of positive emotion. I knew I'd created that experience with my vibration. I'd imagined it with so much love that it had happened. It was simple.

Looking back on that day still makes me smile. I was in the vibration of pure love and gratitude when I wished to tell the band how much their music meant to me. Then I got to meet the band member with whom I connected the most, the lyricist.

When we got home from that epic concert, I contemplated being in the flow and how good it felt. I wondered how to stay in the positive vibe, because I didn't want to lose it to the challenges of daily existence. So I asked, "How do we stay in the flow of positive energy when life gets tough?" Then I got the following message:

Staying in the Flow of Divine Energy

Once we get ourselves into the feeling of connection with the Source of all energy, God, how do we hold on to that feeling?

At one time or another, we all will feel disconnected from love and light. The important thing is to remember that we are always connected. Disconnection is an illusion.

So here we are, all fluffy and happy. We feel loved and secure. Then the world happens. It only takes one decision based on anything other than love, and off we go, down, down, down that spiral. Suddenly, everything is off-kilter.

We have had a reaction to something going on around us, and we have allowed ourselves to lose our focus on love. Anger, frustration, fear, and anxiety then take over, pulling us off-balance and out of the feeling of the flow of divine energy.

We are always connected to divine power, whether we choose to perceive it or not. The sooner we recognize what is happening—that we are falling out of alignment—the sooner we can get back on track. We must make a conscious effort to focus on the little things in life that bring us joy and happiness. Little by little, the whirlpool of negativity loses its grip.

We can decide to pay attention to our emotions and choose to respond, not react.

We can take time to figure out what causes the worst reactions. We can find the triggers and the real cause of the negative shift leading to imbalance. How?

We can pay attention to how we feel. When we feel bad, we have been triggered to a survival mode in which positive thoughts are nonexistent. But we have the power to change this. We can locate the idea that caused the emotion and learn to redirect that thought. But we must begin with the breath. Deep breathing takes us out of survival mode and into our inner place of divine power.

When we breathe slowly and deeply, we can feel the energy within shift from fear and illusion to clarity and faith. We can breathe and flow in that divine energy until we can examine the situation from a higher perspective of love. Here we find the view of compassion for ourselves and everyone involved.

The flow is the experience of unconditional love. From this place, negativity has lost its grip. We can decide upon a different response to those triggers in preparation for when they surface in the future. Because they will appear again and again until we have mastered this skill. We can use a predetermined response to the triggers when they do appear. We can breathe and connect to the energy that creates worlds. We can learn to respond to the stimuli with love instead of reacting to them, and they lose their power to affect us. The negative triggers atrophy as we find a different muscle to use—the muscle of unconditional love.

With continued practice, we will see a challenge as an opportunity to offer a positive response that provides love to all concerned instead of allowing it to be a trigger for an adverse emotional reaction stemming from fear. We are more balanced when we learn to see our reactionary behavior as fear. We can take time to respond with love instead of anger or frustration. When we respond to a stimulus with love instead of fear, we flow with it and grow with it to the greater heights of joy. When we breathe, connect, and love deeply and freely, we feel the divine energy take us to where miracles happen regularly.

I was able to stay in the flow. I was floating high on life for a good while, thanks to my connection with God and the magic of the power of vibrational attraction. I was good at flowing in the love vibration when things were going well, but life is life.

Eventually, it was time to practice the concept of response versus reaction, which had been given to me in the earlier message of light. I am going to give it to you straight, my friend: that concept was not easily mastered by me. I was slow to assimilate the information, and I had many opportunities to practice. Creating the habit of flowing from love instead of fear was a challenge for me, but it was not impossible, as you will see.

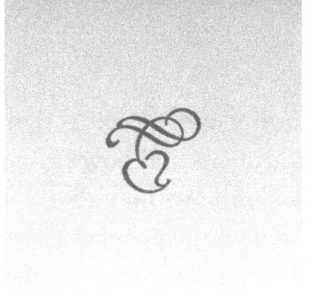

Chapter 15

Love, Fear, and the Unhealthy Ego

People-Pleasing

One of my best teachers in life regarding staying in the flow of love instead of fear during personal interaction was my experience as a scout leader. I started the group with the help of my friend, Tricia. It was my opportunity to give back to my community, and it involved directly spending time with my daughters and their friends. It was a grand adventure!

I will be forever grateful for those years in my life. I met people who would become lifelong friends. I also interacted with some of the most brilliant minds I'd ever encountered before, and I'm not just talking about girls' parents. My group of girls were incredible too.

When we started the group, I did it because I thought I would be helping the girls in my community to learn, grow, and develop important life skills. (Ah, look at the ego on me!) What actually happened was that I grew. I was the one who acquired some valuable life skills by working with them. That right there was a miracle!

The biggest skill I learned through my scouting experience was how to practice love over fear. I have always been a people-pleaser, meaning I have always been motivated by fear of rejection. That didn't change when I became a troop leader.

We had so many girls requesting to be in our troop that I started a second troop with my friends Rosa and DeAnna so I would not have to turn anyone away. I was so afraid of not being liked and accepted that I took on way too much for my own good. At that time, I derived my self-worth from my accomplishments and how I thought others viewed me. I was still working on self-love, and without that, there is no true confidence.

I gauged my value based on the people I served. If my meetings were a success and everyone had fun, then I would allow myself to be happy, and the fears of rejection and failure would fade. The problem is that you can never please everyone, which means I rarely got to be happy.

When all was said and done with a meeting, I spent hours analyzing every moment. I reviewed every word and expression I'd observed, and I obsessively judged myself and my actions harshly. I would naturally zero in on the one moment of the day when I'd noticed anything other than positive emotion coming from either the parents or the kids at the meeting and agonize over that. That was a lot of people to please—two groups, twenty kids more or less, and their parents. And we had meetings every other week for more than five years.

Being an empath added a little extra fun to my experience. I had too much insight into the emotions of the people around me. I was so deeply invested in everyone's happiness at the meetings that I would assume any emotion I encountered other than joy was because of something I did or didn't do in the meeting. Talk about an egocentric way of living. I put so much pressure on myself to make sure everyone was happy that it never occurred to me at the time that people were coming to the meetings carrying their personal lives with them. It wasn't all about me. Go figure! Ah, the things we see in hindsight. But at that time, I was like a little child. I believed any discontent in the people around me was my fault. I bore the burden of failure often enough to make it difficult to withstand. This happens when we derive our sense of worth from the people around us. No good can come from that way of thinking. It's basically impossible to make that many people happy all at once. So after every meeting, I felt defeated. I had to learn to respond to myself and these perceived failures with love instead of reacting to the emotions I felt from others with fear. I wasn't there yet, but working with the two troops was life-changing practice.

Even though I always had people-pleasing tendencies, I never stopped and thought about the root of the issue. Why did I need everyone to like me? I spent a lot of time contemplating the issue. Still, I never actually took the time to ask a real question about it at first, so God found another way to get the answer to me. It came in a message of light from my friend Julie. We weren't even talking about my situation, when she brought up the concept of ego. The subject was not new to me. I knew of the ego. I knew many people who had big ones, and they seemed to think the world revolved around them. As we discussed the topic, something Julie said made me realize I was basically taking that same approach in my scouting meetings. I made the meetings all about me. But instead of my getting a big ego because of my successful meetings, my ego was taking a beating because I failed to make everyone at the meetings happy.

An empath with an unhealthy ego is definitely not flowing in an overabundance of love energy. This causes the shift into absorption mode, which is not good, as we know by now. There is no way for empaths to control what kind of energy they take on in absorption mode. So you can imagine how meaningful my conversation with Julie was to me.

That discussion sparked my interest in the ego. Much of what I'd read about it said that we should let go of ego, but I had no idea what that meant or how to do it. It wasn't until that conversation that I realized I could resolve my people-pleasing problem and my energy-overload issues the same way: by evaluating my ego and understanding its effects on my experience, I could make better choices. So I did what I always do: I walked and prayed about it. This is the message I got:

Letting Go of Attachment to the Ego

> Letting go of ego is not letting go of caring about ourselves and our desires. It is letting go of caring about what others think about us and our wishes.
>
> Letting go of our attachment to our unhealthy ego is not always easy. Throughout our lives, we've been taught "Appearances are important" and "You never get a second chance to make a good first impression." We are taught that we should care what others think of us, sometimes even more than what we think of ourselves.
>
> When we are on a positive path, when the ego is healthy, we are making decisions based on God's love and light. A healthy ego flows from love, and that love shines

through. People with a healthy ego don't act so that others will see the behavior and offer approval. They act so that fulfillment comes from within. When individuals with a healthy ego are told they cannot do something, they do not shrink from the challenge. They instead get it done and prove to themselves that with God's help, they can do anything.

When we make decisions in our lives based on an unhealthy ego, we make them because we are considering what others would think or do in that situation, and we act out of the fear of judgment. The unhealthy ego requires constant encouragement, advice, and approval from others. Without external validation, a person with an unhealthy ego undergoes tremendous stress in almost all situations.

Why listen to the people around us, who are not living our experience? They do not have to live in our skin or with the consequences of our decisions. So why would they know better than we do what is right for us? Some of us get stuck believing that what society thinks is right. It's what we're taught. However, there is ample proof that what the mob is saying or doing is not necessarily always correct. In fact, following the leader or going with that kind of flow can sometimes lead to trouble, especially when the leader is misguided. When others decide they have the right or responsibility to determine the correct way to do things for everyone, they are missing the point of individuality. God created us so that we would be different from one another, so we can learn from our differences and grow together.

Who defines societal views anyway? Are we not part of that society? Why should we let a bunch of strangers decide what is right for us, especially when most are unhappy themselves? Only people with unhealthy egos do that.

We are all guided by God, and that guidance comes to us from within. A person with a healthy ego listens to God and is motivated by love instead of fear. God speaks to each of us through our emotions and points out our motivations. We should pay attention to how we feel, and when we feel bad, we should recognize that bad feeling as direct communication from God. That emotion is God screaming at us from the inside because we ignored him when he whispered. Anxiety is always God warning us against thoughts or actions that are not aligned with our highest and best good. When we listen to our inner guidance, we can let God help us decide what is right for us with confidence and with love for ourselves, instead of making decisions based on popular opinion and fear of rejection. When we make choices based on what others think instead of listening to our own inner guidance, we diminish our potential and devalue that guidance. Why would we believe that another human being would know what is right for us better than God?

When we go forward to make choices, we should leave what others think out of the equation unless it affects them directly. When we are unsure, we should ask God for guidance, not our insecure friends with their own problems to solve. We have to live with the consequences of our choices. Our friends and advisers have to live with theirs.

The only one to judge should be God, and he's not condemning.

When we ask for God's intervention and guidance and have faith, we will receive it. All we have to do after that is follow that guidance.

Try it! See what happens.

I decided to try to start making choices based on my inner guidance rather than on popular opinion. I chose to look at my motivation for the meetings, which was love for my girls and for the kids in the community, rather than focusing on whether or not my efforts were well received. Then I started noticing the nineteen happy girls at the meetings. I began having fun with them rather than fixating on the one unhappy kid who would have chosen that attitude no matter what I did. Somehow, that message helped me to develop a sense of confidence in the decisions I made, because I was now making them from the perspective of a healthier ego. I began to make my decisions for myself and not because of some misguided need for the approval of others. Wow, what a difference!

Flashback

I was clearly in the flow of some incredible energy. I was living my life. I was asking the questions and getting the answers that were helping me to grow as a person. There is so much to learn about this incredible world God has given us to explore. I think it was because I was in that flow of positive energy that I finally got insight into a life experience that had been coming for a long time. Working with the scouts, I learned something new every time I had a meeting or a field trip, but one trip was particularly enlightening, a field trip to a state park with beautiful rock formations. It is a place with some old and powerful spiritual energies. Anytime you get into the untouched or lightly touched wilderness, you will encounter powerful vibrations.

When we first got to the park, I felt fine, but I began to experience a strange sensation as we hiked into the mountains. As I focused on the headcount of my adventurers, I started to feel as though I were walking through a giant cotton ball. I felt light-headed but not dizzy, and the air took on a fuzzy kind of glow. As we continued into the steeper terrain, I noticed a slight humming sound in my deaf ear. The cotton sensation was physically tangible all over my body now, not just in my head. The humming sound became louder, and I recognized the sound. I had heard it before, more than thirty years prior, on the night I'd slept at my babysitter Ruby's house when I was little. It was the same rhythmic chanting, drumming, and thrumming sound that had awakened me in the night all those years ago.

The Messages of Light

The moment I made the connection in my mind that it was the same sound from my childhood experience, I felt a surge of energy run through my body. Suddenly, I was in another time and space. It was dark outside, and I heard the chanting and the thrumming continue. The sound got louder and louder, and my body began to vibrate along with it. It was as if it were coming from inside me. It was so powerful and intense I felt as if I was part of the heartbeat of God, just as I had when I was little. Then I began to see translucent figures artfully and passionately dancing around a fire under the light of the full moon.

Suddenly, I saw, right in front of me, the opening to a vast cave. I realized I was standing in a space similar to what I had seen in what I'd thought was a dream when I was little. As a child, my only point of reference for a dark, vast space had been a parking garage because I had never seen a cave in my limited three-year-old life experience. The vision I had during the field trip was of that place or one like it. In my mind's eye, I could see people around a fire on the plateau at the mouth of the cave, and I could hear the echo of their chant vibrating through the ethers. I was looking in on a ritual that connected them to God, and I was part of it. I could feel God in me and all around me in the vibrations echoing through the ages.

The humming and chanting I'd heard all those years ago had come from them. Just then, I felt a strong vibration move through me as if to attune me to the energy I was sensing in this connection ritual. What I felt was intense and powerful. I felt infused with inspiration, energy, and vitality. I felt a familiarity with this energy on a cellular level. It was the energy of another world long ago, and I felt God there too, in the energy from that time. I felt a sense of wholeness and wonder in that divine energy. I was fascinated by the feeling of love coupled with relief that washed through me. I was in the flow of a divine current of peace that felt overwhelmingly good and brought me to tears. That was definitely God.

A fraction of a second later, I was back in my body, with my troop of explorers, but with a clearer understanding of that childhood experience. I was thrilled to connect the dots, so to speak. Because of that field trip, I was given the opportunity to interpret an experience that had stayed in my memory from my early childhood.

When reflecting on the hiking experience, I got a message of light. I was given some insight into that experience, and it turned out it was from a past life. I resonated with the vibration because I had once lived it. That epiphany explained a lot.

When Ron and I were first dating, he gave me a tour of his house. On the wall in the hallway was a picture of a beautiful Native American woman. As I walked past it, for a split second, I thought I was looking at my reflection. I have blonde hair and blue eyes in this lifetime, so that didn't make any sense. But when I saw that picture, I was instantly transported to a sandbank by a sizable, still body of water surrounded by unspoiled nature. When I looked at my reflection in the water, I saw the girl from the picture. She had beautiful golden-brown eyes, long dark hair separated into two braids that hung down over her shoulders, and golden-brown skin that matched her eyes.

When I looked around in the vision, I saw that behind me was a handsome young boy who also appeared to be Native American. He didn't look like Ron, but energetically, he felt like him. When I came back from that split-second vision, back to the picture on the wall in Ron's house, I realized the woman was me, or at least someone who looked a lot like me in that past life.

Looking at that picture, I saw a flash of a moment in a past life in which Ron and I had known each other. In the vision, I had the feeling we were more than friends. It was hard to tell because the vision was brief, but it felt like love. I love the idea that Ron, in this life, would be drawn to a photo of a girl who looked like me in a past life. I took that as another sign we were connected on a spiritual level and meant to be together. These are things that make you say, "Hmm." Right?

Empath Problems

I had already resolved to let go of my unhealthy ego's hold over my self-worth. I chose to focus on faith. I understood the concept, but the application was next to impossible. You see, my ability to sense what others were feeling was getting in the way of that. It's tough to ignore what people might be thinking when you can feel what they are feeling. Think about that for a minute.

My empathic abilities were causing me to become overwhelmed. I was so busy living my life that I forgot to take the time for myself. That self-care time was important because it kept the empath in me flowing divine energy out toward others. It kept me from absorbing the human energy of the people around me. That concept, at the time, was still not clear to me, but God knew what he was doing. He gave me experiences from which to learn. I was living the life experience that would help me find the clarity I sought. I was still learning how to sort through what I was feeling, and I was still looking for guidance on those feelings. I was experiencing powerful emotions—a lot of them—but which ones were mine? How much of what I felt was actually being picked up from others? How could I deal with emotions coming from energy that wasn't mine to begin with, and what could I do with that energy? It was affecting me intensely. The constant bombardment of emotions and energy was causing me to develop severe anxiety.

I hadn't yet discovered how to differentiate whether the negative energy I sensed from others was because of me or had anything to do with me at all. How could I know if it was me or just that person's mood at the time? Wherever I went, I felt as if every emotion I encountered were directed at me. That's great when people are happy, but it's a terrible experience when they are not. There are so many different people in crowds, with just as many differing vibrations, that I found myself easily overwhelmed by emotion. The more people I was around, the worse I felt. Upon entering busy, populated spaces, I felt as if everyone in the area suddenly stopped what he or she was doing to turn and scream at me. Even if people weren't looking at me, their energy was coming at me like a train. I was frozen on the tracks, destined to receive the full impact of their grief, anger, shame, loneliness, and rage. It happened every time I went out into the world, and I felt there was nothing I could do about it.

Before my abilities were amplified by Reiki and the babies (batteries) I carried, I had little trouble in large groups. I loved going to sporting events and concerts. Those things were fun for me. Crowds were only uncomfortable for me when we were packed in like sardines; otherwise, I was fine. Things changed as my sensitivity grew stronger. I began having full-blown anxiety attacks before gatherings, in anticipation of the discomfort I was sure to experience. My anxiety would continue throughout the whole of each outing. After a while, I started to experience anxiety whenever I was around other people, not just in crowds. I even began to have anxiety attacks before and during my troop meetings. Things I once had enjoyed became difficult. I started to have to pray to get to and through all the public events I was committed to attending. My ability to sense emotion was battling with my inability to process it. As I said, I felt as if all emotional energy were directed at me, wherever I went. I had no reprieve.

The empathic abilities made me feel as if I were a sponge. I soaked up all the energy in whatever room I entered, regardless of whether it was good or bad. The problem was that I had no way to wring out the sponge. This was already exceedingly difficult to manage because I lived in a home with five people. Add to that the fact that I was constantly coming into contact with hundreds of people in small, enclosed spaces, and it's no surprise I was in a state of exhausted confusion regularly. Those events became a living nightmare because I had such trouble finding emotional balance before, during, and after any social interaction. The feeling of contentment in social situations was unavailable to me. Unfortunately, those events happened more and more often as my kids got older, and I had little time to recover my energy between them. To say I was getting overloaded is an understatement. That's what happens to empaths in fear vibration. They go into a superpowered absorption mode.

Whenever I was around people, I felt emotionally exhausted and energetically drained, no matter how much I wanted to be there. I started to believe there was something wrong with me. I wanted to know why I felt so bad after social interactions. It seemed wherever I went, I felt assaulted by negativity. I felt heavier with each interaction, and I didn't know how to release it.

I could have cleared the energy with Reiki and positive prayer, but I wasn't doing that. I was analyzing my emotions and feeling like a victim to the energy around me. I was ignoring any and all of the invaluable tools and techniques I had at my disposal. I was focused on the problem. I forgot to ask for help in finding the solution.

Before I knew it, I was part of my environment, not just physically but also emotionally and energetically. I was becoming part of the problem. I caught myself feeding into negativity on more than one occasion. OK, I am sugarcoating it: maybe *I* was the negativity in the room on more than one occasion. I had a lot of negative emotions to learn to deal with at that time, and I had no clue what I was doing. As I said, I didn't know that most of the energy weighing me down was from interacting with others. I unconsciously took on whatever emotions the people around me were feeling. My body didn't know that the happiness, sadness, frustration, joy, rage, or desperation I experienced wasn't all mine.

Eventually, the stress of it all—well, let's just say it kicked my butt. I fell into a spiral of negativity that terrified me. I will spare you the details of the dramas I created in this chaos, but there were many. You're welcome!

I will, however, share with you the messages I received to help me learn the lessons from those experiences. This message of light came to me while I was thinking about how I had become part of the negativity around me. This message seemed to be explaining to me how that negativity happens and how to deal with it.

Modern-Day Plague: Negativity

Why do we find it so easy to focus on the things in our lives that cause us to feel anger, fear, anxiety, and stress? Those emotions leave us weak and drained. Some would say they arise from the shadows. They sneak up on us when we least expect it. Then it becomes challenging to get rid of the nasty feelings. Soon we find ourselves thinking about and discussing nothing else. The more we focus on the negativity, the more it grows. The snowball of thought becomes an avalanche of emotion that is completely out of our control as it grows, consuming everything in its path.

The negative energy spreads like a disease, like a contagion. Overwhelmed by the negative energy, we begin to lash out at everyone we meet, spreading the disease.

Here's how it goes: Some rude person cuts you off on the freeway and almost causes an accident. But rather than being grateful there was no accident, you become furious. You arrive at your destination enraged. While you stand in line at the store, you see the cashier smiling and talking to the person in front of you, and that's annoying because you are still thinking of the idiot on the freeway. You become increasingly irritated, and suddenly, you are the rude one. You lash out at the cashier, spewing something that takes the smile right from her face. You snatch the receipt and storm off, thinking about rude, inconsiderate people, while the cashier you just emotionally assaulted is still working with people; only now she's not smiling. She's thinking about rude, inconsiderate people and morphing into a lousy mood herself. Now she's rude and insensitive to the following fifty people or more who pass her way that day.

Meanwhile, you've gone about your day in the same negative manner. You sit with a friend later, discussing the rude, inconsiderate people in the world, and she tells you the story of her day. She was having a wonderful day until she met a horribly rude cashier at the store.

Negativity spreads like disease only faster. We allow negativity into our lives by choosing to put our attention and personal energy into it. The same is true for positivity. The more attention we give to the things we appreciate, the more love and light we welcome into life.

We must turn our attention to the things that make us feel happy and loved. That is easier said than done, but it is doable. It takes practice and effort, but we have all the help we need and a limitless supply of amazing and beautiful things to choose from.

Taking it one step at a time, think about the previous example.

We've all had days when everything went south, resulting in emotional exhaustion. What could we do differently?

The first step would be to focus not on the rude driver but instead on the fact that there was no accident and that the crisis was averted. You can't help your initial reaction, but you can respond appropriately to the situation when you pause to consider your own choices at the moment.

Take a deep breath, and find something—anything—good to focus upon. If you can't think of anything immediately, that's when you pray. Even if the prayer is "God, help me find something positive to focus on," you are breaking the momentum of the negativity. You have stopped the spread of the contagion. At that moment, you have vaccinated yourself from the disease that is the modern-day plague: negativity.

Side note: The preceding message was written many years before our world was hit with a pandemic, but if you think about it, the message holds true. The only things that spread faster than the coronavirus itself were the fear and negativity surrounding it. Everyone was affected.

Right after I received that message, I heard someone talking about negativity. The individual said something like "If you're feeling bad in social interactions, look at your friend group; look to your left, and look to your right. If neither of those people is spewing negativity, it's probably you." Oh my, did that hit home! I was doing the "Poor me" thing. Again. The good news was, it was not my first time with that emotion. I already knew where to start to shift my vibration. Just like when I was a teenager, I would say (stay) positive. I would have to at least say positive things out loud, even if I couldn't actually stay positive within yet. At least that way, I wouldn't be adding to the negativity around me.

As the empath in me explored and analyzed all the various emotions and vibrations in the world around me, I noticed one particular emotion that seemed to be coming from me as well: guilt. This was an emotion that plagued me. Since everything I did had to be perfect but never was, I felt guilty for letting people down almost all the time.

I asked about it on my walk, and this is what I got:

On Guilt

They say guilt demands punishment. For those who truly experience it, guilt is punishment.

If that were true, then I had been in prison for decades. I punished myself for every mistake I ever made, never mind the guilt I absorbed from others as an empath. I continued to focus on the concept of guilt as I contemplated. I was trying to figure out how to deal with it, and to do that, I had to understand the nature of guilt. So I asked for a message of light, and here is what came to me:

How do we free ourselves of the energy of guilt?

Emotions are the guide. Guilt does not come from love; it comes from self-judgment. Pain and shame do not come from love. They come from focusing on fearful thoughts of being judged. The decision to focus on the fear of rejection and the fear of being unworthy of love will make us feel as if we are at a distance from God, because God is love. When we judge ourselves, we are not coming from a place of love. When we experience the negativity associated with self-recrimination, it is not a punishment from God. It is only the energy we put out returning to us so we can learn from it. We punish ourselves when we choose to believe that we are the mistake itself instead of the person who learned from it.

To honor ourselves and the love that we are, we should pay attention to the way we feel. We can see what kind of energy we are putting out to others when we do. We can use this guidance to flow love and light into situations instead of the energy that causes us to experience guilt. When we think a thought and feel bad, it is certain the idea is centered on a judgment of some sort. Love feels good. Guilt, pain, and shame arise from fear. Fear feels bad. The fear of enduring the pain will sometimes prevent us from facing that fear and healing it. Instead, we defensively turn that fear around onto someone else in the form of judgment, making the other person responsible for the way we feel. This does not help us to feel better. In fact, it makes us feel helpless and weak, like victims. We are powerless when we choose to believe that someone else is responsible for our feelings. In this case, we have to wait for the other person to comply with our desires in order to feel good. This rarely happens without a fight. But when we take ownership of the way we feel in response to other people's actions, we have the power to shift our own reality. We realize that people are people, and they will behave as they will, but we have the power to choose to respond to them with love. We will never feel guilty about interacting with another human being when we flow from love.

> Whoever does not love does not know God, because God is Love.
> —1 John 4:8 NIV

Just as I was finishing up translating that message of light complete with Bible scripture, I got the following message about God's love. It seemed to be a continuation of the previous message, so I kept flowing with the vibration. The words seemed to write themselves. By sending me these messages, God was washing away all the fear, pain, guilt, and shame the human in me felt, and the empath in me had absorbed, and replaced those emotions with love. To me, that was a miracle. I realize now that every time I opened to receive the wisdom of God, I also opened to receive the love of God, which healed me and realigned my vibration.

God's Love

You can't flow God's love through you without getting God's love on you. God is love. Any act of love is a tribute to honor our Creator and his creations. As we love and comfort one another, we receive the same energy in kind, for God's love is pure and unlimited. As we tap into the flow of this love by sharing it with another, we become one with its energy. We then are not wielding the energy; God's love is wielding us. We become instruments of love. We become tools of creation, manifesting beauty and light, for all beauty and light stem from God's love. What better way for God to reveal himself in our world than through the kind and loving acts of his children, who are guided by his hand?

> Give, and it will be given to you. A good measure, pressed down, shaken together, and running over, will be poured into your lap. For with the measure you use, it will be measured to you.
> —Luke 6:38 NIV

This may be the secret to a happy life right here. You get what you give, or, in the immortal words of the Beatles, "In the end, the love you take is equal to the love you make." Learning not only to be a giver and receiver of love but also to flow in the vibration of love itself has its perks. There is no guilt, shame, anger, or blame when we flow in love. It's a beautiful flow of energy that makes this life worthwhile. That leads me to this next message of light. When we flow in God's love, we actually get to enjoy the gift of life.

The Gift of Life

Life is a gift. Life is the process of growth and evolution. In this life, when we no longer quest after the knowledge and wisdom found in the unknown, the waters of our life become stagnant. We become bored. We stop trying. Why bother when there is nothing exciting to anticipate? If only we could continue on in life with the wide-eyed wonderment of the child we once were, there would be no limit to our growth. There is always more to learn. The mysteries of the universe are infinite. So when you think you have it all figured out, ask a new question. Learn to savor the journey. Expect the exhilarating "Aha" moments yet to come. They bring the tides of change and growth.

Have you ever really stopped to look at the intricate details in the world around you? Look at technology, for instance. Notice how tiny the elements are that make our lives simpler. Where did the inspiration come from that allows us to talk to one another through the air in writing, sound, and images? Now those same things that used to be in science-fiction novels are a reality. Technology continues to advance at an exponential rate just because someone is always asking a new question.

Many of us have become lazy. We have lost our passion and drive. Frankly, we have lost our faith in our own capabilities and potential. We say or think things that would lead us to believe we are incapable of achieving the feeling of success. We say, "Oh, I can't do that. Those people are extraordinary. They are gifted. That's not me."

The fact is, life is a gift, and therefore, we are all gifted.

Why do we doubt that if we tried, we might succeed? Probably because of past perceived failures. Too often, we feel discouraged, as if we've been handed a raw deal, but is that really the case? How raw is the deal really? Every experience is the opportunity to learn and grow. We are just as capable of looking for opportunities as we are capable of focusing on failures and difficulties. When we look for an opportunity, it will present itself. Then we can run with it, instead of watching it run away because we were too afraid to try. We are all capable of diligence and determination.

Ask yourself: What do you want to do with this gift you've been given? How will you use your abilities? It's up to you. Will you be the child who appreciates and takes care of a gift? Or will you be the child who trashes his toy and wonders why the world is so unjust? Will you watch the waters of your life become dark and stagnant, or will you let the waters of growth and opportunity flow?

Learning to See Miracles in Everything

After that download of messages and the energetic boost that came with them, I decided I wanted to be the child who took care of and appreciated her gift, this incredible gift of life. Everywhere I went, and in everyone I encountered, I looked for the miracles. Everything was a miracle to me. I do mean everything. I refused to get sucked into negativity for longer than a moment. Knowing this, God, with his infinite love and dazzling sense of humor, decided to help me strengthen my ability to see miracles in an interesting way.

My spirits were high. I had just dropped Kira off at her elementary school, and I went on to arrive at Aja's preschool early enough to play, as we always did. However, it was too cold to play outside that day, so we went into the classroom instead. I took a seat in the rocking chair in the reading section of the colorful kindergarten classroom, and my adorable little Aja sat in my lap. We cuddled as I read Christmas books to her until the other kids began to arrive. I kissed her goodbye, taking in the scent of her hair, and she ran off to play with her friends.

I was walking back to my car in the warm glow of mommy bonding, when I suddenly remembered something. I intended to take Aja's teacher a natural cold remedy I'd left in my car. (Keep in mind this was a time before a sneeze or cough caused mass panic.) I looked at the time on my phone. I had somewhere to be, but I decided to grab the medicine and take it to her anyway. I hurriedly headed back toward the school, when *whoop*—suddenly, my feet were in the air, the world went spinning, and I was laid out on the ground like a gymnast on a failed dismount. To me, it happened in slow motion. I saw the world spin. I saw a blue sky and clouds above me. I saw frozen yellow grass. I saw all of that at the same time as I felt my hip hit the ice on the ground and, with it, my pride. As if that weren't enough, the slow motion continued, and my hand crashed to the ground, barely in time to slow the impact of my chin on the icy concrete.

The Messages of Light

Dazed, I gingerly rose from the ground, noting the shift in my mood. My first thought was *Wow! It's true what they say: no good deed goes unpunished.*

The negative thoughts continued to spiral as I walked into the classroom and handed the teacher her medicine. I was embarrassed, and by then, I was running late, so I considered leaving without saying anything about the ice patch, but my training kicked in. I was looking for miracles in everything, so I thought, *What is the miracle in this?*

Instantly, I got a flash in my mind's eye that answered my question, and I went straight to work. I got a custodian to stand by the ice, and I went to the administration to tell them what had happened. Their concern was for me and any injuries I may have sustained, but I quickly dismissed those concerns and got straight to my own. You see, the flash I'd had in my mind was of a mommy walking with a baby in her arms and holding hands with her older child, when she stepped on the ice. You can imagine the rest of the vision, but please don't.

Thank God the scene in my vision was averted. I was the only one hurt by the nasty patch of black ice. My physical injuries were minimal, and miraculously, the damage done to my pride was healed entirely when I found the miracle in the situation. And of course, as soon as I shifted my focus, the person I was supposed to meet that morning called to say she was running late too. Everything was in perfect alignment—except maybe my spine. I left the school that day feeling as if I had just gotten off a roller coaster featuring strong g-forces, but boy, did I learn a lot! You can't go wrong by doing the right thing.

I found myself contemplating the morning's events later that day on my walk, when I received the following messages of light.

The first one would have been good to hear before I fell on my face, but then again, what would the lesson have been without the hands-on (facedown) experience?

> Slow down! Do not walk so fast you cannot see or feel where you are headed. Take your steps through life with purpose.

Take Time

Take the time to look around. What are we in such a hurry to do anyway? When we rush, we allow chaos to take over. We experience anxiety, and we feel out of control. When we rush, we subscribe to the illusion that time is limited. Time will expand to meet our needs and desires; we only have to believe that. Time only exists in the physical realm, and we are much more than these physical bodies. What we create here in the physical realm is limited only by belief. We can think that time is restrictive or believe that it is expansive and offers freedom. What we experience depends on our focus.

What makes us feel rushed anyway? Does it have something to do with worry or fear? Fear is created in our existence when we choose not to trust in God's timing. God's timing is perfect. How many accidents happen each day because someone is in a hurry? Have you ever stopped to think that the only reason you weren't in an unpleasant situation that day might have been because of God's timing? You may have thought you were running late, but you were perfectly safe because of the delay. It's just a matter of retraining our thoughts. When we are in a hurry, we are choosing to focus on someone or something at our destination that elicits fear or frustration. We spend our energy imagining the negative consequences of our tardiness, making things worse. We can instead decide to focus on love and light. Ask that we arrive in perfect timing and that the outcome be for the highest and best good for all involved. We can redirect our focus to love and what makes us feel better about a situation instead of what makes us feel worse.

Taking our time gives us more opportunity to focus on choices to be made and allows us to make those choices in clarity. When we take the time to look and see where we're going, we have time to decide. We can choose to stay on that path or to find another. We don't have to live our lives haphazardly in a rush. That vibration can only bring more people and events in the energetic flow of chaos. We then end up meeting others who are rushed, frustrated, and even angry, unless we take time to choose a different vision for our future.

We can choose to look at our blessings and appreciate them. We can ask to feel relaxed and happy. Whether we are on time or not, our energy level can be light and peaceful when we do this. When we walk into a room, our peacefulness will be contagious to those who also have made choices out of love, and it will repel those who haven't. Those who haven't taken time to choose from a place of love and have subscribed to the illusion of chaos will inexplicably be called away or have something else to do.

We should take time to look around and see the beauty in life. We can act with purpose to find this beauty. When we give our attention to the divine elegance around us, we experience a wave of absolute peace and serenity that we certainly don't feel when we are rushing. Take time to sit in the shade of a tree. Take a beat to listen to birds singing. Take a second to notice the colors around you. We have to seize the moment by choosing to see it. We can smile. We can enjoy the sound of the breeze as it whistles through the trees. We can let our energy fly, and we can soar and sing with the birds. Life is a song, and it's ours to compose. We should soak up as much of this love and beauty in the world as we can and then take it and share it with others. When we do, we will see it grow.

When You Are Not in Alignment with the Message

I had the opportunity to read the preceding message when I was not in the mood to hear it. I read it when I was in a foul disposition because I'd failed to take time for myself. In that negative vibration, I was annoyed.

From the place where I stood, the last thing I wanted was to look at some blissful and seemingly wholly unattainable experience of life. It made me feel even more distant from the rest of the world, like an outsider looking in. Reading something out of my vibrational grasp just made me angry, and it caused me to think, *Come on! Really? Like it's that simple.*

My first instinct to something I'm not aligned with is to react; I close the book, change the channel, or even leave the room.

The thing is, even if the message is annoying when it comes into our experience, we are close enough in vibration to see it. Once we see it, we have a choice to use the information and grow from it or be annoyed now and grow from it later. Either way, we are growing!

So I chose to embrace the information rather than be annoyed by the vibration. I didn't create excuses for my lack of positivity, as I would have in the past. I know now that if I put off the growth, I will continue to struggle. If I welcome it, I may have some growing pains, but ultimately, I will feel better sooner rather than later. The fact is, I know how I feel is based on my focus. I like to feel good, so I decided to focus on what makes me feel better: helping others.

In helping others, we also help ourselves.

Chapter 16

Embracing and Understanding My Gifts

The Unexpected Journey

If someone had told me when I was younger that I would grow up to be someone who was extremely sensitive to energy and emotion and that I would see, hear, and communicate with spirits, I would have thought he or she was crazy. I mean, really? Like I would talk to dead people? Like the kid in *The Sixth Sense*? Please! Not me! No way. That idea would have seemed ridiculous, if not impossible, to me then. Adding to that insanity, the idea that I would actually tell people I could do it would have been ludicrous! That would have been too "out there" for even my open mind to believe back then.

But contrary to those beliefs of my youth, there I was, doing just that. I was talking to dead people. Even crazier, plenty of living people knew I was doing it. The more I followed my guidance by relaying the messages from spirits to their loved ones, the stronger my ability became.

I wanted to help people. But with my amplified ability, there came a feeling of immense responsibility. As I mentioned before, everyone we meet has someone on the other side who would love to talk to him or her, and I wanted to help them all. It started to become all-consuming. Not only did I want to relay their messages, but I felt I had to do it. I felt it was my duty, not just an ability. Those minimissions were becoming problematic for me.

I had no control over when the spirits would pop in, and the visits were becoming increasingly frequent. I also had difficulty in managing the two different conversations going on at the same time when the spirits did decide to pop in. I often found myself communicating with the spirit at the same time I tried to converse with the living person in front of me. It was especially tricky when the living person had no clue why I was acting so distracted. Imagine you're having a conversation with someone, and the person you're talking to suddenly changes his or her focus to something or someone you can't see and starts interacting with it. Have you ever seen someone talk to thin air? It's strange!

Being an empath was no help either. Remember, I could sense emotions profoundly. I had so many things happening to my body and mind all at the same time that I became overburdened with it all. It was so confusing. I was trying to determine if what I was experiencing was my own emotion or if it was coming from the person in front of me. On top of that, I had the spirits talking to me too!

I continued to worry that people would think I was insane, because I was kind of acting that way. During many conversations with people, I found myself staring off into space and nodding or shaking my head in response to the spirit that no one else could see. I began to worry about how people might react if I spoke to them about the spirits trying to reach them. I began to question and doubt my capacity to manage my ability while retaining my sanity.

So I made an agreement with God to help me stay sane. I decided I would just tune the spirits out unless certain conditions were in place before I was prompted to speak. First, I asked to be sure the person would actually want to communicate with his or her loved one. Second, I prayed I would only be prompted to speak about the spirit when the information would be shared at the perfect time for all concerned. Lastly and most importantly, I asked that the message I offered would be well received. Without those conditions in place, I wouldn't say a thing, because I was afraid of judgment. Yep, my vibration had shifted back to that. Old habits are hard to break sometimes. The funny thing is, I had no reason to believe that the messages I had to deliver wouldn't be well received, because they always were. I had no evidence to the contrary, except what manifested in my mind because of my fearful thinking.

I understood the concept of "What other people think of me is none of my business," but the application of the idea was increasingly troublesome while I was busy sensing other people's emotions and learning to overcome my insecurities about them. I was still sorting things out, but I knew for sure I was on an unexpected journey of self-discovery.

The Rosary

As I continued to explore the hidden depths of the power within me and how it related to the world, I was given the opportunity to practice. It was early in the summertime, when I got an unexpected mission. It was another opportunity to strengthen my skills. Now that I think about it, nearly all my spiritual tasks were unexpected. I mean, it's not as if I had access to God's schedule. I just decided to be a willing participant in whatever he had planned, and I trusted my guidance to alert me to when I should get involved. I asked for clear prompting.

The time for me to get involved came around. I was prompted. It happened when I invited my friend Patricia and her daughter to come over to hang out with us at the pool. My friend and I were sitting by the pool, watching Kira and Aja play together with her daughter, Camilla, in the water. We were talking, when I was prompted to ask her about the man standing beside her.

This man was the first spirit to appear to me since I'd made my pact with God for clear guidance, prompting me to speak. I knew this was it. I was being clearly prompted, so there was no getting around it. He had been there for a little while, waving his arms in the air, trying to get my attention. It seemed he had something important to say, so I spoke up and talked to Patricia about him. In retrospect, I realized it was the first time I'd skipped the part where I worried about what the other person might think. This time, I went straight to telling my friend what I saw. Ah, the power of intention. I'd made that agreement earlier, so I knew that clear prompting meant I would be safe from judgment.

When I knew that my distraction was obvious, I explained that I saw a man standing beside her. When she looked over her shoulder to see who was there and didn't see anyone, she nodded to me in affirmation, as if she knew exactly what I was talking about. She leaned forward and looked at me intently as if to say, "Go on." As I engaged with the spirit, I began to see what he wanted me to see.

The first thing he showed me was what he was wearing, and I described it to her. I had no idea why that was important, but as I shared the information, I could tell it meant something to my friend. He continued giving me bits of information that seemed to be random to me, but Patricia seemed to understand almost all of it. I had no idea who the man was to her or why he'd appeared, but I knew I had to honor my ability by following my guidance. So I shared more of the details he offered.

I told her I could feel his love for her, because I could feel it. Yay for being an empath. I knew he was someone close to her. By the depth of the love I was feeling, I thought he must have been her father or grandfather. My empathic ability came in handy. What I felt gave me a major clue.

As I spoke, her eyes welled up with tears. When I was done talking, Patricia explained that I had just described her father, who had recently passed away. At that moment, I could also feel how much she loved her father. There was an energetic connection happening. It was as if he were holding her and rocking her in his arms while she released her grief through her tears. The love between them was so profound I felt as if I were intruding on a private and deeply personal moment between a father and his daughter.

The exchange between the spirit and me continued as he kept his love energy focused on his daughter. He had a message for Patricia and the rest of his family. As I delivered the information he offered, I could sense pure joy on his part. He was able to confirm for his family that he was happy and at peace. I also felt a sense of relief coming from my friend as she openly received the love her father was showering on her.

The interaction continued, and I went on describing what I saw. The spirit and I were communicating but without words. I could see him, but I couldn't really understand him. It was like two people speaking different languages while trying to have a conversation. So he made gestures to show me what he was trying to say. I was focused on what he held in his hands. He kept holding it up and then pressing it to his heart. It was a rosary. I could see that clearly as he held it up in my view. So I asked my friend if he had been a religious man, and she said he had been devout. That made

The Messages of Light

sense to me, but I could tell by his actions that that wasn't the message he was trying to get across. He shook his head, indicating "No."

Then he leaned forward, lifting his chin, as he looked me in the eye in the same way his daughter had when she encouraged me to go on earlier. I could see the family resemblance. I could tell by the intensity in his eyes that I was missing the point of the message. That wasn't what he wanted to say about the rosary. He kept clutching the rosary and holding it up to his heart. So I asked if he'd prayed the rosary every night, because he kept indicating he held his rosary at night, every night. He did this by holding the rosary up, placing it between his hands, and then putting his hands by one ear. He leaned his head over his hands and closed his eyes, indicating sleep, with his hands still holding the rosary.

Patricia didn't know what to think about what I was saying and said she had never seen him pray the rosary at night, much less every night. I could feel confusion coming from her at that point, but I did not sense doubt. She was trying to figure out what he meant. I explained I was sure it was a rosary, and it was dear to him. After a while of repeating the same message about the rosary, we moved on. I wasn't getting anything new on that subject. Not wanting to break the spell because of my uncertainty, he gave me more information proving to us that I was indeed speaking with her father. He offered guidance, love, and other messages of light for his family. Still, that day, we never figured out what he meant about the rosary.

I was still curious but ultimately OK with not knowing what the rosary meant. I was happy I'd dared to speak up when I was called. I was also pleased that I hadn't freaked out when the biggest part of the message, the part about the rosary, didn't seem to make sense to my friend. I was really growing from the experience. I also realized it was the first time I'd communicated with someone on the other side whom I hadn't met face-to-face on this side first. I was learning so much. I was in awe.

With the messages of light delivered, Patricia and I spent the rest of the afternoon getting to know each other better. At the same time, our girls played together, splashing around in the pool.

A few weeks later, my friend invited our family to dinner at her house, and of course, we accepted. A beautiful older woman was seated in the kitchen area when we got there. When she saw me, her eyes got big, and the smile that crossed her face was so bright it was contagious. I couldn't help but smile in return. Then I heard her ask her daughter in Spanish, "Is this her?"

Patricia saw the look of confusion on my face. It wasn't a language barrier, because I understood clearly what she had asked. I knew she was referring to me. My first thought would have been, *Uh-oh! What did I do?* had she not been smiling so warmly at me. Then I received an incredible honor. Before my friend could explain, the woman wrapped me in an embrace so loving that I almost cried. Then she said, "Thank you! Thank you!" this time in English. Then my friend explained to the confused onlookers—my husband and daughters—what was happening.

The woman was thanking me for delivering the message from her husband weeks before. Apparently, the information was healing and helpful beyond any measure I had known. The beauty of the peace on this radiant stranger's face and the warmth of love in the hug she gave me were worth every minute of my struggle it had taken to get there.

Can you believe the story gets better? Years later, I shared this text in its preliminary stages with Patricia, and she told me of the miracle of the rosary story. It explained precisely why her mother had embraced me with such adoration. The rosary message that neither she nor I could decipher had been for her mother.

The day we received that message of light from her father, my friend went straight home and told her mom the story of communicating with him through me. Apparently, when she told her mom about the rosary, her mother knew exactly what her husband was talking about.

She explained the message about the rosary by simply saying, *"Hija, me llamo Rosario"* (Daughter, my name is Rosary [Rosario]).

When he kept holding the rosary to his heart, indicating how dear his rosary was to him, he was trying to give me the name of someone he loved: his wife, Rosario. The Spanish word for *rosary* is *rosario*. We were communicating without words, so he found a way to tell me whom he was talking about. He was indicating that he loved his wife, Rosario (rosary), very much. He was also trying to explain that he still holds his wife in his arms. He was trying to say that he was still with her and that he would always love his Rosario.

I am still in awe of how that little miracle came about. Back then, talking to a spirit wasn't as easy for me as having a simple conversation.

Most of the time, it was like trying to play charades. The spirit offered visual clues and sometimes words, but it was up to me to interpret them, and I wasn't particularly good at that yet. Interpretation of information from the other side takes practice.

My insecurity did ease up after that experience, even before I learned about the most awe-inspiring part. So instead of fearing my gift or viewing it negatively, I decided I wanted to understand more about it, and I practiced using it. I wanted to use this gift to offer comfort to those who had lost someone to the transition of death. Many people I knew were suffering through that kind of loss. I wanted to know what I could say to someone who has lost a loved one. I wanted to offer something to help others understand the transition from the physical world to the spiritual realm. I prayed about it, and this is what I got:

We Have Just Changed Form

> We have just changed form. We are no longer hindered by a physical body. We continue to exist. When you have a thought, a memory, or a conversation about us, you summon our energy. At that moment, we are there with you, standing in the room or sitting with you, smiling, reenacting the event, reliving the memory, holding you, and comforting you. Those moments in life that are difficult to bear—when your heart feels heavy and when you feel like you don't know how you can go on, but you do—are the times when we come to you. We surround you with love. We offer you comfort and peace and support you so that you can go on.
>
> We come to help you release your grief. So go ahead and cry when we wrap you in our energetic embrace. Then occupy your mind with thoughts of love. Consciously focus on designs for a happy and fulfilled future, so you can go on. When you call on us to help you and to be there with you, we come. We are with you. Grieve for your loss, but remember that we are not gone, only changed.

We are still present in a different form. Keep us in your thoughts, and we are just a breath away.

In this expanded dynamic, we will make new memories together. We will send you signs, and you will know they are real. There is so much to this universe to learn about and to understand. Be open to the beauty of the love that surrounds you. Fill yourself with love. It carries you through the deepest waters of sorrow. Rest in the comfort of knowing that we are at peace and that we are still with you. Be open, and you will feel the truth in these words. Sorrow is leaving you now. Receive the comfort and peace, the sweet release of your grief. Fill the space with joyful memories.

Remember me, and I Am with you always.

Going On about My Business

At that point in my life, I was still just trying to get my bearings. I was learning how to strengthen and control my abilities as an empath and use them to help people. The more I answered the call of my higher purpose, the more calls I got. My next adventure was a self-empowerment class I was roped into teaching by my sister-in-law, Kathy. The group I would be teaching were girls just about to go into high school, and she felt that a self-empowerment class would be perfect to prepare them for that transition.

The problem was that I wondered whether I was equipped to teach self-empowerment. Again, we go back to concept and application. I understood the idea of self-empowerment, but was I the right person to be teaching it?

Self-doubt was in the house.

I took everything so seriously! I mean, I guess that was mostly good, but it was a lot of pressure. I was terrified. I had no idea how to connect with the girls. I wanted to speak to the girls on their own level, but their mothers were sticking around for the course, altering the dynamic. Talk about a challenge!

It's a miracle I didn't run screaming from the mission. Instead, I prayed about it, and inspiration took over. I realized the miraculous timing at play.

I had just written about my angsty teenage years as part of my mission to write my story, so those feelings and emotions were still fresh in my memory banks, and because I had already accessed a higher perspective on the topics, I actually had something to share that might be of value to them. I was able to tap into those feelings from my youth to ask pertinent questions. Then I took my usual walk to connect, and that was when I got the messages that would be the topics of discussion in the class. It was as if God were writing the course for me.

What follows are the messages I shared with the class, with a little explanation of what I was contemplating when I got them.

For the first message or key point in the whole workshop, I had to ask, "What is self-empowerment?"

> Self-empowerment is the power to make a choice using your own internal compass. It's the ability to think for yourself and act according to your individual ideals. Self-empowerment, simply put, is acknowledging that at any moment, in any given situation, there are endless possibilities from which to choose. To access personal power, one must simply make a choice. We each have free will, so no one else can choose for us unless we give him or her the power to do so. So take a deep breath, and make a choice.
>
> Choose to be happy.
> Choose to do good things.
> Choose to be helpful.
> Choose to be kind.
> Make a choice to recognize the moments and the opportunities within them that will bring you closer to those goals.
> Choice, not chance, determines your destiny!

After I got the first message of light, they began to flow. I realized you can't teach self-empowerment without teaching self-love. Nowadays kids and adults get a little confused about the whole self-love thing. They confuse courage for conceit and authenticity for awkwardness. So young people will diminish themselves and alter their perspectives and actions to fit in with the group. They are so busy trying to be loved that they forget to love themselves. I was thinking about that, and I got another message:

Self-Love

You cannot love yourself too much. Self-love is the key to self-confidence.

Confidence and arrogance are in no way the same. Arrogance is an expression of insecurity. Confidence comes with honoring a commitment to the higher self. Take time every day for self-care. Meditate, pray, exercise, dance, or play. Get to know yourself on a deeper level. You may just love the person you meet.

Continuing on in my contemplation, I thought about how teens tend to define themselves based on the opinions of others. I know I did. They are afraid to be their authentic selves, because they might be rejected. Teens—and adults, for that matter—are also really great at self-ridicule. I was thinking about that, and this is the message that came to me:

Permission

You don't need anyone's permission to be who you are. You exist! God created you! That's your authority. Be your authentic self, no matter what pressure exists around you to be like someone else. No one can do you better than you. Trying to fit in is hard, so don't try to fit in. Try to be the best version of yourself. That's actually doable, and it's way easier.

Give yourself permission to be human. Learn to forgive yourself for not already knowing what you just learned from your mistake. What we call *mistakes* are simply learning opportunities. Instead of punishing yourself for every imperfect choice, chalk it up to experience. Resolve to let that lesson teach you to make different and better choices in the future. Love yourself for learning.

The messages were flowing now; everything I ever had gotten wrong in high school came rushing through me like a river of information. The next message that came to me was a concept I understood well and had spent many years training myself to apply. While growing up, I'd heard adults talk about how teens should learn to keep their priorities straight, but the lists of priorities back then were different. They were always a variation of the following: school, good grades, extracurricular activities, work, and family. I never once heard an adult tell kids they should prioritize their own happiness and well-being. Self-care was not a big thing when I was a kid. I was contemplating all that, when the following message of light came in. It is a concept that never gets old, so I teach it often.

Priorities

Priorities—it's essential to have them, and it's even more important to be one. Be number one on your list of priorities. Self-care is the key to happiness and fulfillment, because it raises your vibration. When you fill yourself up with love and energy, you have plenty to share with others. People will be drawn to you because your energy feels good. Without self-care, which translates to self-love, we become the needy friend who drains the energy of the people around us to fill up our own energy reserves. We become energy vampires, sucking the life from our friends, our family, and even perfect strangers.

I started to see that the picture unfolding was looking more like a spiral staircase. Certain concepts and challenges from my youth kept coming around. Each time, I had the opportunity to level up and get new inspiration. With further information, I could see the situation from a higher perspective. This was no exception. Because I was challenged to teach this class, I was forced to focus back on my youth. This time, I was able to see the situations differently. My views and beliefs then evolved as I looked at my experiences from a new perspective—a perspective that came from the knowledge of experience coupled with the wisdom in the messages of light. In thinking about my teenage years, I realized my biggest struggle was dealing with judgment. It wasn't just judgment from others that bothered me. The self-inflicted judgment riddled with criticism was the most challenging thing for me to bear. That struggle didn't go away as I got older, as you, my dear reader, well know. This was a concept I was still working on. The opportunity to teach it forced me to explore my fear further. Maybe if I had understood the nature of judgment better when I was younger, I wouldn't have struggled so much. So I asked about it, and I got another message about judgment that I felt might be helpful to the teens.

Judgment

You wouldn't be caring if you weren't comparing. Comparison always leads to the judgment of the other person or yourself. Neither is productive. Judging another is an avoidance technique keeping you from personal growth. When you judge yourself, you are holding yourself in a negative vibration by subscribing to an illusion of inadequacy. Do not compare yourself to others. You are not here to be the best copy of another person. You are here to be the best version of yourself. Only your own personal guidance will get you there. Following the advice of others without considering your own purpose and desire for fulfillment will only lead to distress. Make sure that what feels right to you is always factored into the equation. Do what is right for you.

The information was still flowing. It was crazy in a cool way. As soon as I had a thought about something I'd experienced as a teen, the wheels started turning, and I cranked out more messages. This is another concept I wished I had known when I was young, and it was another step along the spiral staircase of life lessons. This is a concept I had already viewed from multiple perspectives. This was another opportunity to view it yet again from another angle: the opinions of others.

This message gave me more insight into a big issue in our world today:

What Others Think

Many of us spend time making our decisions based on what other people think. We worry about looking strange or less than intelligent to our peers. Some of us spend countless hours criticizing ourselves. We actively seek out flaws and imperfections so we can correct them before anyone else notices they exist. The problem is, the flaws we seek we find.

We judge everything based on what society at large deems to be perfect. What is perfect? No two definitions of an ideal life are alike, so why do we all strive for sameness? We place value in the opinions of others over our own. We draw energy from the feeling of acceptance, while our energy is drained at the thought of being rejected. The worry and concern we experience open the floodgates to more harmful and self-destructive thoughts. The negative thoughts ultimately give way to self-destructive behavior.

We give so much value to what others think that we ultimately unknowingly give away our power. Sometimes we give our power over to someone we really care about, such as a parent, spouse, or friend. Other times, we give our personal power away to others who would wish us grief. Whether or not anyone realizes that it is happening, it is. There is a real and obvious exchange of energy in every human interaction. We are funneling our power to other people and forgetting to look to the Source to replenish what was lost. Other people don't need our energy. They have their own power. However, they may prefer it when we give them our energy because it's easier than learning how to replenish with spiritual energy on their own. The energy they are looking for isn't from another person anyway. It's from God. God has plenty of love, ample energy, and infinite power, and guess what: he loves to share. Fill up with this love, and share it!

Here's a thought. God created us. God is the perfect Being. God is the Creator of all things, and God does not make mistakes. God created each of us individually with thought and purpose. His creations are all perfect in their own ways. To see this perfection in ourselves, we need only look for it instead of looking for flaws.

They say, "Nobody's perfect." We say, "Nobody is perfectly like one another." God is the definition of perfect. When we accept ourselves as we are, perfect creations of God, and recognize that we are made as we are meant to be, perceived flaws and all, we can accept the energy God is offering, and we have a chance at happiness.

We must acknowledge that we have choices. Where we go from this moment is a choice. We have the opportunity to draw the limited energy from the people around us through drama, or we can learn to draw strength from God. It's a choice. We can continue in the current state with self-loathing and self-destruction or gain power from God by looking for the beauty and good in ourselves and others. God created us in his image, after all.

As the energy continued to flow, I began thinking about schools and the cliques that form from bonding over a common enemy or mutual distaste for something. Teens—and many adults—will tolerate one another's presence, but they judge all along the way. How much easier would it be if teens learned acceptance instead of just tolerance? This is the message that resulted from that contemplation:

Acceptance

Acceptance is not a synonym for *tolerance*. The meanings of these two words are entirely different. Acceptance of ourselves and others is more than merely putting up with or dealing with the way we find ourselves and others to be. Acceptance is finding love, joy, and beauty wherever we look. It means looking for and seeing the light within us and embracing it. Then we look for that same light in the people, situations, places, and things in our experience. All the life around us radiates light. When we accept this light, we can bask in it, drawing it into ourselves, and be filled. The dark and empty spaces within are illuminated, and we see that we are whole, complete, and perfectly imperfect.

My connection to God was so powerful at that point that the information kept washing over me like the waves of the ocean, drenching me with wisdom. I thought about how many kids, including myself, developed anxiety issues as teens. I thought about how I'd felt the need to have some kind of control over my life when I was growing up. I had overthought everything and worked myself into a tizzy over things I could do nothing about. Then I got the following message:

Let stuff go! Don't micromanage for the Big Guy.
God didn't need our help to create the universe. Don't doubt his ability to solve your problems when you've asked for his help. When you let go of your issues, genuinely let go; the magic of creation will unfold. Most people say they've let go of a problem but then continually focus on it anyway. That is not letting go. That's like planting a seed and then going back later to dig it up to see if it is growing. Let it go. Trust God.

If you're thinking about something all the time, you haven't let it go. Every time you think about a condition or situation you are unhappy about, you're giving it more power over you. If you can't think about it without feeling distressed, take a deep breath, and align to get a clearer perspective, or think about something else.

Of course, I could not end the message-gathering session without spending at least a moment on the ever-present fear of failure, a concept that caused me and a lot of other people distress. And the message that came was the following:

> Don't give up. Don't ever quit. The only real failure is the failure to try and sometimes try again.

That was the last of the cascade of inspiration that filled my mind and my spiral notebook with wisdom to share with the teens in my self-empowerment workshop.

Teaching Self-Empowerment

Teaching self-empowerment for young women was a fantastic, life-affirming experience. As I drove to the class on the first day, I prayed for the highest and best good for all concerned so that the class would go as God intended. Then I began thinking about how much I had already learned and healed just by exploring the topics I would teach that day. My mama always says, "You never teach anything you don't need to know yourself." I know what that means now, but my first reaction to that concept was "How can you teach it if you don't already know it?" The answer is that every time you teach something, whatever it is, there is an exchange of energy and perspective that elevates the consciousness of both parties. You explain what you do know, and you end up learning something new on the subject. When two or more people come together in a quest for knowledge and expansion, respective vibrations rise, and they obtain access to higher consciousness: God.

> For where two or three gather in my name, there am I with them.
> —Matthew 18:20 NIV

By the time I arrived to teach the class, I was feeling fully connected and in the flow of confidence and peace. I listened to my power music all the way there. The Red Hot Chili Peppers' song "Midnight" was still in my mind when I rang the doorbell. Then I entered the house, and I quickly learned that teenage girls still intimidated me. I was met with the energetic greeting of girls who clearly had someplace else to be—any place but there. Don't get me wrong; they were sweet and kind girls. They were simply teenagers who probably would rather have been sleeping on a Saturday morning before nine o'clock instead of having to be there to learn about personal power. I can see the irony in that statement even as I write it.

At first, the energy of the resistant and discontented girls knocked me back a bit. Instantly, I got nervous again and insecure. But then I took a deep breath or three. I remembered this was a fabulous opportunity for me to personally apply the exact concepts I would be teaching the girls that day. At that moment, I saw that I, a fully grown adult, was terrified of teenage girls! This was probably because I remembered what it was like to be one. In that instant, in my mind, I was a teenager again. I recognized that I cared what the girls thought of me, and I admitted to myself that I was afraid of judgment again.

Once I faced my fears head-on, they dissipated, though they didn't go away completely. The breathing helped too. I was still nervous, but somehow, I could move through the feelings instead of getting lost in them. Then I focused on my purpose in being there. I was meant to be of service. No one had said it would be easy or comfortable. I thought about the message "What Others Think" and continued to breathe and center myself. From then on, I was able to stay connected to the flow of energy from God. I noticed this time that as I streamed the energy from God through me and out to my audience, I wasn't overwhelmed anymore by the girls' vibrations. I could still sense them, but I was no longer absorbing energy from other people. This was a big revelation for the empath in me. As long as I was flowing the divine energy out to my audience, I wasn't absorbing their energy or feeling their emotions as my own.

I could tell it was helping. I could feel the energy shift as I progressed through my presentation. My empathic abilities were serving me instead of hurting me. That was some serious progress!

I decided to use my experience just that morning as an example of claiming my power. I talked about how nervous I had been when I walked into the room. I told the girls I'd had to take a few deep breaths to reset, and then I was able to share how awesome it felt to step outside my comfort zone. I told them how I'd learned to make the most of the situation, and in going there that morning to teach them about personal power, I found a new strength of my own. Something about revealing my authentic truth made them more open to what I had to say. Once they were smiling, I knew I was exactly where I was meant to be. And would you believe the energy grew even more powerful?

I found out during our break that some of the girls had to go to a different high school than their friends, and they weren't happy about it. They had all been living with the feeling of uncertainty and insecurity I'd described myself feeling when I entered the room. I was happy to see that several of them resolved that day to face their fears and move outside their own comfort zones toward opportunity instead of resisting it. It was amazing that they realized they would be OK at whichever school they attended. In fact, many decided that day to stop battling their parents, at least on that topic. That, to me, was sort of a miracle.

Excitingly, one of the concepts I was teaching the girls also struck a chord with one of the moms who stayed to audit the class. I found it fascinating that the topic that got her attention wasn't even supposed to be part of the presentation. The information I shared was inspired by the lyrics to the Red Hot Chili Peppers song I'd listened to on the way to the event that morning, "Midnight." I was thinking about how kids competed for things, such as homecoming queen and student council president. Their personal identities seemed to take a beating when they sometimes didn't achieve a particular goal.

Words spread throughout the song in different verses—"Never waiting when I know there's only one," "Just a minute while I reinvent myself," and "Make it up, and then I take it off the shelf"—became part of the lesson. I talked about how important attitude is when entering a competition. The act of competing for something in and of itself can inspire growth both emotionally and spiritually when approached in a healthy manner. I explained that winning is great, but when the situation determines that there can be only one winner, the act of reaching outside your comfort zone is the real win. Competing with yourself, and only yourself, to be better that day than the day before is the true measure of success. Lasting fulfillment doesn't necessarily come from a big trophy or accolades or even from our peers. Those feelings are great but limited. The novelty of the trophy will wear off, and friends will have other priorities, so that energy fades too, but the self-love that comes from growth and expansion is unlimited. We reinvent ourselves with self-love when we decide to compete only with ourselves to be better today than yesterday. We get to decide who we are from that place of love and strive to be that person. We "make it up and … take it off the shelf" every day. Sometimes we even do it on purpose. That's the law of attraction.

Somehow, the message inspired by a song miraculously flowed right into the lesson about the message: "The only real failure is the failure to try." It added a new perspective on failure. We learned that even though we may fail by societal standards, in trying, we are still winning because we are learning grace and self-love through the process. That message got the attention of an adult in the room.

To me, it was a miracle. This mother, who was not necessarily the intended recipient of the information I was sharing, came to thank me for helping her with an issue she'd been contemplating. She said the concept I'd taught was also applicable to something she was dealing with in her career. She said it had given her a whole new perspective on her situation. She said she felt better about her future because of what I'd said. I was shocked.

A message of light had been delivered! The song I'd heard on my way to the presentation had been a message of light. I had been so focused on reaching the teens that it never had occurred to me that a parent might also be inspired by what I had to say.

This following-your-guidance thing is really cool. I facilitated some positive change for others by saying yes to teaching that class. I also got to experience some exponential growth myself by tackling something that previously terrified me: talking to and teaching new people.

By the time the class was over, I was fully invested in the concept of the highest and best good. The magic is real! I floated on a cloud of bliss for a month. The idea that I may have helped someone by following my guidance and conquering my fear was inexplicably fulfilling. There are no words. It's just something you have to experience for yourself. When you give of yourself, you also receive.

I was praying about that very subject when I received my next message of light. This one was for me!

I asked, "How can I help them?"

"Teach."

"How can they free themselves?"

"Faith."

"How can I comfort them?"
"Love."
"Who are they?"
"You. You are all one! You are connected. You cannot perform any action without affecting the group as a whole. Any act of love raises the vibration of all involved."

Well, gee, that was profound. It kind of put life experience into perspective for me. It made me realize that what we do is important. Every act of self-love affects the vibration of everyone around us. Conversely, every act of self-destruction affects the vibration of everyone around us too. Maybe that's why the Golden Rule is so important.

> Do to others as you would have them do to you.
> —Luke 6:31 NIV

This is an energy thing and an empath thing. When we are kind to one another, we amplify one another's energy, effectively raising the vibration of the whole. We know what happens when we are not kind, so I won't even go into that, and empaths, those who can feel what other people feel, are less likely to intentionally inflict harm on others, because they would feel that too. Maybe that's why God made us all empaths and is turning up the volume on our gifts now—so we as a society will actually practice the Golden Rule instead of only talking about it. He's correcting the course of humanity for the better.

It's as if we, who can sense other people's emotions, were given this gift so we can learn to fine-tune our individual vibrations. When we feel the emotions and energy around us, we can mindfully choose to flow divine energy to ourselves and through ourselves out into the world. This enables the energy within us and the energy around us to shift and rise to a higher vibration. This is our opportunity to create our own heaven on earth.

Raising Vibration

After the previous message was written and interpreted, I was offered up a little reinforcement to the lesson. My little empath child, Aja, proved the point. It was as if she got the message too, as if she intercepted the transmission. She was sitting on the floor playing, when suddenly, she stopped what she was doing and looked at me. Her eyes were expressing wisdom well beyond her years. Then she got up, still looking at me with those wise little eyes. Aja didn't say a word as she walked over to me. I felt as if she read my mind, and I was reading hers. In my mind, I heard her say, *Here—let me show you how to do it. This is how you raise a vibration, Mama.* Then I got a seemingly spontaneous hug from my baby girl, except it wasn't spontaneous. It was as if she were telepathically communicating with me, and her actions at that moment solidified my belief in the magic of the entire exchange. It was a pure act of unconditional love, and it definitely raised my vibration.

Spontaneous hugs are some of the best things in life. My heart melted when my Aja randomly gave me that hug. She raised my vibration with a single act of love. All I was looking for in reassurance about that message came straight through my little girl that day. In that spontaneous hug, there was no need and no judgment, only love. I was so flooded with joy that I had to write about it. This is what came out:

Another Moment

Another moment has come and gone,
and had you asked me yesterday,
I don't think I could have seen
the beauty I see today.
You see, today I got a hug.
Someone's happy I am here.
So now, in tears,
my heart is full.
Free of sadness, free of fear.
For today I know that I saw God
reflected in her eyes.
With no agenda, no demands,
just love with no disguise.

With that divine energy flowing through me, I felt I was ready for whatever came next.

Christi Conde

A Miracle for the Mission

Kathy, the person who'd pushed my reluctant self out into the world to share my gifts (thank you, Kathy), gave me another mission that would help me grow. She asked me to talk to her class about how to see miracles in everything. I was working with kids again, and this time, I had full freedom to speak about God because of my religious audience.

It was surreal to find myself standing outside in the grass of an old church, surrounded by beautiful, openhearted children. Talk about a moment of awe! When I looked up, I saw that I was standing in the shadow of the church's cross, and I felt humbled and honored to be there. Just before I began to speak, while I was taking in the details of the experience in that holy moment of wonder, I felt an infusion of divine energy begin to flow through me. I felt a connection to the energy of Jesus, who, in my personal experience, was the greatest teacher of all time in the ways of relating to God and the universe he created. At that moment, I felt a closeness, a comfort, and a feeling of joy I hadn't really felt since the day I sat on my swing and talked to him as a child. He was there with me, guiding me. I felt elevated. It was as if I were floating out of my body, but at the same time, I was there among the wide-eyed and eager children and ready to learn. It was thrilling to experience that divine vibration of love and light. He was infusing me with all the love and wisdom I was supposed to share.

That day, I talked to the children about God and the importance of following his guidance. I explained that the most important thing about guidance is that it can help us only when we follow it. Then I talked a little about how to listen to their hearts to determine good choices. I explained that God lives in our hearts and that he communicates with us through our emotions. I encouraged them to tap into their emotions when contemplating any choice. I told them to look to their hearts for answers, and the answers would come. If the thought that came next felt like love and light, that was God saying, "What you are focused upon is for your highest and best good. Keep looking at that! Keep taking steps in that direction."

I also explained that when they got an anxious feeling inside, an intense voice of warning, that was God saying, "Hey! Either what you're looking at or the way you are looking at it is not for your highest and best good. Look for a better choice or a better perspective on the situation."

I emphasized the importance of listening to their gut, but in this case, divine instincts can be felt in the heart.

We talked about the miracles in life and how we can see them whenever and wherever we look. Then they asked me about the most recent miracle I had seen or been part of, and I told them a story of a miracle that had happened to me just the day before. I love how God always gives me stories to illustrate the messages at the exact perfect time for me to use them. This one was about listening to my gut and the miracle that came from it.

The day before I was to talk with the kids, I was heading to one of my scouting meetings, and when I looked at the clock, I realized I was incredibly early. I had a little extra time to fill. At that moment, I thought, *You should get your car washed*. Notice I didn't think, *I should get my car washed*. The fact that the inspiration was talking to me was an indicator that it was guidance and not just a random thought. Then the image of a nearby car wash appeared in my mind just as I happened to be approaching the street that would take me there. It was perfect timing. I turned toward the car wash and drove to the intersection where I had to make a U-turn to enter the facility. I was taking my time, minding my own business. I was casually getting ready to make the turn, when I saw a huge black truck driving in the lane I was about to turn into. It wasn't close, but it wasn't far. Usually, in a situation like that, I would err on the side of caution and wait, but something in my head said, *Go! Go now!*

I didn't argue. I just went, knowing there must have been a reason I had God screaming in my ear. After I pulled into the car wash, as I was waiting in line to pay, I saw the same big truck in line behind me. My first thought was *Oh, maybe that's why they told me to go. If I had waited and he had gone first, I might have been late to my own meeting.* So I said thank you for the assistance, thinking that was why I'd gotten the guidance. Then I heard in my deaf ear, "That's not it! Pay attention!"

I felt a heightened sense of awareness amplified within me at that moment, and I did pay attention. There was a sense of urgency in the vibration behind the message. Whatever was going on, it was important.

When the machine told me to pull forward after the wash was complete, I cautiously eased out of the car wash into the area where the vacuum cleaners and trash cans were. I moved my vehicle slowly as I scanned the area for whatever I was supposed to see. I am glad I did. When I looked to my left, I noticed a toddler outside the vehicle his mother was vacuuming. She hadn't seen that her little one was out of the car and was toddling right toward the pathway leading out of the carwash tunnel. He was walking toward my moving car when I saw him. I stopped my car at once, probably with a screech of the tires, even though I was driving slowly. I don't know if it was my stopped car or my waving my hands and screaming over the roar of the vacuum cleaners that got their attention, but I somehow managed to get the attention of the mother and the car wash attendant simultaneously. Then the empath in me went on a roller coaster of emotions. I immediately felt a jolt of alarm coming from both the mother and the car wash attendant. I saw the mother look up as she noticed her toddler was no longer in the car, and I felt a wave of panic hit me so hard I almost fell over. Then I felt her relief when she saw my vehicle was stopped. When she quickly scooped up her son and shot me a meaningful look of gratitude, I could feel that too.

As I got back in my car, trying to regain my composure, I looked in my rearview mirror to see the huge truck in line behind me coming out of the tunnel. That was when I understood, and I heard the message, "That's why." The truck was so big the driver would not have been able to see the wandering toddler so low to the ground. If the truck had gone through the car wash first, then something terrible might have happened.

I was in the middle of thinking it was a miracle—a possible tragedy had been averted—when I heard the voice in my head say, *Thank you. That little boy has important work to do. Good job!* and I knew the mission was complete.

Take it for what it's worth, but I like to believe it was a miracle, and I also believe I helped it happen simply by listening to my guidance. The kids thought so too. Their openness to the existence of miracles inspired me. Many of the children there that day not only decided they would look for miracles but also outwardly offered their hearts to God, stating their desires to be part of miracles as well. How cool is that?

The Uninvited Guest

Inspired by my work with the children, I continued every day to try to be the best version of myself. I have to say, at that point, I was doing a decent job of it. I focused on all the good I could do to help others in order to keep my personal struggles at bay. I did have times of deep internal chaos, just like everyone else. I learned that being spiritual or being able to communicate with the spirit realm does not exempt us from the human experiences of pain, insecurity, or fear. We came here for the full human experience, didn't we? The contrast of discomfort only makes the joy in life more delicious. The trick is always to find ways to heal and clear out old energy as we navigate through the pain in our experience. When we do this, we make room for the joy vibration to take its place.

I continued to practice Reiki on myself, and I began to treat more people with Reiki professionally. I also continued to exercise and practice self-care to the best of my ability at the time. My focus on self-care served to strengthen my spiritual muscle even more. My ability to sense energy, emotion, and even energetic entities was becoming more powerful. True to form, whenever I focused on spiritual growth, I was given another cool experience from which to learn. This time, I was given a ghost experience.

What's the difference between a ghost and a spirit? I was about to find out. I got a call one day from my friend Veronica. She was experiencing some strange phenomena at her house, and she wanted to know if I could help. She said her son had noticed some odd occurrences in his room at night, and her housekeeper was scared because of the things she kept seeing. For a second, I felt afraid too because of the unknowns. I didn't want to be messing with any dark energy.

I quickly checked my faith with a big, deep breath and a prayer and then scheduled a time to visit when no one else would be in the house besides my friend and me. When I went over to assess the situation, Veronica gave me a tour of her home, and I instantly felt his presence. I could feel a swirling and shifting of energy like a breeze coming in from an open window. But there was no breeze and no open window, just a shift in the energy, and it gave me a sort of goose-bump sensation. As we continued to explore the house and the energy in it, I realized that seeing this spirit would be trickier than I'd thought. He was an expert in camouflage. He kept hiding in the rooms we entered. He was following us. I could feel him, but I could only catch glimpses of him. It seemed he was hiding from me. My first clue was the feeling of uncertainty I sensed coming from him. The empath in me sensed the energy and emotion of a young person. It was as if he didn't want to show himself because he was afraid I would make him leave.

First, I saw something shift out of the corner of my eye as if he were ducking behind the couch. Then, in the backyard, he was behind a tree. More than a few times, I felt him following us on the tour of the house as if he were hanging back and observing. He had no interest in communicating with me that day. He was just sizing me up. It seemed *he* was afraid of *me*. Then I realized this spirit had human emotion. It didn't feel as if he had the high, fast, pure energy of love and light that my papaw and the others I'd communicated with before had. My ability to sense energy helped me to feel that this spirit hadn't moved on. He was stuck there. He was not at peace yet. Thanks to my empathic abilities, I realized he was an earthbound spirit, a ghost.

That realization was huge. I'd just learned the difference between spirits in the light and earthbound spirits. The ones in the light felt light, peaceful, and free, while the earthbound spirits, the ones we call ghosts, felt heavy. They experienced fear, insecurity, pain, and shame just as the humans around me did. I was able to distinguish the difference between them through either the energy or the emotions I sensed from them. This was another time when being an empath proved to be a blessing.

So there I was, grasping a more in-depth understanding of the nature of spirits, and I was getting it. Here's the recap: Not all of the entities I can sense are in the light. Some are stuck in the in-between. They are still on the earth plane energetically but without physical bodies. If a spirit still has an energy that feels like human emotion to me, if the energy is anything other than love and light, it means that spirit is still earthbound. It hasn't crossed over into the light, a.k.a. heaven. I guess it makes sense that not all entities I encountered were in the light. Learning the difference gave me an opportunity to understand more about energetic beings.

After Veronica gave me a tour and I had a better feel for the situation, we made another appointment for the next day to see what we could do to handle the intrusive energy. That afternoon, I went for one of my

The Messages of Light

walks. This time, I was looking for clarity. Boy, did I get some clarity! The strangest thing happened. I was thinking about the boy, wondering what had happened to get him stuck between heaven and earth, when suddenly, I started seeing pictures in my mind. It was like a movie playing out in my head.

I saw the boy. He was young, around six or seven. He had mahogany-brown hair and golden-brown skin. He was dressed primitively, and he had an animal-skin cloak wrapped around himself like a blanket for warmth. He was in a small room, sitting by a round fireplace oven. A man in the room stood by the door, and a woman was with him. In the vision, it was obvious they were the boy's parents. The boy watched the crying woman with a look of sadness on his face as the man angrily left the room. I could see the boy and his mother looking longingly out the window as she sobbed. The boy went over to his mother to console her as they watched the man load up his pack and ride off on the only horse they had. I got a sense the boy's father was heading out on a dangerous journey, and the boy's mother somehow knew he would not return. It seemed the argument had been because the father refused to heed his wife's warning.

The vision seemed to flash forward as the scenery changed, and I saw the same boy, years older, standing by the door. The woman was crying again. I got the sense she was highly intuitive, and she could sense the danger on the horizon. She was begging the boy not to go. She pointed at the distant sky, as if warning him of a storm. The boy refused to listen, just as his father had all those years ago. The boy was tall. He stood a full foot taller than his mother, and he looked like a confident and powerful man, but I could tell he was still young. His youth and inexperience were being overshadowed by his need to prove himself. I could tell he wanted to support his mother and make his ancestors proud. He was indicating to his mother that he was a man, and he was going to do what he had to do to prove it. After a while, I saw him lean down and press his forehead against his mother's, as if he were relaying some sort of unspoken communication. Then he picked up his pack and walked down a long and winding dirt path through a canopy of trees.

When I saw the boy again, he was outside, walking by a large, wide, lazy river. He turned away from the water, surveying the landscape, and as he did, I saw that he was looking at a mountain off in the distance. It was in the direction opposite where his mother had pointed when she warned him about the storm.

Time lapsed again. Days, not years, passed this time, and the boy was hiking up an arroyo. I looked around and noticed he had been hunting. He'd hung what looked like a string of rabbits and squirrels from a nearby tree, and he was busy doing something. I couldn't tell at first what it was, then I saw that he had killed a large deer, and he was tying it to a sort of basket made of wood branches—so he could drag it home, I guessed. He seemed to be in a hurry. He kept looking up to the sky. Then I saw it. As he looked out toward his home in the distant valley, I recognized the view. He was on the same mountain where my friend's house was built.

As I looked closer, I saw the reason for his concern. A storm was coming. His mother had warned him, and now he had to race against time to get home. The boy hurriedly worked as the rain began to pour. Soon there appeared to be a river running through the arroyo where the boy was standing. It was what we call a flash flood. The boy struggled to climb up the side of the slippery slope, only to lose his balance and fall down the hill. As he was sliding through the shrubbery, feeling cactus needles piercing his skin, he grabbed on to a bush with both hands to stop his descent. The rain continued to pour as he clawed his way back to his original starting place. By that time, the river had taken on a life of its own. He grabbed on to the roots of the tree where his game hung, and he tried to pull himself to safety. He pulled himself up to the tree, but as he attempted to stand, the low branch he grabbed to support his effort gave way. He flew backward into the shallow but raging water, hitting his head on a rock.

The vision was gone as quickly as it had come, and I was back to my reality, walking the hills by my home. It seemed I had been entranced for a long time, but the details had been revealed in a vision lasting only seconds. I was struck by the experience. It had felt so real. It was as if I had been there in that time, watching it as it happened. Then I thought, as I usually did when I got incoming, *Where did that come from, and how did I tap into that? I'm not even in the room with the spirit. How did I get that information?* The explanations that followed my question were the following two messages of light about the nature of earthbound spirits and how to communicate with them. The information surprised me. It was like nothing I had ever seen on television or heard from others before. Yet the information resonated with me in a profound way.

About Earthbound Spirits

Imagine a giant cloud of light. That cloud of light is heaven, Source energy, or God by human standards. Everyone who has ever lived, all of us living now, and even those who haven't been born yet have a part of themselves there in the light. Those with and without physical bodies have a part of them that exists there always. This means everyone. This is where our infinite souls live. This is where all souls merge with the great Creator God. Imagine that each soul is a beam of light, an extension of God's light (souls exist without physical bodies too), and when someone is ready to be born into a physical body, that beam of light extends outward from the Source of all light and into the physical plane. The picture here is a giant cloud of light with billions of rays of light extending toward earth. On the end of each beam of light is a physical body, a soul within a frame. Those beams of light, our souls, maintain a constant connection with the Source of all energy. When the connection to the Source of that light is active, the physical body will thrive. When an injury occurs that disrupts the physical body's ability to survive (death), the soul usually returns to its Source. The spirit goes into the light. There in heaven, the spirit is reunited with God and all his or her loved ones who were waiting for him or her on the other side.

Sometimes spirits, or souls, will remain focused on the earthly plane even without physical bodies. These are commonly referred to as ghosts or earthbound spirits. There are many reasons souls will stay focused on the physical plane. Some don't realize their bodies are gone, and they wander around, invisible and confused. Some of them realize they died but stay focused on their human emotional pain or the pain of their loved ones' grieving, so they cannot find the light. Some of the earthbound spirits are just afraid of what will come to them on the other side, so they do not look for the light. If humans believe they are undeserving of heaven when they die, they tend to stay focused on the earth plane as well. These earthbound spirits remain on the earth plane until someone who can communicate with them finds a way to guide them into the light.

Communicating with Spirits

Each of us has a divine consciousness that exists within us. This consciousness can travel the column of light that exists between the physical body and the cloud of light we call heaven, where the answer to every question that could ever be asked exists. This is where the consciousness of every person who has ever lived, every person who lives now, and every person who will ever live exists. All are in perfect unity with the energy of God.

When we meditate or pray, our divine consciousness travels higher up the column of light. The higher the consciousness travels, the more we have access to information from God. Being able to communicate with God allows us access to the wisdom of the ages, and it is helpful for all things. It is especially helpful when trying to help a spirit into the light. Here our divine consciousness can find the higher selves of earthbound spirits. Here we get the details of their lives and the information required to help them transition into the higher flows of love and into the light.

When we get a vision, our consciousness has traveled up that column of light and received information from the Source. Once the information is received, it is relayed back

> to our human minds. Our higher consciousness does this so that it can help us to help someone else.

Long story short, everyone, living or dead, has a higher self that resides in the light. Those who meditate and pray often tend to be able to navigate the column of light to a level of higher consciousness and gain answers directly from the Source of all energy, God. In my situation, my higher self in the light talked to the boy's higher self, which was also in the light. It's possible his mother's higher self was in on the communication too, from her perspective in the light. Even though a large part of the boy's consciousness was trapped on earth, a part of him was always with God. In his confusion brought on by death, he lost his ability to access his higher self and the guidance of the eternal aspect of him that would have led him to the light.

How does consciousness live on without the body? Answer: God.

That's why I could communicate with him without being in the house. I saw the whole thing from a higher perspective. I traveled to a higher plane of consciousness, where his higher self, who had been safe with God all along, told my higher self the story. How cool is that?

Let me say here that this is not the only way to communicate with earthbound spirits. It's just the way I do it. If I can do it, everyone can do it. Psychics and mystics are better at it because they practice their own methods to communicate with spirits regularly.

With another major epiphany embraced, I moved on to the next pertinent question about Veronica's and my little earthbound friend: "Why?"

Why hadn't he gone into the light when he died? The answer: he was concerned about his mom. His dad had gone off on a hunting trip years ago and hadn't returned. The boy felt it was his responsibility to take care of his mother in his father's absence, and they were almost out of food when he left. He was worried about what would happen to her if he didn't return to her before winter came. He was so focused on his mother when his spirit left his body that he didn't notice the light and therefore didn't go into it.

The boy had been stuck there for a long time by our standards. Judging from the changes in the terrain from the time in my vision to what it looked like in this time, it must have been at least a few hundred years.

The next day, I returned to Veronica's house with a better idea of what to do next. We went through the house room by room again, this time with lit sage to clear any negative energy in the house. I sent Reiki energy into the corners of all the rooms to replace any negative energy with light energy. Veronica held a white candle. We used it to amplify the divine energy of our prayers, asking God to keep the space filled with pure light energy.

Room by room, I noticed that the spirit boy was getting closer to us. He wasn't keeping his distance like the day before, so I began talking to him. Soon enough, he started answering. He began showing me pictures. Maybe it was just the way they communicated with me, but it seemed spirits liked the game of charades. The boy showed me through pictures and visions why he'd decided to come inside the house. It had something to do with the fact that the backyard—his usual spot and where he'd died—was being renovated. It was as if he'd decided that if they were going to mess around in his space, he would go mess around in theirs.

Once he did, he discovered he liked it inside. That was why he hid from me. He was afraid I would make him leave. As he warmed up to me, he began showing me pictures of his experiences in the house. He showed some electronic toys he was fascinated with. He liked to play with them at night. He discovered that the lights would come on when he got close to them. It was endless entertainment for him to go through the house to see what he could affect. He liked to move things around too, so my friend and her family would notice he was there. He showed me different scenes of the family who lived there, and as he did, I could sense his affection for them. The spirit seemed to have a longing to be part of the family.

He was interacting with me more freely by then. We must have established a rapport. When Veronica and I got back to our starting place at the heart of the home, we said another prayer for the household and for him. Then I explained what had happened to him, and he seemed to understand. It was as if I helped him to fill in the gaps of his own memory. When he remembered what had happened and understood how much time had passed, I thought he would be ready to go into the light, so I told him to look for the light, but he didn't want to do it. He wanted to stay to protect my friend and her family. I then explained that he could still do that but in an unlimited way from the other side. Then I reminded him of his mother and told him she was waiting for him. This time, when I told him to look for the light, he laughed because it was suddenly right there. It appeared out of thin air the moment he looked up.

Before he went in, he gifted me with another vision. He showed me a giant column of light streaming from the heavens that opened like a doorway when it contacted the earth. Then I understood his protective nature. In the doorway of white light was the silhouette of a woman. I knew it was his mother because I had seen her before. But as the vision became clearer, I saw it. I looked at the woman and then at my friend, and I got it. The woman could have been Veronica's long-lost sister! OK, maybe not, but there were enough similarities between Veronica and his mother that it was easy to understand why he may have felt a need to protect her.

Then our little spirit friend went to the light and stood next to his mother. They raised their hands as if to wave goodbye, and as they did, white light shone from their hands. The light grew brighter with their combined energy, and the room went white as the blinding light went out with a blast that covered everything. The wave of light started with the room we were in, but then it went out in all directions. It illuminated the entire house, and then the wave of light washed over the entire neighborhood and went out in all directions from there. Everything it touched was tinged with a golden hue. It felt as if the two spirits were sending out a blessing like a blast of unconditional love. Then the doors to the light column closed.

Moments later, I felt him again. This time, I felt nothing but love from him. He was in the light. He was free. Then I saw him. His energy was vibrating at such a high frequency he looked like a wave of light flowing around the room. He looked like a dolphin playing in the ocean. He told me to thank Veronica for everything and promised he would continue to watch over her. He said the house was so charged with divine energy that others would not be able to come into her home unless they were in harmony with the divine energy of love. He said if they tried, they would be so uncomfortable they would have to leave. And he was right! The week after the spirit said he would protect Veronica's home and family from anyone with negative intent, someone actually had to leave her house abruptly. This person suddenly started feeling unwell after being inside the energetically charged space for only a few minutes. Would you believe that this person, who used to visit regularly, never returned to Veronica's house again after that?

Veronica's home and family were protected by the divine energy of God and this amazing spirit. We'd helped an earthbound spirit cross over into the light, and he became a guardian to Veronica's family. I left that experience with knowledge that I rely on to this day. It was a life-changer. I realized I can help the stranded spirits I meet to cross into the light. How cool is that?

Being Called

Not long after my first ghost adventure, I was asked by Kathy to help with a gathering for her class. Kathy always encouraged me to do my spiritual work. She believed in me. In fact, she believed in me more than I believed in myself sometimes. But whenever she called, I answered, even when I was a mess.

Now, keep in mind that I was a bit of an emotional wreck a lot of the time back then. I was just finding my magic in the midst of my personal madness. I was struggling. Amid my empathic abilities sometimes getting out of control, regular life stress, and writing my story, I found myself confused and overloaded with emotion more often than not. Just because I haven't gone into detail about my personal drama and trauma doesn't mean it wasn't there. I started to exhibit self-destructive tendencies and went deep into the abyss of self-loathing. But whenever it looked like I was losing my connection to my higher self, Kathy or another of my earth angels stepped in and pushed me in the direction of healing.

Working with Kathy's class was an incredible experience. The kids were amazing. They inspired me in ways that no one else had. I understand the call to be an educator now. The reward is great. The Father Yermo kids were open, kind, and beautiful inside and out. They were genuinely loving.

This time around, the experience with them seemed to be all about helping me. For some reason, I was more inclined to reach out to help someone else than I was inclined to do the work to help myself. It was my unworthiness complex: "I'm not good enough to feel better or heal, but you are, so let me help." God found a way around that. He sent me to the kids at Kathy's school again.

While I was brainstorming for activities for the kids to do on the retreat, I was struck with divine inspiration when I got the following message: "When you feel broken, take the pieces, and make a mosaic."

I know now that I needed that message more than the tweens I was working with at the time, but of course, I missed that back then. With that burst of inspiration came the idea for an activity we did during the workshop. We gathered different-colored construction paper. On the pieces of paper, the kids wrote down problems or troubles they were having in their lives. This is powerful in two ways. First, in order to write a problem down, you must face it. Second, there is a feeling of release in getting the problem out of the mind and onto paper. Looking at problems on paper offers up a new perspective. Our fears are rarely as scary on paper as they are in our imaginations.

Once the children wrote down a few problems on the brightly colored paper, they got to tear up the paper. Talk about a gratifying experience! The kids enjoyed that part of the activity. Some of those papers were ripped to shreds. This gave the children a sense of personal power over the problems or circumstances in their lives. Doing something so focused and proactive destroyed the feeling of helplessness they may have had about the situations before, when the issues were just a jumble of fearful thoughts creating chaos in their minds.

Then, as the message had instructed, we made mosaics. The kids took the torn-up pieces and glued them together on a template designed to create a kaleidoscope of colors. The children had their choice of templates. Some chose the image of a heart. Others decided to place their torn-up problems on a cross. Some created beautiful sunsets with their colored papers. I, who was doing the activity alongside the children, chose a butterfly to represent the transformation I knew I was undergoing at the time. Some wanted to be even more creative. They designed their own template page on which to paste the colorful paper.

This activity proved their ability to turn their problems into something beautiful. It was practice in creating a new perspective with which to view their life experiences. It was an excellent activity that granted me new insights into my own life. Instead of letting my past continue to wreak havoc on my present, I decided I would make a mosaic with the lessons of my youth.

As I continued to write my story, I began to dissect the seemingly terrible experiences of my life and take from them only the positive. I tore up the thoughts that no longer served me and turned them into something beautiful. I realized that for every unpleasant experience in my life, there was something good to come from it as well. It is God's world, and nothing happens here that good does not also come from. That something good for me was my spiritual growth and healing.

I decided to focus on finding the miracle in every situation. That is how we turn something awful into something beautiful.

Snapshots of Minimiracles

In that particular workshop, finding the minimiracles was easy. I began to collect beautiful little moments in my mind. They are like Polaroids in my memory. The first happy memory of the experience is the moment when I saw the same kids from the previous year with giant smiles on their faces.

I was outside, standing in the grassy area where we would begin the experience. I was taking in the atmosphere. I was in a holy place, and I could feel it. At that point, I realized I was standing in the cool shade of the shadow that came from the cross that sat atop a beautiful old church. The energy was surreal. I couldn't believe I was about to teach the children there for the second time. Talk about a feeling of awe. I felt so honored to be there again that it almost didn't seem real. However, I was knocked back into reality in the next few seconds.

I saw the kids coming around the corner, and I noticed they looked pleased to see me. I was in a state of joy when I saw the smiles spread across their faces as they waved hello to me from a distance. My happiness turned to a brief moment of surprise as the slow-moving line of students broke into a swarm of buzzing children running in my direction. Then I felt a brief moment of shock as my feet went out from under me, and I saw the blue sky. I laughed almost hysterically as I realized I had been tackled in a group hug. As I rose from the ground, still laughing, Kathy's expression almost knocked me back down again. I laughed even harder as I saw the look of horror on her face when she saw what had happened. Thank God I was standing in the grass! For me, the experience of being tackled in a group hug turned out better than fine. To be met with a wave of love from children that literally knocks you off your feet is a priceless gift, and I treasure that moment with so much joy it's difficult to describe. To me, it was nothing short of a miracle.

Another precious moment in the photo album in my mind was captured when I read the following message of light to the students. The miracle for me was in the reaction I not only saw but also felt from my young audience.

I received the message of light on a Sunday morning. It was the day before I was to go talk to Kathy's class. I was swimming in my doubt. I believed I had nothing new to offer, even though I had already been given the coolest activity ever, the mosaic activity. Whenever I was called to do something like this, I experienced some kind of doubt or fear about it beforehand. I needed inspiration for the kids and for me at the event, so I did what I always did: I walked, meditated, and prayed. This is what I got:

Being Called

> You are being called,
> not to change who you are
> but to be who you are.
> You are perfect in God's eyes!
> Do you really want to be the one to tell God
> that he didn't do it right?

> We are each called to be who we are. As we go through each day, we encounter opportunities to express who we are. This can be our biggest challenge in life.
>
> Do you know who you are? You are a daughter or a son—this we know for sure. Are you also a brother, a sister, or a friend? These are ways of describing yourself to others. This is not who you are but part of the reason you

are here. We are here to be love and to support the people in our lives so that we can all expand in consciousness. This is part of your purpose and what you came to do with this life. Who you are is much more significant. Who you are makes a difference in the world! You are a living, breathing extension of God. You are part of all that is beautiful and miraculous in this world. You are unique for a reason. You possess talents and extraordinary gifts that only you can offer the world. So be who you are.

Trying to be what other people think you should be will lead to confusion because you have so many roles in life. You mean so much to so many different people. So let them see the real you, not the person you think they would love. Do not change who you are to fit in. If you become a false version of yourself in order to be loved, it will be impossible to accept when people express their love for you. You will always know that the person they love is an illusion, a character you are playing, not the real you.

No matter what you do, stay true to you!

Just be you! Be unapologetically you!

God created you. You are precious to him. You are perfect in his eyes. He created you the way you are for his reasons. You are a miracle! Accept that you are special and that you are being called to show the world just how special you are. Let God shine through you, and watch how his miracles unfold around you. Answer the call, and let God's love flow into the world through you.

Hush. Listen. God is talking, and he is calling you by name.

When I got that message, I thought it was for the kids. I'd prayed for inspiration for the children. I wanted to offer something of value to the children so I would feel more confident about what I was teaching them. Again, I was given something to teach that I was supposed to learn. That message, like the one about the mosaic, seemed to be about helping myself too. I was being called to be my authentic self, just as the children were.

And just like the children, I was going to have to figure out who that was—again.

As I stood there after reading my message of light to the students, I looked around at their hopeful young faces, and I noticed a girl was crying. She had been deeply touched by the message. Later, she even sent me a thank-you note that made me feel genuinely happy to have made a meaningful difference in her life. It is gratifying to be part of a child's spiritual growth. I keep her note close to me because it reminds me that no matter how bad I felt about myself at that time, I was able to reach someone in a positive way by letting go of my fear and allowing the energy of God's love to flow through me. Isn't that what it's all about? We must learn, grow, and eventually use that wisdom to help others.

The final snapshot in my memory of that experience is probably the most profound. I was asked to help with a gathering for the kids. Part of my role was to help with the re-creation of the stations of the cross. For those who are unfamiliar with the stations of the cross, it is a reenactment of the path that Jesus took as he carried his own cross to his crucifixion. In this experience, the children were the actors, and the performance was presented to friends, family, and the school staff. Kathy organized the whole thing, and I spent the weeks before the retreat focused on making the wardrobe for everyone who took part in the reenactment, from Jesus and Mary to the Roman soldiers and Pontius Pilate.

What happened during the reenactment was awesome to experience and witness. The kids were funny. They were giddy and noisy as they waited outside the seminary chapel. I experienced a brief moment of concern that they would be unruly and that things wouldn't go well. Of course, my anxiety proved to be unnecessary, as anxiety usually is, because God was in charge.

When the chapel doors opened and the procession began, I was overcome with the presence of the Lord. Apparently, so were the children. I watched the expressions on their faces as the energy washed over them. They went from jovial and giddy to suddenly profoundly serious. I was so in awe of the experience that I felt as if I had floated out of myself. I was watching the whole thing from a higher perspective. The silent observer within me was fully engaged. The reverence the children exhibited was nothing short of inspiring. I could see how deeply they were all feeling the experience, and I could feel how profoundly they were connecting with the energy of God. His presence was real for them. I noticed a few of the children weeping, and they weren't just acting. Then I saw some of the parents were crying too. After that, it was over for me; I was sobbing like a baby too. It wasn't sadness we were feeling, although the re-creation of Jesus's last day on earth is difficult to endure. We were feeling a sense of comfort and release. We were feeling the peace of his presence. We were enveloped in the awe-inspiring energy of the Creator of all things. It was both beautiful and overwhelming. We all experienced a sort of closeness, almost a feeling of oneness with God, Jesus, and one another. It was tangible and undeniable.

Everyone left that day feeling like a new person, reborn in the energy of the divine. Everyone felt the unconditional love of God in a new and profound way.

Chapter 17

Concept versus Application

We Are the Creators of Our Own Life Experiences

Of course, the positive energy I felt from that divine experience with the kids in Kathy's class was short-lived. And when it ended, it was as if I had energy whiplash. I was flying high on the energy of the beautiful experience of divine connection, but when it was over, without something to distract me from my negative and fearful thinking, I bottomed out again. I was at the most challenging part in the making of my mosaic. I was at the part where I had to look at my problems to tear them apart, but it seemed that as I looked at my issues, they were tearing me apart instead. Healing takes a lot of work, and the longer you wait to get started, the more stuff you have to heal. I was delighted the children were given a chance to start young. I had a lot to work through, and I was tired. My negative thought processes were relentless. Trying to overcome the constant rush of negativity coming from my own mind was exhausting. There was nowhere I could go to escape myself. Eventually, I hit an energetic wall. What came next was not pretty.

Hell is real. I have been there. I created my own hell. I did it with my choice of thought and my choice in action. There was no escape from real-life stress, the energy I absorbed from others, and the strain I put on myself with my negative thoughts. When I was overwhelmed, all the Reiki in the world could not fix it. Why? Reiki cleared the energy out, but I immediately replaced it with the same thoughts that had caused the energetic dis-ease in the first place. Energy is like water. It moves fluidly.

When you move a vibration out of a space, it must be replaced with a different vibration. Otherwise, the same energy will just come back and refill the void when the emotional tide returns. This is why now I do so much energetic coaching before I teach a student Reiki. The energy clears and heals, but because of free will, we are free to go back to practice the lessons as many times as we want. I guess I needed practice.

Nothing could correct my distorted view of my life. I compounded the stress of whatever recent event I faced with whatever pain I experienced from the memory I was working on in my book (mosaic). I should have been dealing with one issue at a time. When the overwhelm from the overload of emotions hit me, I went right back to dumping the harmful sludge into my system by making poor choices based on fear. I fell into the flaming pit of my own personal hell, and I chose to pitch my tent there. When I was alone with my thoughts, I roasted in the fires of my own self-loathing and self-judgment. I had good all around me, but all I could see was the ugliness within me, and all I could feel was the pain my thoughts evoked. I still joke about how I spent so much time roasting my marshmallows in the fires of hell that I never got to eat them. I spent most of my time watching the beautifully roasted bits of goodness drop into the flames, char into coal-like black lumps, and then fizzle away.

This hell of which I speak is a metaphor for the torture I was subjecting myself to with my negative thoughts. My perceived unworthiness and my obvious willingness to suffer because of it created my misery. I chose to suffer instead of applying the concepts I'd learned that would allow me to enjoy all the good I had right there in my life. I had so much beauty in my life, but my thoughts would never let me appreciate it.

This was all by my own choice. I am the thinker of my thoughts; my thoughts didn't think me into existence. I used my struggles as an excuse to view myself as a victim. The "Poor me" mentality was my default mode, as you may recall. I bought into the illusion that I was too weak to handle the overpowering emotions I experienced every day. Even though I had survived 100 percent of all my previous struggles. I was still a people-pleaser, with most of my validation coming from outside myself. I was feeling victim to the emotions of those around me. I was constantly bombarded with energy because my empathic powers were out of control. I was in constant fight-or-flight mode because I was stuck in the chaos of my own mind. Life experiences can be hard by themselves, and I was making them a thousand times worse with my negative mindset.

To make a long and awful story short, this went on for so long that I resorted to alcohol to numb myself in those times of complete overload. Of course, that just added more weight to an already heavy load.

When I drank alcohol, it had a much stronger effect on me than before I had children. Remember, my energy was already amplified by Reiki, and I'd carried two babies in my womb, also supercharging my natural abilities. I didn't know—and was about to learn—that the same energy that enhanced my natural gifts and abilities also amplified the effects alcohol had on me. One glass of wine felt like three, and because alcohol lowers inhibitions, my impulse control went out the window. Guess what happened then. My one drink turned into three glasses of wine, and those three glasses felt like nine to me. Not good.

What happens when someone who talks to spirits gets drunk and checks out of focused consciousness is this: a signal goes out into the universe that invites any of the earthbound spirits in the area to take the temporarily unoccupied vessel for a ride. Earthbound spirits still crave life, and some are willing to borrow any vessel that isn't already occupied with a fully focused consciousness. This is what happens to many people who get blackout drunk; they walk around and say and do things that are completely out of character because at that particular moment, it's not really them. That's not to say that people who get drunk are not responsible for their actions in blackout mode, because they are. They chose to drink alcohol, which created the problem in the first place.

When other beings borrow your body for a while, they leave a residue of awful-feeling negative energy all over you and inside you. The more often someone gets drunk, with or without a spirit borrowing the body, the worse the hangover.

Alcohol is a chemical that affects the central nervous system. The more it is consumed, the more difficult it becomes to find a moment of happiness. When our nervous system is out of balance, we are not making enough of the biochemicals that create health and wellness. It's science, not theory.

Unfortunately for me, I used alcohol as a crutch. I did it long enough to hold myself in the pit of hell, even to the point that I believed I wouldn't get out. I believed I deserved to feel the way I was feeling. So I chose to keep torturing myself for past decisions instead of making new and better ones. It wasn't a conscious choice, but it was a choice nonetheless. Boy, did I suffer! And do you know what else? I spread that pain around me like a contagion and then suffered more because of the discomfort I caused the people I loved.

Eventually, I realized that the hell I was living was manifesting from my own design. Our thoughts create our reality. My bag of marshmallows had been in my hands the whole time. I consciously chose to try to roast them and then drop them into the fires of hell instead of just enjoying them as they were. Then, one day, I realized my legs still worked, so I picked up that bag of marshmallows, walked right out of hell, and made s'mores in the life of my dreams.

Just to be clear, my thoughts were the fires, and the marshmallows were my dreams of happiness, fulfillment, love, and peace. When I realized I was the thinker of my thoughts, I was able to turn down the flames. Then I walked right out of the hell of my own creation and created my own heaven on earth. Read on to see how that happened.

As I said before, this book aims to illuminate and amplify all the love and light in life experience. I have omitted the hundred or so pages about the personal pain I inflicted upon myself and others. I deleted the details of my suffering, the excuses I made for myself, and all the attempts to justify my very human behavior. I will, however, share the lessons and messages I received in my times of struggle, because I know they are meant to help others just as they helped me.

This poem is a message that came to me in a moment of deep despair, and what happened with it was another miracle.

Darkness

There is a silence in the darkness,
so quiet it rings in my ears.
This silence is deafening.
It's impossible to bear.
It rips through my soul.
It hollows my heart.

The Messages of Light

> It shakes me to earth.
> It tears me apart.
> The pain runs so deep
> it crushes my bones.
> It hurts more than death.
> It's feeling alone.
>
> I'm down on my knees
> with nowhere to go.
> I'm lost in the darkness;
> I'm so far from home.
> So I turn on the light
> by saying a prayer,
> and the Lord, he rescues me
> from the depths of despair.
> He lifts up my heart,
> and he opens my eyes.
> I bask in his comfort,
> in the love and the light.
> The darkness then dissipates,
> until it is gone.
> It is then that I realize
> I was never alone!

That poem brought me back, if only to the concept of God's unconditional love. I knew I wasn't alone, but sometimes it helps to get that reminder.

As I said before, no matter what I was going through with my personal struggle, I always tried to serve a higher purpose. So when I got a call to teach a level-one Reiki class, I did it, even though I felt awful.

Every time I teach a class, something amazing happens to me: I learn and grow as much as the students I teach. I get to see the magic that creates miracles firsthand.

The woman who came to me at that time to learn energy work with Reiki was a soldier. She had just returned from a tour in Afghanistan. She had been deployed in the early 2000s, after the attack on 9/11. She had seen some serious stuff over there. She was healing and trying to move forward, and she wanted to learn Reiki to improve her self-care routine.

As we went through the course and worked with the energy, we both started to feel better. Then, toward the end of the class, something interesting happened. I was suddenly prompted to share my poem with her. That was unusual for me, as the poem was deeply personal, but something inside me told me I should show it to her. As I read it aloud—it was handwritten in my spiral notebook—I could feel her strong connection to what I'd felt when I wrote the poem. When I looked up after I was done reading it, I saw that she was crying.

She excused herself, and I sat there at the table, wondering if she'd had a good reaction or a bad one. I also doubted my instinct to share it with her, until she returned. Her response was a good one. The poem gave her confirmation that God was with her in her personal darkness. She connected with the emotion on a deep spiritual level, and she asked me if she could get a copy of the poem. She said she wanted to share it with friends who were still on deployment in the midst of the war in Afghanistan and Iraq. This poem was a message of light intended to help others, not just me. That, to me, was a miracle.

Even in the light of miracles, I was lost. When the magic and awe faded, I was left with my inner critic. Instead of being happy that something I had written could be used to inspire and help others to get through their own darkness, I focused on how I had no real reason to be such a mess. The soldiers whom the poem was going to had seen more pain and suffering than I could ever imagine. Yet I was wallowing pitifully in my failures, feeling sorry for myself, thinking only of myself and my pain. When I recognized how disproportionate my pain seemed compared to theirs, it made me feel even worse.

When I prayed, I felt connected, but all I could do was dwell on my mistakes back then. The struggle was real for me. Prolonged stress would trigger me, and a step backward would trigger my self-loathing. I couldn't look in the mirror, because I hated the person I saw. So I just kept praying. It was all I could do to get through the day. I tried to release the negativity and tap into something better through prayer and meditation, and one day I got this message to help me do just that:

Freedom of Release

Release is accomplished by flushing the strands of energy that tie us down to the world of illusion with love and light. The strands of energy holding us in a lower vibration are connected to people, places, and events that have hurt or saddened us. Many will choose to cut the cords to eliminate any connection to the people or the past events. This is so that the people on the other end of the cord stop siphoning our energy. This way, others' energy doesn't creep up the cord and into our vibrational fields and ultimately bring us down again.

Cutting cords is an activity done in resistance. We say, "I want to cut this out of my life," and the universe that God created gives you more of *this* because of your attention to it. This is the power of magnetic attraction. Energy is tricky. When we cut a single cord, ten more grow back in its place. God's universe runs on vibration. Vibration doesn't do exclusion, only inclusion. If you include it in your thoughts, you include it in your vibration. The act of cutting cords is an attempt at exclusion. It doesn't work well. Cutting a cord may help you cut a negative person out of your life, but it doesn't clear the vibration. So any new person coming into your experience at that time will be a vibrational match to the person with whom you cut the cord.

Any lesson in God's universe will repeat itself until we learn to respond to it with love. Love clears the energy. When we flush the strands of energy tying us to our pain with light and love, the person who receives the energy is our past self, who was hurt. We send the energy through the cord. Instead of thinking about the person who hurt us, we send the energy to the past. We send it to the version of us who was injured in that event. Our past selves fill with love. That love then abundantly overflows onto the other person or people involved. It's like time travel. We can't change the details of the past, but we can change how we perceive and process the emotions from those events. We can rewrite an event energetically, offering ourselves and the other human(s) involved the love we wish we had shared in the first place. When we pray, meditate, and send love to our past selves and anyone who hurt us or was hurt in the situation instead of cutting the cords, we shift from vibrationally throwing our hands up in exasperation to flowing love to all involved. This is an act of honoring ourselves and the value of the experience. This naturally releases the weight of the negative vibrations and allows our consciousness to rise up out of the illusion. This gives us a clearer perspective from which to learn and grow.

Flushing the cords with love and light instead of cutting them heals us and shifts the vibration. If a person is intended to remain in our experience, the cord will run clear with divine energy. Then the interactions and energetic exchanges become beautiful and fluid. If the person is only supposed to be in our lives to help us learn from that particular situation, the cord will naturally retract when it is flushed with light. The lesson of greeting all circumstances with love and a higher perspective is learned. We are freed from the attachment to the human illusions brought on by the exchange.

How do we flush the strands with light? Imagine golden light—God's love—flowing into the top of your head. See and feel it cycle through your entire body, moving down the spine and then back up the front of the body. Breathe. With each breath, the light within you grows stronger and brighter, until you are so filled with the vibration of love that it overflows the physical body, creating a feeling of weightlessness as the light fills the buoyant, bubble-like space all around you. Recognizing you are safe and loved, imagine a beam of light supplied by God moving through you and then through the cords connecting you to others. Imagine the light growing so bright that any darkness in you, the cord, the person, or the circumstance is blasted away and replaced with light. In doing this, we send others exactly what they were trying to get from us in the first place: love.

When the weight falls away and our vibrations rise, we can find the miracle in the situation. God's world is perfectly balanced. For every tragedy, there is a wonder to be seen. For every mistake, there is a lesson. For every terrible experience, there is an equally good one out there to be had.

When we remember the blessings in our lives and pay attention to the good around us, we let go of our ties to the energy holding us down. It is impossible to experience fear or negativity while in the vibration of gratitude or positivity.

We are here to soar, experience life, and find the joy in it! The Lord's Prayer says, "Your Will be done on Earth as it is in Heaven" (Matthew 6:10 NIV).

That means our job is to bring God's love in its fullness to earth as it exists in heaven. God lives within each of us, and it is our job to share that love and light with the world around us.

A lousy circumstance or event can weigh us down and incapacitate us, or we can learn from the experience and use the knowledge to propel ourselves forward. When we look for the good in a situation, it will guide our energy upward to a better, happier place of being.

Empaths can use this same technique. We can use it to keep the vibration around us filled with God's energy so that we don't absorb the energy from the people around us. Pay attention, fellow empaths! This is the trick: negative energy can't get anywhere near you when you overflow your energetic field with God's love. You can still sense the energy around you, but because your proverbial sponge is already soaked with God's love energy, you don't absorb it.

Begin with breath. Breathe slowly and deeply. Make your exhalation twice as long as your inhalation. After a few breaths, your nervous system will move into balance, and you should be calm enough to access the energy of the divine. Flow that love! Flow so much love for yourself that it overflows onto the people around you. Watch as it washes away the fears and insecurities. Everyone just wants to be loved, and the squeakiest wheels need the most attention. Send them love, and watch what happens.

Look at it this way: this is our chance to change the vibration in any room. This way, God's energy gets all over the people around you instead of your letting their energy get on you. If only I had known then what I know now.

Another Reiki-Related Miracle

I have never advertised for private clients, so to me, every new client is a miracle. Every class I've taught has a purpose outside my limited human scope of knowledge. God has a curriculum and a plan for my classes. It's never only about learning energy work. It's always about something deeper and more critical, not only to my students' growth and expansion but also my own. Often, I get to see the miracles with my clients and students as they happen while we are together in a session or a class. Other times, I get to look at the magic that resulted from the mission later. Just when I needed to keep my focus positive, God sent a message of light. I got confirmation that I was supported through a simple phone call.

It was an ordinary day. There was nothing particularly special about it, except for a conversation with one of my students. She had taken first-degree Reiki with me a few months prior, and she was calling to thank me and tell me of her own personal miracle because of it.

Thanks to my student, I was about to hear proof that everything will fall into place when you put God first. She made it her priority to flow from love, and because of that, she got to watch miracles happen. The phone call reminded me of all the concepts I'd taught her, because I needed to remember them myself. It gave me proof that the messages I delivered in class were truly divinely inspired.

This amazing student not only understood the concepts of energy I'd taught her in class but also applied them to real life. She called to tell me she had just returned from a long trip, and when she told me of her adventures, I was in awe of the series of miracles she'd experienced.

She said she had been praying about her grandfather. They were close, and she wanted to do something nice for him while she still could. He wasn't getting any younger. She said her grandfather had told her once of a dream he had of going back to visit his childhood home, a place he hadn't seen in more than seventy years. Since her grandfather had shared his wish with her, she said, she couldn't get it out of her mind. The more she thought about it, the more it became her dream too. Eventually, she began to consider what it would take to make his dream a reality. It was an exceptionally long trip and an expensive one. She had no idea how she would manage it, but she said she prayed for a way to make the journey happen anyway. She asked for the highest and best good for all concerned, and then she went out every day and looked for signs that it could be done.

As she told me the story, I could hear the excitement rising in her voice, and I could feel my vibration rising right along with hers. She said the first thing she focused on was transportation. She had to find a way to get there, and she knew there was no way her car could make the trip. So she prayed about it and left it to God to develop other options for her. Not long after that prayer, an unlikely volunteer offered to drive her there. The volunteer was someone from her past with whom she had some unfinished business. She almost rejected the gift because of the way it came to her, but she said she remembered that we'd talked about not being emotionally attached to how the prayer was answered, so she accepted the help. God always has a plan. I could see the miracles unfolding already. I sat listening to the story with wild anticipation. The fact that she chose to accept the offer makes the story even more miraculous by adding the element of her own healing to the mix. How cool is that? She set out to do something good for someone else, and God added a special perk just for her. She got an opportunity to heal an old rift with someone who once had been dear to her, and she did.

Next, she needed money. She prayed about it the same way, asking for the highest and best good for herself and all concerned. Would you believe she received more money than she needed, also in a miraculous way? Someone she knew was so moved by her desire to do good for her grandfather that the person offered to finance the whole trip. How cool is that?

She said the biggest miracle was the look on her grandfather's face as he first caught sight of his home. There was a flicker of youth and a flash of childhood joy on his face that she had never before witnessed. She said she had never seen him so happy, and she had never been so happy either. The trip gave her more than just a sense of joy and fulfillment; it gave her a feeling of deep and profound connection, both with her grandfather and with God, who orchestrated the events on their behalf.

As she reached the end of her story, I felt as if I were floating. I was lifted spiritually to a place of bliss and total peace. I was in a place of complete and unwavering faith where only love and light exist. I recognized the feeling of being in God's presence again. I felt the overwhelming sense of awe that makes you so happy you cry from the serenity of connection. When in his presence, you release all the grief you once held so tightly. It's humbling and awesome. As I recognized the feeling and basked in it, I heard a message. It was a Bible passage: "Again, truly I tell you that if two of you on earth agree about anything they ask for, it will be done for them by my Father in heaven" (Matthew 18:19 NIV).

This is the concept behind the miracle. It explained why my student's dreams came true so incredibly. She prayed for someone else's dream to come true, and because two of them dreamed the same dream, it happened. Our Father in heaven provided it. How amazing is that?

Want to know what the miracle was for me? I mean besides the fact that her grandfather's lifelong dream came true—as if that weren't enough. I learned that the concept of cocreation was in the Bible and that it works. I got a message of light reminding me of something I had forgotten. It was a lesson I'd thought I had already learned: it's not enough to understand a concept; you have to actually apply it for it to work.

I was full of gratitude for the experience her phone call had given me. I was happy to be part of something so beautiful, and that was enough to keep me moving in a positive direction for a while.

The Spiral Staircase

I knew I wanted to believe in myself and ignore all the rest, especially my fears and self-recrimination. I wanted to build from within and become strong enough to rid my vibration of the negativity. But how could I ignore the negativity when it was coming from me? I couldn't. It was frustrating! When I wasn't busy teaching Reiki or distracted by the inspirational stories of my friends and students, I focused on my mistakes and my inner darkness. If enough trouble stirred up around me or within me, I escaped with alcohol. The cycle continued. I felt like a hypocrite. I understood the concepts I was teaching others, but I was not applying them in my own life for any significant amount of time. The things that used to inspire me and make me happy just made me feel hollow and empty. I felt stuck.

I was confused. The lessons that came to me through messages of light kept repeating themselves in different and sometimes more challenging ways. Life doesn't get easier; we get stronger. However, I was exhausted because I felt there was no end in sight to the difficult lessons. These were not always easy lessons to learn the first time through. Having to repeat them over and over again after confidently teaching them to someone else made me feel like a fraud. It seemed that just when I thought I had a handle on things and had a concept figured out enough to teach it from a place of certainty, I would come upon another challenge about that very subject. It was as if God were encouraging me to practice what I preached. After a while, I believed I was doing a poor job of it. I felt like a failure every time I made a mistake or had a human moment. I was supposed to know these things already! I gave myself no leeway. My standards for myself were unrealistic. To make things worse, I went to the dark side in my mind. There I punished myself and suffered the way I believed I deserved instead of following my guidance and redirecting my thoughts.

Eventually, after I suffered enough to temporarily satisfy my self-loathing, I decided to do something about it. I went for my usual walk to pray and connect, and of course, when I did, I got a message of light.

I had a vision that showed me what was really happening. It was an elaboration on a thought I'd had before. When I was receiving the messages for the self-empowerment class, I thought about how I kept repeating certain life lessons in different situations or with different people. Each time

I did, I learned something new that would enable me to see the situation or myself at the time from a higher perspective. Every step I took to navigate a challenge and overcome it was a step up the spiral staircase to a new level of consciousness. Each repetition of a lesson in my life gave me a unique opportunity to apply a concept I'd learned and to see the miracles that would come from it. When I applied the concept, I ascended to the next floor up. If I failed to apply the concept, which happened often, it felt as if I were tossed off the staircase altogether and would have to start all over again from the beginning. The scenario itself is exhausting to think about.

The truth is, I never lost the knowledge I obtained as I grew. Sometimes I just failed to apply it. In this case, I wasn't thrown off the staircase. I just got stuck at a particularly arduous step. During this contemplation, the vision showed me what I probably looked like to God.

I saw myself as a child who needed a step stool to reach the step. God was there all along, offering me the concept that would easily become that step stool—if I would apply it. But no, not me. I was the kid using my head as a battering ram to break through to the next level of consciousness instead of simply using the tools at my service and ascending. This was not only exhausting but also painful, and it didn't have to be, because the concept—the step stool that would boost me up to where I wanted to go—was right there for me to use the whole time.

In the brief vision of a stubborn child, I suddenly understood what my guidance was telling me: "This is what happens when you fail to apply the concepts you've learned. It doesn't feel good. You get stuck repeating old, painful patterns of thought."

I realized that emotional drama or perceived failure didn't cause me to fall down the staircase to the subterranean level of hell. It just felt that way for a moment. The higher you are on the staircase, the more terrifying it feels when you look down. Once you feel the bliss of connection, any vibration that is out of alignment with that feels like falling off a cloud and landing on your head. It hurts! My problem at the time was that the more I bought into the illusion that I was falling on my head, the more I focused on the pain I felt instead of the fact that I survived the fall every time. I focused on my struggles instead of the strength I developed when I overcame them. The good news is that I was actually getting stronger, even if I couldn't see it yet.

The Human Condition

In life, there is always loss; it is the human condition.

Nothing puts life into a better perspective than death. My wallowing in self-pity and self-loathing was interrupted by life. Actually, it was the end of life—the deaths of several people dear to me over a brief time again. It was another round of three departures. It was painful, and the empath in me could feel the deep grief of all the people around me. I thought of the families who were left behind; the children who'd lost their fathers; and the parents, siblings, and friends who were suffering. I could feel the pain around me so profoundly that my perspective shifted again—but this time not how you might think. The losses made me think about how fleeting life truly is and how important it is to do something worthwhile with the time we have.

I realized I wasn't as bad off as I thought. Compared to those of the people around me who were grieving, my problems were minute. I chose to give my attention to the thoughts that were hurting me. My pain was self-inflicted, which meant there was something I could do about it.

Understanding that my thoughts were creating illusions that were pulling me out of vibrational alignment, I decided to intentionally look around me and see the blessings in my life: my children, my husband, my parents, and my friends. Our relationships were far from perfect, but they were beautiful and precious to me. From this perspective, I was much better equipped to face the energy of grief around me.

The death experience is inescapable; if you live long enough, you will know someone who dies. That's the thing about life: no one gets out alive! Sometimes you have to laugh. It's good for you! It raises your vibration. For me, the higher my vibration, the easier it is to connect with those on the other side. And let me tell you, those in the light have an enthusiastic sense of humor. Why wouldn't they? They don't have pain or suffering where they are. So laugh, and you'll feel them laughing with you.

In all seriousness, the death of the human body is real, and it is painful to lose someone we love, but it is not the end. I know this because it's been shown to me. It seems that's what I do, right? I talk to dead people, and because of that, my experience of death is different from the experiences of most. When spirits leave the body, I can usually still contact them. To me, they really aren't gone. Even in death, they have much to teach us from the other side. I was thinking about that when I got the following message from the loved ones we recently had lost, which taught me more:

Loved Ones Lost

Loved ones lost, especially those we've lost tragically and unexpectedly, may cause us to doubt God's love and protection. We may choose to distance ourselves from God. We may even experience anger or hostility toward God. The feeling of loss is overwhelming. We humans need someone or something to blame. The pain is too much. There are no thoughts of tomorrow because today is already impossible to bear. Each breath we take is torture. The only question we have for our Creator is "Why?"

We feel alone, and we miss our loved ones terribly. We are not as far from them as we think or feel. The pain we experience as those abandoned, both by our loved ones and by God, keeps us from recognizing that the connection is not lost. We feel we are grieving for what our loved ones are missing in this world, but in truth, we are grieving for our own loss of future experiences with them. Grief is human, and it is possibly the most difficult emotion to bear, but through it, we can grow.

When our tears have slowed and our state of shock has begun to fade, we can then find our loved ones again. Our loved ones continue to exist; God has merely changed their form and way of expressing themselves to us.

We are not as far from them as we thought. When we can accept the situation and trust that everything is as it should be, we can feel their presence. They are not gone at all, just different.

When we become open, they appear to us, and they comfort us in any way we will allow. Sometimes we will see them in our dreams, in the smile of a child, in the beauty of a sunset, or in the delicate wings of a butterfly.

In those moments, they whisper to us of the joy, beauty, love, and life that is never-ending. Where they exist, there is no pain, only love.

The process of arriving at this realization is always unique. For some, it may take years, while for others, it may be weeks. There is no schedule; there is no timeline by which we should conclude our grieving. There is, however, the life that we are blessed with, which we must treasure and value. This life we are given is a gift, even when it is painful.

In time, we begin to grasp that although we feel the loss, the evolution of our loved ones is a miracle. We realize that the physical body was no longer needed for the purpose intended. It was no longer of use. But the soul carries on, and it is not restricted by physical boundaries and limitations. Those who are no longer confined to the physical world are moving on in their purpose. They flow in a vibration of purity and strength that is unfathomable to our physically focused minds. We who are left behind are charged with the duty to carry on. We can honor our loved ones by learning from what they taught us in the time shared with us. Each of us is here for a reason. We show respect by remembering the impact a loved one has had on the world and continues to have on the world. This is when the beauty begins.

So look for them. They are everywhere. Our loved ones are present in every loving thought and in every hug, sunset, flower, rain shower, butterfly, bird, smile, kiss, and laugh. When you think of your loved ones, they are with you, enveloping the entirety of your being with love. Create memories and experiences with them in new ways. Take time to think of them, feel them, love them, and honor them. They are a gift to you from the God who loves you. Breathe it in, smile, and hug those who are still here for you to embrace.

Christi Conde

Death: It's a Part of Life

As time went by, my powers of perception continued to grow, and when Lodi, my mother-in-law, was ready to cross over, I was certain I would still be able to reach her. The amazing woman who had given birth to the most wonderful man on the planet died peacefully in the night after briefly coming out of an Alzheimer's haze she had been in for fifteen years. Yes, you read that right: we got a miracle. The day she died, the hospice nurse told us it was time to say our goodbyes because she'd had an event that morning, and it wouldn't be much longer. I had no idea the event the nurse spoke of involved Lodi's returned ability to speak. Lodi hadn't spoken in years, but she spoke to her family that afternoon. She made eye contact, and she knew whom she was talking to. With her atrophied vocal ability, she struggled. Still, she was able to say several times what sounded like "all of you." When she said it, we all knew her last words to her family that day were "I love you."

There are many miracles when someone leaves his or her human body behind. With Lodi's death, those miracles reminded me that there is much more to this world than what we see with our human eyes.

This experience started with some curious timing. Lodi was a devout Catholic, and she died on the Wednesday in the middle of Holy Week. It made a world of sense to me that she would choose to go during Holy Week. It's a time spent in reverence and prayer, a time when we commune with Christ and honor his sacrifice. Did you know the church doesn't perform funerals during Holy Week? That meant Lodi got an extended celebration of life. Her children got to have time to truly honor her memory and celebrate the gift of having such an incredible woman for a mother. Her accomplishments before her diagnosis were admirable and inspiring and too numerous to count, and she would continue to demonstrate great feats even without a physical body.

Lodi taught me much from the other side. I kept catching glimpses of her around my father-in-law after she passed. Lodi wanted to stay with her husband. She wanted to comfort him and to comfort her family. Her family in the light surrounded her, including her mom, dad, and sister, but Lodi's sole focus was on her family here on earth. She wanted to stay close to her loved ones. I didn't know it at the time, but Lodi wasn't going anywhere just yet. I get why she wanted to stay. It's understandable. She'd missed out on fifteen years of communication because of Alzheimer's. She was trying to make up for lost time, but it definitely made for some interesting antics later. Stay tuned!

Another thing we found incredible was the date of her death. Lodi died on April 20. Lodi's mother had died on April 21. Her sister, Faye, had passed on April 22. They all died in the same week, years apart, on April 20, 21, and 22. The coincidence was too much to ignore. The timing lends credibility to the idea that there is much more to this universe than we can ever know, much less understand.

I wanted to understand. As soon as I could after I found out Lodi had left her body, I went for a walk to connect. I wanted to talk to her and see if she had anything to say. When I got back to my notebook, Lodi gave me this message of light for her family:

Take Time

Take time to remember.
Take time to laugh.
Take time to treasure
moments from our past.
Take time to grieve.
Take time to cry.
Take time to mourn,
but this is not goodbye!
For love we share,
it has no end.
All earthly boundaries
it does transcend.
When you call me,
I am there.
I can hear your every prayer,
for I am at my Father's knee.
I am peace. I am love. I am free.

Exploring this experience with Lodi was incredible because I learned more about what happens when the soul leaves the body. I didn't realize it at the time, but in her case, she kept her soul focused on this physical plane for a little while. In other words, she didn't cross over into the light right away by our human interpretation of time. She stayed earthbound for a little bit, and the longer she stayed, the more confused she became. I have to say, though, she had me fooled when we wrote the poem together. It sure felt like she was in the light, but I found out later that she wasn't there yet. What I felt coming from her when she gave me the poem was the combination of the energy of her higher self, who was actually "at [the] Father's knee," and the power and depth of the fifteen years of unexpressed human love she was feeling at the time.

Alzheimer's had halted her ability to communicate the extent of her love for her family. This woman loved profoundly and powerfully, so when she got a chance to express it through me, I was overwhelmed. It was so powerful and beautiful it felt like divine energy to me. I thought she was in the light, because I felt so much love and peace coming from her. Maybe she thought she was in heaven. She was free of the limitations of the body that had betrayed her for so long. I can see how that feeling of freedom might be misinterpreted as heaven. It was a definite improvement from the feeling of confinement she experienced because of her disease.

It wasn't until months later, when she energetically fried our air conditioner, that I realized she hadn't crossed over yet. Mr. Conde, her husband, was taking care of our dogs while Ron and I took the girls on vacation. We lived just around the corner from one another, so it was easy for him to stop by to check in on our pups.

That day, Mr. C. came into the house to feed the dogs, and Lodi followed him. The longer spirits take to cross over, the more confused they become. She was walking/floating along behind him, trying to talk to him. She didn't know that he couldn't hear her. She thought he was avoiding her. You see, when Mr. C. was at home, he spoke to her out loud when no one was around. Maybe that added to her confusion, because she thought they had been having two-way conversations the whole time. Well, he wasn't speaking to her then. He was focused on feeding our dogs. The more she tried to communicate, the more it seemed he was ignoring her. Eventually, after about the third or fourth attempt at getting his attention, she decided to yell his name. Her frustration caused her to build up energy beyond her ability to control it.

The last time she screamed, "Tony!" she stamped her formless foot and shook her bodiless fist, and all the energy in the house was drawn to her location. That surge of energy funneled into the nearest electrical device, the air conditioner. Zap—out it went!

That was when I knew she was still hanging out here on the earth plane. Spirits in the light don't do that. They play with lights to say hi. They don't fry them out.

When I realized Lodi was still earthbound, I contacted her, and I tried to help her go into the light. She refused and said she knew she could get to the light at any time. Lodi had been devout, faithful, and loving for her whole life. She believed that Jesus had died for her sins so her human mistakes would be forgiven. In fact, Lodi told me she could see the light when she looked around. Still, she wanted to stay with her family. She had been restricted for too long by a body that didn't function. Now that she was in the spirit state, she could be with her family, even if they didn't realize it. She felt compelled to stay.

So she did. She stayed for her husband's birthday, so he wouldn't be alone. Then she hung out for Mother's Day. After all, it was her day, and her children needed her there. Then Father's Day came, and she wanted to be with her husband for that day too. Family gatherings were a chance to be with everyone together at once. On her own birthday, which was three months after she left her physical body, of course she had to be there at her birthday party. She was the guest of honor. She knew the whole family would want her near that day. Of course, they did, but they also wanted her to find peace.

Whenever I encountered her, she was less thrilled about her new state than before. The novelty of being free of the physical limitation of a restricted body was replaced by sadness because she could not interact with her family anyway. I have found that disembodied spirits keep their human characteristics. They aren't really free of the pain just because the body is gone. They continue to vibrate at the same frequencies they vibrated at when they were alive. The problem is that the longer they stay focused on the earth plane without a body, the more they feed off of the human energy around them. They absorb it. The longer they remain in the in-between, the more confused they get. The worst part about that is that they do more harm than good when they try to help the loved ones left behind from this vibrational flow. They accidentally end up amplifying whatever human emotion is active in the person they are trying to help. If the human loved one is struggling or worried about something, the spirit's energy amplifies that vibration. Suddenly, the worry the human was experiencing devolves into terror. It's like plugging the human vibration into a high-powered battery. The spirit is the battery. I learned that spirits can usually only amplify a vibration that is already in a living human. They don't implant new energy into the people they visit. The exception is when a spirit borrows a human's body when the human has consumed too much alcohol or drugs, which happens more often than you might think.

The longer a spirit lingers between worlds, the more its vibration shifts down toward the negative end of the vibrational scale. For some spirits, that negativity could just be sadness, while with others, it is anger. In Lodi's case, she fit the description of a spirit growing sadder and more disheartened the longer she was here. She wasn't borrowing anyone's body to reexperience life. Still, she was accidentally starting to amplify the sadness, frustration, and confusion in the people she cared about when she was near them.

I wanted her to have the experience of peace she deserved, so I tried to explain that she could do much more for them if she just crossed over. Moving into the light would free her from that sadness, and she wouldn't accidentally amplify that sadness in someone she loved. She wouldn't feel limited, as she did in her physical experience. She heard me and understood, but she was on her own schedule. She reminded me that all things happen in divine and perfect timing. So I tipped my energetic hat to her and took a step back to watch with a new level of respect and admiration as her story continued to unfold.

The time eventually came for Lodi to cross into heaven, and I got to see what she meant by "divine and perfect timing." It was more beautiful than I could have imagined. She crossed over into the light during a mass. It wasn't just any mass; it was the perfect one. You see, my father-in-law, a devout Catholic, requested a special intention prayer be said for Lodi during masses on Mother's Day, her birthday, and their wedding anniversary. Each was more beautiful than the one before it. The third one was the charm, because she went into the light that time. The ideal circumstances lined up so that the miracle could happen in the most remarkable way. I feel honored to have been witness to it.

I watched as she appreciated her beautiful family who gathered at the church to honor her and pray for her that day. There was so much love in her vibration that she glowed. She was in awe of how large her family had grown. They were all praying for her. Lodi's children, their spouses, and her grandchildren and great-grandchildren were all gathered for her. We had all been together in her honor many times before, but something about that day was different. She wasn't trying to be part of the human experience anymore; she was saying goodbye.

As I sat there between my husband and my daughters, I felt a shift of energy. I looked over to see Lodi virtually sitting between Ron and Mr. C. Her vibrant glow seemed to envelop them in a cloud of fuzzy pink light. Every time I looked over, she was sitting near someone different, and her glow surrounded that person too. She was whispering her love to each of them. After she'd made her rounds, kissing each one of them on the forehead, there was a moment when she disappeared altogether for a second. I guessed she was out in the world, kissing the foreheads of the family members who weren't present at the church. When she returned, she sat next to her husband, basking in love and peace, and her warm pink glow seemed to surround us all.

This mass was unusual compared to the first two masses held for her. The priest nearly forgot to mention the names of those for whom we were praying. He remembered just as he was preparing the Eucharist. It's almost as if someone whispered in his ear to remind him. He stopped what he was doing, called the altar girl over, and had her hold up the paper listing the names of the loved ones for whom we were praying. He read them over the Eucharist he had begun to prepare. When I heard Lodi's name—actually pronounced correctly for the first time in any of the masses—I looked for her. Instead of sitting with her family, she was floating toward the altar.

There the priest was holding the round wafer, the body of Christ, over his head. A bell rang, and the wafer transformed into a sphere of sparkling white light. There was a flash, and I watched Lodi go into the light. I looked over at my husband at that moment and saw a look of surprise flash across his face.

I asked him later what he had seen that surprised him, and he said he could have sworn he saw his mother's face in the stained-glass portrayal of Mary, the Blessed Mother, just above the altar. What is the chance he would see his mother's face at the exact moment I saw her go into the light directly in front of the stained glass he was looking at? He didn't realize what he had seen or why until I explained what I had seen. I could sense he believed me when I told him how the Eucharist had turned into the light for her. It makes sense. She always had been a faithful Catholic. Of course she would find the light, the doorway to heaven, in the Eucharist, which had offered her so much peace in her life.

Moving Through Emotions

Life keeps moving, and the world keeps turning even while we grieve. The many experiences I had with spirits teaching me from the other side were amazing. They helped me process my grief, and they helped me understand much more about the nature of the energy of spirit. Even though I was learning and beginning to understand, there was still such a heaviness in the sadness around me that I absorbed it eventually, and again, the heaviness became part of my vibration.

One day I was thinking about how to manage the energy of sadness that I was experiencing. I wanted to learn how to process it in a healthy way. I was praying for clarity, when I got the following message of light:

Sadness of Loss

> There are many occasions for us to experience sadness with good reason. There is no shame in being sad. The question is, how long do we choose to experience that emotion? Sorrow, especially in the loss of a loved one, must be experienced. It must be felt like the raw and painful emotion that it is, but then it must be processed and dealt with. The loss we experience will never be forgotten, but in lingering in the depths of pain, we lose focus of our blessings.

We must grieve, but in grieving, we must act. We must honor our loved ones. Speak of them and to them often. They can still hear us. When the tears come, let them. In doing so, we release the energy holding us in darkness.

When we honor our loved ones by thinking of them or speaking of them, they come to us. And when they do, we experience a wave of release because the loved ones on the other side are actually hugging us. They come to us and energetically envelop us in the vibration of love that continues to exist even without the physical body. When one is in a state of grief, crying is the most natural reaction to the hug, especially when it comes in the flow of divine energy. It offers immediate relief from the deluge of sadness. An energetic hug from our loved ones opens the floodgates so that we do not drown in our grief. That's why our loved ones hug us from the other side. A hug will almost always get the tears flowing.

Tears are God's gift to us. Tears are cleansing, and they effectively wash away the muddy waters of sadness. When the water runs clear again, we can see with fresh eyes the beauty in the world that was brought about by the life of the one we love and miss so much.

Keep On Keeping On

Unfortunately, as I said, I absorbed the sadness all around me—the joy of being an empath. I had no idea how to release it. It was building up. Over a few years, there were so many I knew and loved who died that I found it difficult to honor them all in the ways they deserved. Despite the fact that I knew the ones on the other side were fine, there were so many I missed that I felt if I gave in to the release of my tears, I might never stop crying.

With my focus centered on death and loss, it was no surprise that my next Reiki class involved two people who had just recently lost a loved one. It was the same loved one. My new students were a mother-and-daughter pair.

I'm not sure what prompted them to reach out to take the class together, but I know it was supposed to happen. I'm guessing an angel must have whispered in Yvonne's ear. Throughout the two days of Reiki instruction, we spent our time immersed in the energy of learning and healing. I had the opportunity to explain my understanding of death to them—that it is really not the end. Then I shared the messages I was prompted to share, including two of the earlier messages: "Loved Ones Lost" and "Sadness of Loss." I was in awe of how it happened again. I received a message of light, and then the perfect recipients appeared in the next class. How crazy is that?

As if the miraculous timing of the messages weren't enough, God and the loved one in question sent one more beautiful message of light that could not be ignored. It came as a result of a figurative tap on the shoulder I got as the class was ending. I had just presented my students with their first-degree Reiki certificates, when I was prompted to take a picture of the pair. I had never taken a photo of any of my Reiki students before. But it occurred to me that they were my first mother-and-daughter pair to take a class together, so I wanted to commemorate that with a photo. We went into the backyard to have a more scenic backdrop for the picture. As I stood back to snap the shot, Yvonne mentioned something about her father. She thought he must have been happy watching them together. Suddenly, a giant yellow-and-black butterfly floated into my camera's view at that moment, as if to say, "Hi! I'm here." The butterfly seemed to linger, floating around them as if enveloping them in an energetic hug. I thought it was a miracle because the message of light I had relayed to them talked about an energetic hug.

Yvonne's eyes welled up with tears when she realized her father had just sent them a message of love from beyond. I know it might sound strange to think the butterfly carried a message, but it was more than just a butterfly floating through the yard. It brought with it a different kind of energy. The air took on a magical quality. A sense of calm comfort enveloped us. It is hard to describe, but his presence was strong, and I wasn't the only one who could feel him. They could too. That happens with Reiki. Heightened senses are a natural side effect of working with universal life-force energy. It clears out the energy weighing us down. It clears away the haze of confusion clouding our vision, and we begin to see the world through a different lens—the lens we choose.

I saw that the look of joy and surprise on Yvonne's face was matched by her mother's. I also felt a magical sense of awe coming from them with my trusty empathic abilities. They knew the butterfly floated around them for a reason. There was no question we had just seen a miracle. The timing was divinely inspired for sure. It would have taken Hollywood fifty takes to get that magic right. With us, it happened naturally with the magic of God's miracles. No retakes necessary!

The miracle didn't stop there. About a week later, Yvonne called me in a state of surprise and awe. I could feel her energy even before she told me what had happened.

She was feeling a little stressed at work, but more than that, she was missing her father. She had a lot to do that day, and it was important work that needed strict focus, but she couldn't focus. The overload of grief coupled with work stress began to take over. When she was just about to cry, she started talking to her dad in her mind, telling him something to the effect of *I wish you were here*. At that exact moment, she looked out the window to see what looked like the same large yellow butterfly we had seen at my house the week before. It was the only butterfly outside her window at that moment. In fact, it was the only thing she could see.

The butterfly wasn't flitting around in the bushes; it was straight up, hovering outside the window. It stayed there floating for a long time, as if to say, "Hello," in a way that was impossible for her to miss. She could feel her father's presence profoundly and as powerfully as the day she had felt him at my house. She could feel his love. He was supporting her, and he was giving her an energetic pep talk in his own way. They were making new memories together. She felt as if her father had just told her not to worry and that everything would be fine.

It was another miracle to her and me, and it keeps happening. It's her dad's way of popping in to say hi. It's their new thing. She still calls me sometimes to tell me that her butterfly has shown up for her. When it does, it always seems to be a sign of comfort or support, and it always appears at the perfect time for her highest and best good.

Christi Conde

When the Music Fades

I was excited and honored to be part of that beautiful experience. It was a miracle. Miracles always made me feel better for a while. The problem was that when the magic and wonder faded, I reverted back to my negative thinking. Annoying, right? Don't worry. Eventually, I figured it out.

I berated myself for everything, including my inability to hold a positive vibration. After the most recent miracle with the mother-and-daughter pair, I thought about how undeserving I was. I was gifted with amazing experiences with people outside my home, but I couldn't be the person I was supposed to be for my own family. If not for the miracle breaks and messages of light in my darkest times, I don't know how I would have survived that part of life.

I felt out of control. I wasn't using any of my tools that came to me through the messages of light long enough or consistently enough for them to actually work. An old saying kept playing in my head: "Those who can't do teach." My unhealthy ego had begun to assault my consciousness. Every negative cliché I had ever heard, whether it applied to me and my situation or not, popped into my head.

Unfortunately, I started to believe I was the teacher who couldn't do. I stopped enjoying the things that used to make me happy, including my volunteer work. As rewarding as it was to work with my girls' scouting groups, it wasn't enough to help me overcome my energetic deficit. I didn't feel capable of maintaining a flow of love strong enough to keep myself from absorbing the energy around me. I was in desperate need of approval and validation, and it wasn't the job of the people around me to supply it. I realized the girls I was working with deserved a leader who was not a flailing energetic mess. I was caught between honoring my commitment to the kids and honoring myself. I knew I had too much on my plate and had for some time. I was slipping into a version of myself I did not recognize. I think my ego was too unhealthy to let me see what was happening. I was so lost I had to pray for guidance.

When I prayed, I got my guidance. I went for my walk, which usually lasted about an hour, and while I was out there moving, praying, and soaking up the sunshine, I got my answers. It was a funny exchange in

The Messages of Light

retrospect, but at the time, I felt as if I were being scolded. The conversation went something like the following.

"Dear Lord, please help me. I feel so lost and out of control. I don't know what to do. I feel like I am so busy volunteering that I don't have time for my own family. Definitely not myself."

The guidance I heard was "Then give up the scouting troops."

Naturally, I decided to argue for my limitations. "It's not that simple," I said. "There are a lot of girls who depend on me."

Then the scolding came in: "Has your ego gotten so unhealthy that arrogance has taken over? Do you think you are the only person suited to help these girls? Do you honestly believe I would tell you to do something without a plan already in place?"

At that point, I bowed my head in embarrassment, as would anyone being reprimanded by God. The message was received. I knew I could not continue to serve from the proverbial empty cup. I knew I wasn't doing anyone any favors by filling that empty cup with siphoned human energy either. Through that message, I realized I was not the only person who could do what I was doing. I mean, it was a national organization. Clearly, someone else could be entrusted with my precious group of girls.

So I said in a sort of childishly snarky way, "Fine then! Who?"

There was a sort of energy shift, and I felt I was being laughed at but at the same time adored. I felt as if I were being kissed on the forehead and told, "Aren't you cute?" But in that moment, I got a flash of the person who was supposed to take over. It was Rosa.

I thought about it for a minute and realized that was the "Aha" moment I was looking for. Her daughter was in the troop, and she was already a group leader. She was spiritual, and as I said before, she was kind. I had known her since our children were small, and she knew the side of me I was trying to nurture. I'd relayed messages to her from her mother on the other side before. If anyone would understand my desire to focus on my spiritual gifts, it would be Rosa. She was perfect. The only question remaining was whether or not she would accept the responsibility. The training sessions, the preparations for meetings, and the meetings themselves were a considerable commitment of both time and energy.

I'll give you one guess as to her answer! Yep, Rosa accepted, and in fact, she said she would be honored. So yay for flawless divine guidance. I know for sure the guidance was divine, because it turned out better than I could have possibly imagined. She took over the troop, and many years later, even after her daughter has graduated from high school, this amazing woman is still actively involved in the organization. How cool is that? She's gone above and beyond and continues to do so. See, divine guidance is truly flawless when you dare to follow it.

I admit my heart broke the day I told the girls I would be leaving the group. They were warm, loving, and understanding, but some were clearly sad, even though the troop would continue without me. It was difficult, but I had to trust that it was the right move. I was being called in a different direction, and I knew I had to go.

I stayed involved in some of my other activities, so I could be near my daughters at school, and that enabled me to keep an eye on the girls from my scouting groups as they grew. I am proud of every single one of them. They have grown into exceptional, successful young leaders of our world community.

Writer's Block

So there I was. I had given up something important to me so I could focus on practicing my spiritual work and writing my book. The sad thing was, I had no idea how to write the book. I had collected quite a few messages of light by then. I had written a lot about my life, but what I wrote did not feel inspired. I was in no mental or emotional state to write anything positive or inspirational. I tried. Believe me, I did. The only thing that came out was the negativity I had within.

I still got guidance, though. God never deserts us! When I prayed about it, the response was "Focus on healing."

That task, to me, was more daunting than writing a book. A cascade of questions began to flow: "Where the heck would I start? And what about my book? Isn't that a big reason I was supposed to stop the scouting thing?"

I meditated as I walked and prayed, and when I asked about my book, I got a clear instruction: "Make three copies of it."

I argued like a frustrated child. "It's not done! It's not even all typed yet. Most of it is still in spiral notebooks."

The Messages of Light

The answer was stated clearly and firmly: "Make three copies of it as it is. Give one copy to your mom, give one copy to Kathy, and you keep the other. Then forget about it. You will know when to pick it back up again. The time is not now. Trust. You will know."

So I did as I was instructed. I went to a copy shop and copied the typed pages and seven spiral notebooks of transcribed inspired information and messages. A crazy thing happened when I gave Kathy her copy: she noticed that the handwritten pages were almost all in different handwriting. I looked at them myself and saw it too. I thought it was strange because I had written them with my own hand. As Kathy and I examined the pages, we noticed the handwriting seemed similar when the messages fit a similar theme. The vibration of the information coming to me changed my handwriting.

The discovery raised a big question for me: Whom was I talking to? I'd thought I was talking to one entity, God. So why was my handwriting different almost every time I accessed my guidance?

I meditated and prayed about it, and this is what I learned. I was speaking to and receiving information from God, as I'd thought. The information was being relayed to me through various angels, ancestors, and spirit guides who were sent to answer my questions, hence the different handwriting. I had already talked to earthbound spirits and ancestors who'd crossed over, so it made sense that my higher self in the light, who is always one with God, could access any being with the information I was seeking. God was the telephone operator, the telephone itself, and the network connecting the callers. I'd learned this before when I talked to Rosa's mom, but now I had another perspective on a phrase I had heard many times before. In this context, "God is love" has a more profound meaning.

> God is love. God is the love that connects us all to one another on earth and to the love that exists in all the angels, ascended ancestors, and spiritual guides. God is the Creator and is in all creations as well. God is the informer as well as the information itself. God is in everything. God is love.

While making copies of my book, I caught another glimpse into a new perspective on the nature of God. How cool is that?

Again, I was awe-inspired. I know there will always be more to understand about this concept, because the true nature of God is infinite, and our human minds are limited. There is always more to learn and explore in this world, and it can be revealed to us in incredibly magical ways. In this flow, we never get bored, and we don't have to conjure drama to remember we're alive. We get the exhilaration of magic and miracles. We get the joy of truly experiencing the love of God.

I thank God for creating and connecting me to my angels, ascended ancestors, and spirit guides and for having my back all these years. Thank you! I love you!

With that revelation, I put aside writing my book. I tucked it away in my old briefcase, and in its place, I focused on my own healing. I wanted to be able to consistently access that flow of love. I wanted to stop the yo-yo from going up and down so swiftly and dramatically. I began to strengthen my spiritual muscle intentionally. I began to apply the concepts I had long been teaching directly to my own life. As I practiced, I went about exploring what seemed to be a new world of mystery and wonder. The more I practiced prayer and meditation on my outdoor walks, the stronger I became. As I practiced what I'd learned from the messages of light so far—faith, compassion, choosing a higher perspective, and vibrational flow—I got stronger. My visions and communications with God, other humans, spirits on the other side, earthbound spirits, angels, ancestors, guides, and my higher self became clearer. It took some time, but I began to trust myself and my relationship to the energy around me, becoming more and more in sync with divine flows of love. I remembered my true self more every day and began to create the life I wanted in a flow of magic and miracles that I found mind-blowing. I learned that my life experience directly results from my perspective and vibrational flow. I can always choose a new perspective. Therefore, I will always have access to the higher vibrational flows of energy.

Now, don't get me wrong; my life still had some drama in it, as you will see, and I still had times when I chose to dive headfirst into the illusion of fear, but I was never again helpless. When I decided to put myself first on my list of priorities, as I taught in the self-empowerment class, I had plenty of energy to spare to share with others. I began to serve from my overflowing cup. This was another revolution around the spiral staircase.

My Mom

My newfound connection must have given my mom a sense of relief. She was my go-to person for all things—and most of the time, it was all things drama! But seriously, my mom and I always had been remarkably close, and as I got older, we only grew closer. She was more than just my mom; she was my best friend. She was the physical manifestation of unconditional love in my life. Believe me, my intensely emotional self wasn't easy for most people to love, but my mama made it look easy. She loved me and understood me better than anyone on the planet. The understanding went both ways. I knew my mom was a free spirit. So I understood when she left town after living there for only a few short years. I knew her difficulties had nothing to do with me, and she had to follow her guidance. Otherwise, she'd have been miserable.

She was as happy as I'd ever seen her. Her dreams of comfort, peace, and financial security were realized. For a good many years, she was thriving. She had friends, and she was in a job she loved, making good money. She still visited us every few months when she came to do readings at the local psychic and metaphysical fair. My mom was doing what she loved. She was living her best life, and I was happy for her.

Then, one day, I got a call from my mom's boss, who told me my mom was in the hospital. I wasn't totally shocked to get the call, because I had been feeling my mom's energy nearby me all morning. It was as if my higher self were talking to her higher self the whole time. That explains why I heard, "This is not what I wanted!" I kept hearing that in my deaf ear in my mom's voice. I heard it before the call and then repeatedly after.

While trying to tune in to my mom to hear what she said, I gathered my things and got on the next plane out. I was in a weird haze the whole time, and nothing seemed real. I watched myself do all the things one does while traveling, but I wasn't really in my body. My body was on autopilot, and my spirit was wandering the ethers, trying to get a better signal on my mom.

When I got there, the signal was stronger. I knew she was still at least partially in her body, because the closer to her I got, the stronger the signal became. I could hear her loud and clear voice in my deaf ear as I approached her hospital room. This time, she told me, "Don't let them see me like this!" referring to her bosses, Kim and Karen, who were standing outside her door. My mother was a regal woman and proud. She was always done up to the nines (her words) when she was out and about. She never left the house without her makeup on and her hair done. At that moment, she was not pleased that anyone saw her in a hospital bed, especially two of the people she admired and respected most. It was great to be able to hear her, but that made the reality that she wasn't using her body to communicate more real. I could hear her, but her mouth was not moving.

After a long and sleepless night, I was an emotional mess. I was calm and collected on the outside, but I felt lost, scared, and alone inside. I wanted my mommy. So I prayed. I prayed for the highest and best good for my mom and everyone concerned. That was all I could think to do.

Then I got to see a miracle: my mom woke up! As miraculous as that was, what I saw when she woke up was also pretty mystifying. I got another vision, a message of light.

As her eyes opened, I noticed they were out of focus, as if she were looking at something far off in the distance. Then she lifted her arms as if grasping for that thing just out of her reach. She began to sit up as she reached, as if being pulled forward by some unseen force. She sat up entirely in the bed as she grasped for the invisible object. Then it was as if she lost sight of what she was reaching for, and she collapsed backward onto her pillow. She then lowered her arms, as if she were getting back into her body, and she started to scan the room. When she saw me, we locked eyes, and she said, "I missed it." The sadness I saw in her eyes and the emotion of devastation I felt coming from her broke my heart.

I was sad for her because after the fact, I could see in my mind's eye what she had been reaching for. In my heart, I caught the briefest sensation of the serenity that had eluded her. I saw a light. It looked like the train light from the movie *The Polar Express*. It was round and bright, but the light was headed away from her.

I was sorry she had missed it, because it was beautiful based on the emotion I felt from her, but I was also sad for myself ("Poor me"). She didn't want to be there on the planet (with me) anymore. In fact, as she became more lucid, it became clear she was disappointed. She was ready to go. My mom confirmed my perception. When her friend Deb walked into the room and stood next to the bed, my mom looked at the two of us and asked, "Which one of you did it? Which one of you called me back?"

Deb slowly raised a hand and meekly said, "I'm sorry."

My mom looked at both of us and sadly said, "But I was ready."

Things with my mom were never quite the same after that. I was scared I would lose her again, but I was also desperately sad that she didn't want to be there anymore. I took it personally. My feelings were hurt. I began to subscribe to the idea that my mom didn't want to be with me anymore. My self-esteem and self-love took a blow. I was falling back down the spiral staircase again.

I did not instantly lose my understanding of the concepts I'd learned, only my resolve to apply them. I felt as if I went way past my rock bottom to the subterranean landscape of emotional hell again. I felt as if I were using my head as a battering ram to move through my life's lessons. I should have been using it properly as the step stool of understanding that would help me ascend to higher flows of consciousness. Instead, I chose to wallow in my delusions. I decided to feel abandoned and unloved. I went straight into my destructive default of self-loathing and a victim mentality. I went so far to the dark side of thinking that I made my mother's pain and suffering and her desire to be free of it all about me.

When I realized I was being selfish while she suffered, I tortured myself for that too. I felt as if I fell backward on the spiral staircase and landed on the floor of delusion. At that point, I stopped moving up the spiral staircase to a new perspective. Instead, I began to circle back through my old thoughts, beliefs, and expectations in revolutions of insanity. I was upset and angry. I chose to keep repeating the negative flow of thought and emotion over and over while expecting those choices to somehow overthrow the laws of nature and give me a miracle. I was running in circles, going nowhere, buying into the illusions presented by my unhealthy ego instead of ascending to higher levels of consciousness.

Boy, was I lost!

Even though my mom's life was saved, I still felt scared. As I said, things between us changed. I had no idea how to talk to her, because she didn't need or want to hear about my problems, and at the time, my trials and tribulations were all I thought about. Without her help and support, because she was navigating her own struggles, my burdens were heavier, and life was more challenging for me. I devolved emotionally and spiritually. I was a mess.

Because of everything I'd learned, I knew I would never be helpless again. But it was taking everything I had just to survive my self-inflicted pain. Helping myself out of it would be a whole other thing. After the emotional injury of almost losing my mom, my focus of thought caused my nervous system to revert back to survival mode. I couldn't think of a happy thought to save my life, so self-love was out the window. It became clear that I had to find another way to manage my stress. So I started running again.

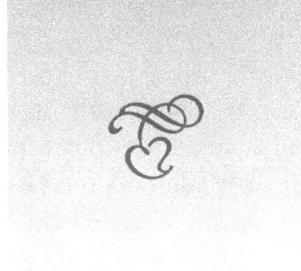

Chapter 18

Recurring Themes and Lessons Learned

Running

I have always been a fan of physical activity and exercise. Being an empath, I found that movement and outdoor play were naturally the best ways for me to manage my emotions as a child. As I got older, my emotions grew with me, so the habit of exercising in one form or another stuck. I worked out with Jane Fonda audio cassette tapes in elementary school. The cassettes had a little paper insert showing the proper form of the exercises. In middle school, I was on gymnastics and soccer teams, exercising regularly and dealing pretty well with elevated levels of tween stress. I was a cheerleader in high school, and I went to the gym regularly. I also used to get up every morning at 4:30 a.m. to run at Album Park when I was a teen. My dad didn't love that his daughter was sneaking out of the house at that time of the morning, but at least I was mostly only sneaking out to exercise. That was when running became part of my life, in the peaceful, quiet hours of the early morning.

Over the years, I ran for many reasons. I ran for pleasure. I ran for fitness. I ran because my coaches made me run. I ran to detox. I ran for stress relief. I ran to feel the power of my physical body, and I ran just because I could. Outside of my usual commitments, if I wasn't walking and praying, I was probably running. I found a sense of release when I ran. Whatever I carried with me when I started a run was shed somewhere along the open road, and by the time I finished, I felt light and free.

I took a break from running for a while in my early years of college for the obvious early adult excuse—too much partying. I had to pick it up again later for the same early adult reason. I had to burn off the fifteen pounds that tried to dwell on my hips and thighs after my first year of college. I complained to Ron about my weight back then, and he said the only way he knew to burn off weight was through running. It was as if a lightbulb went off, and I understood. I remembered how good I'd felt when I ran as a teen, so I started again. I started a daily routine of about a mile or two a day, and I quickly burned off those fifteen pounds.

I used weight training after my girls were born to burn off the baby weight and stave off the baby blues. When my girls were old enough to be left alone with Riane for an hour, I went back to running. I started off just trying to get up one hill without stopping. Eventually, I was running four miles on the streets that paved the mountainside near our home with no trouble. I equated running the seemingly impossible hills to the seemingly impossible challenges in my life. If I could make it up that hill, I could do anything. My theme song was "Going to California" by Led Zeppelin. The lyrics "Standing on the hill of the mountain of dreams, telling myself it's not as hard … as it seems" became my mantra as I ran the hills of my neighborhood. And it worked for a while.

When I got to that point in my life, guilt, shame, pain, and fear were, as I said, overwhelming again. So I ran. It was something I could do for myself. It helped to keep my mind off the fact that I almost had lost my mom and the realization that was even harder for me to take: she was ready to be gone.

The more I ran, the more I loved running. I liked what it did, not just for my body but also for my mood and mind. I loved the endorphins. Running is a natural way to stimulate endorphins. Endorphins are responsible for the so-called runner's high you may have heard about. It's a natural high but addictive nonetheless, and I was addicted. Given the options, the endorphin rush from running was much better than wallowing in self-pity or self-loathing and healthier than numbing with alcohol.

By the way, dear reader, nothing I just talked about healed me. The running was a distraction and avoidance technique allowing the energies of pain and fear to continue to grow within me like a dust bunny. Wallowing only made things worse at that moment, and numbing with alcohol only intensified the pain in the long run. But I had to work with what I knew at the time, and running was it. Running helped me survive, but it didn't help me thrive.

One day my sister-in-law Becca told me she was going to do a half marathon, and I was impressed by her courage. I loved running, but I had no desire to do that much running. The 13.1 miles of a half marathon seemed too much to me. But as I watched Becca train, I was inspired by her determination. We ran together often during her training, and I enjoyed running for the pleasure of running. When my brother-in-law Conrad sent me a picture of Becca at her first half-marathon finish line, she looked so happy and the atmosphere looked so fun that I decided to give it a try.

It took me a year to train for my first half marathon, and it was great. I enjoyed it, and I used the time to connect and pray, just as I did when I walked. Eventually, I was able to run about fifteen miles a week, and I was flourishing. It helped that I had a reasonable goal. I made the commitment to myself to run a half marathon. I didn't care about how I compared to the other runners. I just wanted to prove to myself that I could finish.

Overall, that was a decent year. I had few relapses into the dark abyss of misery from which I was running. By honoring the commitment to myself, somehow, I managed to get to race day. I made it!

Ron dropped me off at the starting line and went home to give the girls their breakfast and bring them back with him to see me finish. The event would take hours, so I didn't see the point in making them sit there for the whole thing.

As I stood there breathing in the early morning air and looking at the balloon-arch starting line, I took in the whole experience. It was like a carnival or party atmosphere, not what I'd expected. The people around me were buzzing with energy and activity. Everyone was happy, excited, and cordial to one another. There were themed water stations and music, with people cheering the runners on through the 13.1 miles of road. I had a blast running that thing. My body felt strong and energetic, and at times, I felt so good it was as if I were outside myself, watching the whole thing from above. I was having so much fun that I was shocked when I got to the finish line and saw my time on the big race clock.

I had run the half marathon in two hours, one minute, and sixteen seconds. That was close to a nine-minute mile! (With that, I began to care about my finishing time. I got a burst of external validation, and I was hooked.) I couldn't believe it because my usual pace was closer to a ten-minute-and-fifteen-second mile. I had been having so much fun that I cut twenty minutes off my expected finishing time.

It was a great accomplishment, but it came with its own problems. Although I was thrilled at my finishing time, I was the only one who saw it. Yes, there were thousands of people there, and there was a record of my achievement; however, I was a little disappointed because I didn't see my family at the finish line. Ron was five minutes away, parking the car, thinking he was twenty minutes early. But I still got to enjoy the experience of finishing, which had been the original goal, right? I had done it!

Interestingly, even after the triumph of completing the half marathon, I was still unsatisfied and sad. Why? Because even though I'd achieved my goal, I had healed nothing. I was running from myself and my emotions, so I reverted to my toxic thoughts when the race was over. I took my attention from the fact that I'd accomplished a goal and decided instead to be butthurt, as my kids used to say. Why? Because it hadn't gone exactly the way I had envisioned it would go.

In retrospect, I realize the sadness of disappointment I felt was an indicator that I wasn't genuinely doing the half marathon just for me. It was clear I wanted my family to be impressed, and they couldn't be impressed if they weren't there to see it. So what did I do that day while I was so high on endorphins and the external validation of my finishing time? I decided to run another half marathon, and I would make sure my family was there the next time! Stay tuned to see how that attitude and approach turned out.

I signed up for the El Paso Michelob Light Half Marathon for the following year. The irony is not lost on me that I was running because it was healthier than escaping my problems by using alcohol, and there I was, signing up for a half marathon sponsored by a beer distributor. Crazy, huh?

Not long after that, I signed up to do the Austin Half Marathon with my best friend from high school, Prissy, and her sister Missy. It was a perfect excuse to visit my mom in Boerne; see Riane; and see other friends from my youth, Tina and Alexis, who lived in Austin.

Prissy and I were still friends after all those years. She was always there for me when I needed her. I still wish I could return the favor, but how can you be there for someone to lean on, when she stands perfectly strong in her own right? That's one of the many reasons I love her. She has always been an example of strength and unconditional love. I am blessed to call her my friend. There are some people who come into our lives and prove that kindness, love, and friendship can endure and thrive in this world. She is one of those messengers of light. I was thrilled to get to see her again!

I was excited about the trip. I talked about it all the time to anyone who would listen. I told random parents at Kira's track meet about the half marathon I was going to run. At cheer meetings for my girls, I talked about running the 13.1 miles. At a booster club meeting, I stayed late with Tommie and Mr. Thompson to show them a Nike video about competition and running. I was on a roll.

At the time, I thought I was helping to inspire people, but all I was doing was leeching energy off the people around me. It was like when I had gotten attention with my "Poor me" approach as a kid, but now I was getting attention with a "Hey, look what I can do" approach. Same game, different strategy. Of course, I didn't realize it at the time.

My pain and fear continued to fester and morph into self-loathing because I was still using the people around me as a primary source of energy. I did it unconsciously, but on some level, I knew that the endorphins from running lasted only so long and that I would need another source of energy to get through the rest of the day. I was looking outside myself again for respect and admiration, and I believed I was getting it through talking about running. Wow, how quickly I realigned with the energy vampire of my youth! I'd thought I was past that. My new approach wasn't any better. This time, I wasn't getting the energy through complaining; instead, I got it through posturing or self-involved conversation. Honestly, I was boasting. Ugh, cringe. Both versions of myself were unhealthy, and in retrospect, I can see how annoying both of them were. I was always going on about myself and my goal. Anytime I was around people, I talked about running, all the while scanning faces for looks of admiration or respect. I was constantly posting my run stats for likes on Facebook and getting a rush of dopamine from seeing the number of people who seemed to care. I was like a kid on the playground, yelling to the other kids, "Hey, look at me!" while showing off for attention.

I can see that I was desperate for energy to fill the void created by my lack of self-love, and I found a temporary fix: external validation. Want to know what happens when we fuel ourselves with other people's energy instead of divine love? Read on.

> There are not enough people on the planet willing to validate you to replace the flow of self-love you can find within.

An Important Stop

Just like that, it was time for my Austin Half Marathon. Ron, Kira, Aja, and I started our trip by flying into San Antonio. It was Valentine's Day weekend. We arrived too late to drive into Boerne to see my mom that night. She said she'd be in dreamland by the time we got there, so we went straight to the River Walk. It was a beautiful night, and there was beautiful scenery to enjoy.

The following day, we met my mom at a charming little bakery on Main Street, where she bought us all breakfast. We had a wonderful time eating, talking, and taking pictures. She was excited to show us around her new little town. Her new family, the company she was working for, had moved their home office, and they had paid to help my mom move too so she could stay with the company. Mom's bosses, Kim and Karen, took good care of my mama. I know they loved her, and I will be eternally grateful to both of them for the kindness and affection they showed to my mother. There are no words.

Boerne was charming and quaint. It was like being transported back in time but with all the modern amenities of life in the twenty-first century. My mom took us to her office to see where she spent most of her waking hours, and I was amazed. The offices were in a beautiful home landscaped with foliage. It looked at least a hundred years old. The trees were gigantic, and they created a canopy that let in little sparkling rays of sunlight. It made me think of a fairy wonderland. I was happy my mom was there in that beautiful environment almost every day. *No wonder this is where Esther and Jerry Hicks lived for a while*, I thought. *It's lovely, and the energy is otherworldly. Isn't it crazy how our paths brought us all here?*

We went to her home, where we visited and talked some more. I got to see how she was living, and again, it made me happy for her. She was doing well, aside from back pain that made it hard for her to do anything physical. She had begun to depend on a walker-type device with wheels and a place to sit if she got tired. My mother, the queen of independence, managed well. It was awe-inspiring to watch. I loved getting to see her show off her granddaughters. She was always proud of them, and it was apparent that day. It made me happy that she seemed to be doing so well after her near-death experience. It did make me sad that we weren't as close as before. I wasn't bugging her with my drama anymore, but I also wasn't privy to much information about her life anymore either. Whenever I asked her how she was or what she was up to, she said, "I work, eat, sleep, and get up and do it all over again the next day." I'd had no idea that meant she got to be in all of that magical energy while she did it. It was truly a beautiful place.

I was fine until it was time to leave. I hugged my mama, and I didn't want to let go. I hugged her as if it were the last time I would ever embrace her. Of course, I did that every time we parted, but this time felt different. As my family walked to the car, I sobbed hysterically. I hadn't realized how much I missed her physical presence until that hug. I cried as if I were saying goodbye forever. The image of her standing there, waving goodbye, brings an ache to my heart. It hurts even now to think of how good that hug felt and how bad it felt to let go.

The drive to Austin, where the marathon was to be run, was heart-wrenchingly long, and because of my sadness, I couldn't access any messages of light. I don't think it even crossed my mind to find a way to console myself or be consoled by my angels and guides. The terribly long trip had me in full-on fight-or-flight mode. Sadness does that to an unoccupied mind—it drags out time, and the grief we suffer seems more pronounced.

Guess what else can drag out time: the attractive vibrational power of our thoughts! The more I thought about how long the drive was, the longer the drive got. My thoughts about how long the drive was taking actually drew the traffic to me. God has a profound sense of humor. By the time we got to Austin, the traffic was so bad that the GPS changed to the walking mode because we were moving so slowly. It was torture. I could have run there faster than we were driving, especially considering the amount of adrenaline I built up in my system with my negative thoughts. Being stuck in the car with no way to expend the energy did not help. I couldn't shut off my subconscious mind. I berated myself a billion times for not trying harder to be closer to my mom over the past year.

By the time we got there, I had analyzed every part of myself and found myself lacking. That's what happens when the survival mode is triggered, and mine was. I suddenly had to face living life again without my mom's presence, and every terrible or scary thought that could occur to me came into my conscious mind. Not fun.

Meeting Up with Friends

Eventually, we got to the convention center, where I was to meet up with Prissy and Missy to pick up our race packets for the half marathon. Thank God for that distraction because my wallowing in sadness was getting pathetic by then. It was fantastic to see my best friend. She looked beautiful, as always, and her sister Missy looked fabulous as well. It wasn't the experience I wanted, because we had trouble finding parking, so Kira and I ran in instead of my whole family coming with me.

I tried to take my time and enjoy the event, but I was too conflicted, knowing Ron and Aja were in the car, waiting for me to come out. My vibration was way off. My sense of unease wasn't helped by the fact that one of the vendors decided to tell me, the day before the race, that the Austin Half Marathon is one of the most challenging half marathons in the country. She didn't say that to the person next to me or anyone else, just me. I wanted to say, "Thanks for that!" but I knew I'd attracted that vibration with my own. I didn't realize that it was a message of light!

When the vendor talked about the treacherous race, what my mind did was even harder on me. My fear triggered a memory. I had a flash in my mind of something I had seen in my first half marathon. The vision was of an older man running in front of me in the half marathon the year before. It was a sight I'd been unable to get out of my head since it happened. It just kept coming back to me. I had seen it when I was training and when I showed Tommie and Mr. Thompson the Nike video. Then I saw it again the day before I was to run the half marathon.

The man in front of me appeared to be a seasoned pro, which was why I was so shocked to see him go down. It was scary. First, he started running sideways instead of in a straight line. His head and upper torso began to lean heavily to one side, and then, suddenly, he collapsed.

Emergency workers were there before he hit the ground. Many runners stopped running and offered to help. It was fantastic to see people stop what they were doing to help someone else, but it was still a disturbing sight that stuck with me. I hated that I couldn't stop thinking about it. I kept redirecting my thoughts and asking my guides, "How is that helpful?" I must have been talking over them, because I never heard a response. The negative thoughts about the treacherous race continued to swell in my mind. With the thoughts came the feeling they evoked: annoyance.

After we got our runners' packets, Prissy, Missy, and I decided to meet up for dinner with Joseph, one of our best friends from high school. That night, I had a wonderful time. We all went to dinner at an Italian restaurant to load up on carbohydrates and catch up on one another's lives.

As I looked around the table that night, I was inspired by the people around me. Prissy and Missy would be running the half marathon, and Joseph was doing the whole marathon, all 26.2 miles. I was amazed and proud to be there with that group of incredible people. Running those distances takes some serious determination and discipline. It was also cool to see my high school friends as grown-ups and parents. I enjoyed the experience and had a deep appreciation for the people around me. Who would have thought that we'd get a chance to hang out together all those years later and that it would be as if we never had been apart? That's how you know you've got good friends.

The joy I had from my minireunion didn't last. When we got back to the hotel, I was a mess. I was nervous, moody, and irritable. I don't know what came over me, but I was not feeling like myself anymore. I just needed to go to bed and start fresh the next day.

Christi Conde

The Half Marathon

The day of the half marathon started off like a dream. I met up with Prissy and Missy in the wee hours of the morning while it was still dark and quiet outside in the downtown streets. Joseph was going with his buddies, who were running the full marathon with him, so we planned to meet him afterward. The view was as majestic as it was humbling, and the skyline at sunrise was awe-inspiring. There were masses of people there, and the energy was electric. I was so excited about all of it that I was posting on Facebook about it right up until the race started. I was soaking up all that external validation like a sponge. I totally forgot about the message of light about the race from the day before: "It's one of the hardest half marathons in the country."

It was about sixty degrees outside and 99 percent humidity when we got to the starting line—the opposite of the weather I had been training in and expecting that day. The weather had made a sudden overnight shift, and I was not prepared for it. It was twenty degrees warmer than the day before, and I hadn't known it when I dressed for the day. I hadn't even thought to check the weather—rookie mistake. I was oblivious about the temperature shift until I was actually in it.

I had been training for the previous months in thirty-degree weather. I had run the half marathon in El Paso the year before in forty-degree temperatures, and the sixty-degree weather was a significant change for me. I was overdressed, to say the least.

When I started running, it was not that big of a deal. I just removed my jacket, drank some water, and kept on running. The drizzle of rain was sweet at first, but I felt as if I were running through water after a while. The humidity made me feel as if I needed gills to breathe, but I kept going at my usual pace.

At about mile six, I noticed people running off to the side to vomit in the bushes. There were many people along the path doing that. At one point, I saw no fewer than eight people lined up at the hedge line of a field, side by side, heaving into the bushes.

I kept going, focusing on the concept of mind over matter. As I checked my pace, I noticed I was running slower than usual. I thought I was working too hard to be going that slow, and I picked up the pace. I could see the mile-ten marker. I kept telling myself, "You're almost there. Three miles to go. Just keep going." But as I kept going, I did not notice that I was running sideways. It wasn't until I couldn't breathe and my legs were starting to give out that I realized I was going down. I was fully conscious, but I couldn't control my body anymore. It was an unsettling experience. I couldn't even drink water, because I threw up every sip.

What had started as a dream turned into *The Nightmare at Mile Ten*. I couldn't think straight. I was in a fog. I talked to my husband on the phone to tell him what had happened, and then, a minute later, I asked an EMS guy if he would call my husband for me. He looked at me with humor and confusion and reminded me that I had just hung up with him.

What ensued was one of the most embarrassing sober experiences of my life. The medical workers put me on a gurney, strapped me in, and towed me to the medical tent. I was on a gurney, wearing an oxygen cannula and carrying and using a barf bag, while being pulled by an ATV in the open air through the crowds on the same route as the runners. Keep in mind I could see everyone staring at me. People were pointing, and some were gawking, some with sympathy in their eyes and others with humor. Yes, I saw people pointing and laughing at me and my misfortune.

Completely depleted energetically at that point, the empath in me was overwhelmed too. I could feel the people around me, and there were thousands of them. I could feel fascination and pity focused on me as I was paraded through the streets past thousands of spectators on the makeshift open-air ambulance. I could feel the other runners' anxiety and exhaustion as they looked at me, the runner down, rolling past them to the medical tent. I reminded them of the challenges of the remaining three miles they still had to go to make it to the finish line. But the worst feelings, the feelings I couldn't escape or ignore, were my own. I could feel the devastation of failure realized. I was horrified but too sick to fully experience the embarrassment and humiliation, until I looked up and saw my family huddled together in concern and my daughters' faces streaked with tears. I will never get that picture out of my mind. Maybe it would have been better not to insist they come. Now they too were witness to my colossal failure. This was not the triumphant victory of validation I'd sought.

Two IVs later, the staff released me from the medical tent. I was dejected and down. I was inconsolable emotionally, and I felt horrible physically. I'd trained for an entire year for that run, and I'd failed spectacularly in the truest sense of the word. I'd managed to be a spectacle on parade. What was worse than being embarrassed in front of my family and the dozens of friends who were there to support us in the run? Everyone I knew or had ever spoken to in the previous year also knew I was running that day. Remember, I'd talked about it nonstop to anyone who would listen. Now all those people too would know I'd failed. Talk about a big life lesson. It's even in the Bible. Proverbs 16:18 NIV says, "Pride goes before destruction, a haughty spirit before a fall." Oh, did I live that experience!

When Prissy and Missy got their medals for finishing, they looked for me at the finish line. That was where Alexis, my big sis, and some of our other friends were waiting to see Joseph get his medal for running the whole marathon and to celebrate with us. Instead of going to the finish line to support those who had finished, I had to go to our hotel room to recover. I missed the party. My poor family. Riane; Alex, my nephew; Kira; Aja; and Ron were all crammed together, watching TV, while I was still retching and heaving in the only bathroom of the small hotel room. The walls were thin. It was embarrassing. I still couldn't even keep water down for most of the day. It was as bad as any hangover I had ever felt, but somehow, I managed to experience it without consuming a single drop of alcohol. Look at me go!

The Energy Exchange

My spectacular failure destroyed my ego, and my guides decided to chime in at precisely that moment with this little message of light: "See what happens when you do things for external validation? You end up with public humiliation!"

Ha ha, I thought sarcastically, and I rolled my eyes even as I sensed the humor and love coming from my guides.

My guides were there to teach me something I was primed and ready to learn, but I still resisted. Here's what they said next: "This is karma. The energy you give others comes back to you. Any energy you are willing to take from others must also be returned to the donor with interest."

No kidding. I was feeling that. Everyone I'd talked to about the run had invested energy into my experience. Whether others were rooting for me or secretly hoping to see me fail, their loans of energy came due. All the people I'd talked to about the race had to know how it had gone. They wanted to see what kind of returns they'd gotten on the investments of time and energy they'd spent in talking to me about it. The people secretly hoping my arrogant ass would go down hit the jackpot. Everyone else lost on that investment.

I would not come home with the inspirational story of finishing the auspicious Austin Half Marathon. Nope, those investors would have to watch me as I suffered through this tremendous growth experience.

I learned much about energy exchange from that experience. The external validation I got before the race was not worth the embarrassment and humiliation I felt when it was over.

I know this was a good thing in the long run—pun intended. But seriously, it was one of the most valuable experiences of my life. I even laugh about it now, but at the time, I was miserable. I kept trying to stay optimistic about it, but that was nearly impossible. Everyone I knew was texting me and asking how it had gone. I avoided answering them for most of the day, because it was too painful to relive the experience via text. Eventually, I had to face my mess, and I answered each of the texts. I had to tell them that it just wasn't my day, and I thanked them for their support.

At that point, the empath in me could tell when the people who asked how it had gone were happy about my karma or genuinely disappointed for me. That sucked because I felt there weren't as many genuinely rooting for me as I'd thought. What had I expected? No one likes someone who toots her own horn, as my mom used to say. No one likes a braggart.

I finally posted something on Facebook about the run. If I am being honest, I posted not so that my supporters would have their answers but primarily so that people would stop asking me how it had gone. My pride had me trying to keep the message upbeat, but I got sympathy instead. That was not what I wanted. I wanted praise and validation, not the extra weight of people's concern. Every call or text felt like salt in an open wound because I was so disappointed in myself. Kindness just made me feel worse. I didn't deserve it!

Coming Up with Excuses

As I lay there in my misery, grasping for excuses for my failure, my mind returned to the EMS responder who had helped me get to the medical tent. Our conversation had given me an excuse for failure that would let my bruised, battered, and still unhealthy ego survive another day. There must have been a scientific reason I'd failed, right? It couldn't possibly have been my own fault, right? The EMS professional who'd taken care of me had been kind enough to explain it to me since my brain clearly wasn't working at the time. You would think I would have known that humidity can cause severe dehydration because the body cannot cool itself properly. I am a registered nurse, after all, but I didn't know. And, now I do.

When I was unpacking the experience and analyzing it from my sickbed, I remembered I had been able to feel the energy of empathy from the EMS responder when he spoke to me. He'd seemed to really get what I was physically going through. And that was where the minimiracles began to present themselves. It turned out he could empathize because he was from my hometown. What is the chance of that? Out of the thousands of medical workers there to help that day, the one who came from El Paso just happened to be the one to help me.

The coincidence alerted me to God's presence in the situation and the guidance I'd ignored all along. The messages of light were everywhere. It occurred to me that the people I had seen throwing up along the hedge had been a sign from my higher self to slow down. I'd ignored it. The vision I'd kept having of the man who collapsed during my first half marathon had been a warning message too. Instead of paying attention to what the universe was trying to tell me, I'd kept pushing away the recurring thoughts. I even had been annoyed with the girl from the Expo who told me it would be difficult. Did I look for the guidance behind the message? No, I didn't. I flat-out ignored it. Instead, I chose to be irritated by her words. There were so many messages! I was getting guidance from all around me, but at the time, I wasn't looking to be guided, because I knew what I was doing—or not! Sometimes you just have to laugh.

Honestly, there was nothing that would make me feel better about the situation, not even the minimiracles. Or so I thought. I was embarrassed and sad, and I was triggered. My lifelong fear of failure had manifested in such a way that I couldn't ignore it, and now I couldn't even run from it! God has such a sense of humor. I mean, it's hilarious now, but at the time, I was in the middle of an internal dialogue of self-ridicule and condemnation.

I was wallowing in self-pity and misery, when in came another miracle, another message of light. I found a note from Aja on the hotel stationery. She must have written it while I was asleep. It said, "I love you!" It was sweet and straightforward, and it made me feel better. It made me feel the love she offered, and it made me want to get over my misery. Once I saw the note and noticed how sweet she, Kira, and Riane were to me, I knew I had to snap out of it. This trip was supposed to be fun, and I was ruining it.

Once I could keep sips of water down, I decided I would make the best of the crappy situation I'd created. After one of the most prolonged and painful yet somehow enlightening days of my life, I agreed to go out to dinner and enjoy my beautiful family instead of wallowing in my self-pity and shame.

External Validation

Once I faced the embarrassment and embraced the lesson, I started feeling better, and more realizations began to flow. That was when I recognized that I had been practicing energy vampirism again, but instead of getting energy through the "Poor me" approach of the past, I'd tried the "Hey, look at me" approach. Interestingly, all my attempts to get energy and validation from others ended the same way: in failure and embarrassment. All my attempts at escaping my pain produced the same outcome: retching, heaving, and being downright miserable.

This was something I couldn't escape. I accepted that anyone I previously had talked to about the half marathon would know I'd failed. So what did I do? I decided I would try to run that same half marathon again the following year. I had to try again. I had to give myself a chance to turn my tragedy into a triumph.

You would think I would have known that my decision to try to run the half marathon again was still based on external validation, but I didn't. Not yet. I still needed other people to be impressed with me to feel slightly good about myself. Here is the difference between concept and application: I understood the concept of external validation, but I hadn't yet mastered the art of not needing it.

The weekend following my catastrophe, I ran the half marathon in El Paso, as planned. I actually finished that one, which helped me to scrape together some self-confidence but not nearly enough.

I was still looking for energy from others, so to boost my ego, I decided I needed to post a picture of myself running. Yes, friend, I was still missing the message about external validation. This was not an easy habit to recognize, much less break.

However, God found a way to make me see it. As I have said many times, God has an incredible sense of humor. When I decided to look through the race photos to see if there were any of me upright, I got a good laugh. I searched for my participant number, and the picture that came up of me based on my number was of a seventy-year-old man. Part of his runner number was obscured, so it looked like mine. So not only had I gone down like a seventy-year-old man I had seen during my first half marathon, but in all the photos I found of "me," I looked like one too. You can't make this stuff up! I had to laugh to keep from crying.

I got the message: my finding no picture meant I wasn't supposed to post anything. Finally, I got it. I realized that somewhere along the way, I had stopped running for the joy of running and started running to gather energy from external sources.

I kept running—I was still in desperate need of endorphins—but I stopped talking about it as much. Without the external validation, I began to succumb to feelings of shame and embarrassment, and I was indulging in self-ridicule. I didn't want the "Poor me" energy, and I stopped trying to get the "Hey, look at me" energy, so now there was a void inside me that needed to be filled. That emptiness was hard to manage. It was a black hole of emotion. I was in it again. I was running around in cycles of insanity.

The Messages of Light

Eventually, I got sick and tired of being sick and tired. I understood that wallowing in hopelessness and self-pity wasn't working for me. I arrived at a place where I felt a powerful desire to center myself. I had to ask a good question about the bottomless pit of despair I was in, and this is what I got:

Perpetual Sadness

Why do we dive headfirst into the muddy waters of sadness?

Some people are more comfortable there. Sadness becomes a state of being instead of a passing thing. It becomes our excuse from responsibility and our method of avoidance. Self-abuse becomes the new normal. And relief becomes the new joy.

How do we get away from sadness?

We must feel it, express it, let it go, and then refocus on creating joy. It's a process.

When we procrastinate and avoid issues that require our attention, using sadness as the excuse, it's like choosing to remain in the dark, debilitating energy. When we decide to turn and face whatever is weighing on us, we break free from its hold over us.

In choosing to face the issue, we can shine the light of love on it, dissipating the darkness by which it is surrounded. Then the illusions fall away, and the beauty of the lesson is revealed.

I had to face that truth. Running from my fear, sadness, and myself wasn't helping. The harder I tried to escape, the more deeply entangled in the emotion I became. Depression felt like quicksand. The harder I struggled against it, the more immersed I became in the despair. Again, I will spare you the details of my self-imposed suffering, but it was there, and the pain was real.

There seemed to be a sequence to the emotions associated with moving out of my depression. Once I started facing my fears, my sadness, and the source of both of those things, myself, things began to shift again. Instead of feeling sad, hopeless, or helpless, I started getting angry. I was mad at myself and the choices I had been making. I told myself I would never again be helpless.

What did I do after making that decision? I chose to be exactly that! I decided to buy into the illusions of helplessness and hopelessness. It was annoying. I couldn't be angry with anyone but myself. I chose to live in sadness, and because I constantly focused on fear and failure, I was also easily provoked to anger.

At that time, I basically vacillated between sadness and rage. Neither is a comfortable emotion to experience. It was not my favorite way to live. I was the architect, and the design I chose was flawed. Naturally, the walls of emotion came tumbling down with the weight of the pain I chose to indulge in. I spent some serious time and energy living in my anger. Eventually, that toxic energy got to be too much for me too. So what did I do? I asked for guidance. I prayed, and I prayed hard. I took my walk, and I tapped in to the higher vibrations. I asked about anger, and this is the message I got:

Anger

Anger will consume you.
It will cut off all your air.
It will leave you weak and breathless.
It will catch you in its snare.
With anger left unchecked,
rage is soon to follow.
And then even the little things
become impossible to swallow.
Anger then controls your thoughts.
It will attack all those you love.
The only way to stop the madness
is to get help from above.
So say a prayer.
Take a breath.
You are not here

The Messages of Light

for perpetual stress.
Emotions are our guidance,
and anger has its purpose.
Growth disguised as difficulty
calls it to the surface.
There are ways to handle it,
but be careful not to dwell.
Lingering in negativity
creates a personal hell.
So when you feel it,
that rush of rage,
remind yourself
you set the stage.
You have the tools.
Remember to breathe.
You can do anything!
Have faith! Believe!
And when your breath
clears the air,
you'll find that anger
feels better than despair.
Anger can be wielded,
and it has a message for you:
Remember, you are powerful!
There's something you can do!
You are never helpless,
and you are not alone.
You can change your focus.
Yes, you can heal your home.
This home that we just mentioned,
it is not a physical place.
It is found deep inside of you.
It's that quiet, sacred space.
So use this guidance now,
this anger that you feel.
Look at it, explore it, express it.

Then let it go so you can heal.
If something makes you angry,
there's always good that you can do.
Channel all that energy,
and help someone like you!

From my personal experience and that message, I learned that anger feels better than hopelessness. Anger is still not ideal, but it's better than giving up. And as the message said, it's important not to dwell. My anger was a stepping-stone moving me into a more empowered vibration. The anger didn't fix anything, but just for a moment, it got me to stop feeling sorry for myself. My anger distracted me from hopelessness.

Connecting the Dots

As I said, anger is not ideal, but anything is an improvement when you are as low as I was. The shift in vibration made me realize that hopelessness wasn't the only emotion I was capable of experiencing. I could feel something else; I could feel better. It was a concept I had given up on for some time. The anger felt better, but I continued to struggle.

Why? My nerves were raw. My nervous system was fried. While I was in the vibrations of pain, fear, and self-loathing, I stopped making enough positive biochemicals to keep myself calm and centered. While my emotions were flooding my system with survival chemicals, such as adrenaline and cortisol, my body wasn't making the serotonin I needed to experience happiness. Because serotonin is the precursor to melatonin, I wasn't sleeping well, which led to physical exhaustion. But the most important chemical I wasn't making enough of was oxytocin, the love hormone. Here's a little-known fact: without oxytocin, it is virtually impossible to feel the emotions of love and trust. So I couldn't love myself because I wasn't making the chemicals.

How did I learn all of that? No, it wasn't through my nursing training. The knowledge came to me as a message of light from my beautiful friend Erica. Now I will take a slight detour to chronicle the experiences that led to this life-changing information. The series of events that had to happen to bring this information to me was miraculous.

The Messages of Light

I met my friend Erica through another friend, Rocio, who came to me through her daughter Sarah, Kira's best friend in elementary school. Sarah was a tiny thing with a lion of a heart. It made me happy that she and Kira were friends, because Sarah was good to my Kira. She even stood up to a fifth-grade bully who was picking on Kira when they were in third grade. Sara was a little fireball of strength. Sarah wanted to join the scouting group with Kira. Her mom, Rocio, had some reservations, so she called me to discuss them. Long story short, we talked for hours, and an instant friendship was formed between us. Rocio was a powerhouse of energy and intellect, and it was amazing to me that this strong and successful woman would have any interest in being friends with me. But she did, and we became friends.

She was there for me after my role in the scouting group ended. She was there for me at a time when I really needed a friend who wasn't afraid to tell the honest truth. Anyone who knew Rocio knew that she spoke her mind. She was her authentic self, with no excuses and no reservations. As painful as it was at the time, she helped me through some of my struggles with alcohol just by calling it like she saw it. It was as if God called her in to deliver firsthand the message of light I was ignoring at the time: "You have got to take care of yourself, and alcohol is not helping!"

Rocio even invited me out to a dinner party at her house to help me remember that there was life outside of volunteering, mothering, being a wife, running, and drinking alcohol. She reminded me of the joys of gourmet food (which she prepared), friends, laughter, and fun. That was where I met Erica for the first time.

Erica had just graduated from PA school and had recently taken her licensure exam. As Erica and I bonded over our mutual love of medicine, Rocio came over. She told Erica, "Ask her," referring to me. Rocio told Erica, her sister, that I might be able to get in touch with Erica's guides to find out if she'd passed her exam. So that was what I did. I took a deep breath and tuned in to the higher frequencies. When I did, I could feel the energies of her angels and her ascended ancestors all around her, offering up a resounding, congratulatory "Yes!" Erica seemed relieved. Later, when she found out her guides were right, she called me to tell me, and that was when we became close friends too.

Over the years, Erica and I talked about everything. Energy and the power of magnetic attraction were our favorite topics. Eventually, she wanted to know more about Reiki, so she took my Reiki classes and became a Reiki master. We had so much fun in class! Erica said she loved learning the energy work in the way I taught it, because I brought in the science to explain the woo-woo, and as she was a PA, the science was important to her.

Now that you're caught up, let's fast-forward to the key defining moment when I discovered how to reset my nervous system and reclaim my health, when I stopped running from my dis-ease. I had just gotten the two previous messages about sadness and anger, and I began to face my fears. But there was a reason I wasn't facing them. My fears were still smothering me. Sure, everything I met head-on dissipated, but then I would immediately come up with another fear to focus on. I was triggered to survival mode, and I couldn't break the cycle. I couldn't think of a happy thought because there were so many scary thoughts to face and overcome first. And how could I be of service to anyone if I couldn't even help myself?

So I prayed. I sat down and talked to God, and the conversation went like this.

"God, please help me. The running and the Reiki aren't doing enough to shift my focus. My thoughts are torturing me. What can I do? I want to feel calm and aligned. I want to be happy and at peace. What can I add to the Reiki to help myself maintain a positive energy flow?"

At that moment, even before the whole question was formed in my mind, I heard loudly and clearly, "Open Instagram."

That was it—short and sweet. The conversation ended with two words: "Open Instagram."

Now, if you're like me, you probably think that answer seems odd, to say the least. I mean, really? God is now answering prayers via social media? But I did as the guidance suggested, and there she was: my beautiful Erica was talking about the vagus nerve. Holy cow! It was a miracle. Everything she said made sense. I couldn't redirect my thoughts because my nervous system wouldn't let me. I became obsessed with the vagus nerve, and I began researching everything about it. What I learned led me to understand how to calm the nervous system, and I discovered the ways

I had already been doing it without realizing it. Whenever I took a deep breath to connect with my guides, I was doing it. The problem was that I was not practicing regularly, as I should have been, so the muscle had atrophied over time. After my first half marathon, I gathered all my energy from talking to other people about running, wasting my breath, instead of getting energy from taking a breath and talking to God.

At least when I prayed, I remembered to breathe.

The series of miracles leading to that discovery were in the fiber of my experiences all along. I can connect the dots that led me to that discovery if I look back. If I hadn't done the scouting group, if Kira hadn't had a best friend who wanted to join it, or if Rocio hadn't been skeptical about it, I never would have met Rocio, and I never would have gone to that dinner party, in which case I wouldn't have met Erica. And what if I had been wrong about her question about her licensure exam? Erica and I wouldn't have talked, and I wouldn't have followed her on Instagram. If I hadn't opened Instagram or if Erica hadn't created the perfect post for me to see at that particular moment, I wouldn't be who I am today. The information was a life-changer. Do you see how God lined up the perfect people, circumstances, and events so I would find the information I did at the exact moment I asked? The messages of light and the messengers who delivered them were always there to be discovered.

Positive Trajectory

> God is always sending us messages of light, sending help from above. Sometimes we see the light, sometimes we feel it, and other times we don't, but it is always there. There is nothing that happens in which good cannot be found. There is a lesson in everything. You are never helpless. You can always do something, even if it's just taking a deep breath or saying a prayer. Have faith!

My personal growth continued, and I began to incorporate everything I'd learned about self-care into my teaching and my doing. I continued to run to stimulate the production of the endorphins I loved so much, but I started adding deep-breathing exercises to the mix. I picked up my spiral notebook again—not to write the book, as I was in no place for that, but I started writing again as a healthy way of processing my emotions. As you know, writing has always helped me to cope with my personal drama and connects me to my higher guidance. This poem is an example of what I mean by that. When I started writing, I was a mess, and by the end, I felt loved and supported by God, my angels, my guides, and, finally, myself.

Mirror

I look in the mirror,
and who do I see?
Just the slightest glimmer
of who I used to be.
I used to be so strong and happy,
not how I am right now,
but I know that I can find myself.
I will! Someway, somehow!
I know I've got a choice to make,
decide who I want to be.
I can choose and choose again
and each time differently.
Each day I will paint a picture
of myself within my mind,
confident, healthy, happy,
caring, loving, kind.
Then I'll ask, I'll pray for help,
and every day I'll grow.
I will make the choices,
decide where I want to go.
I'll use my heart as guidance.
I'll pay attention to how I feel.
When it's good, I'm right on track.
If not, it's time to kneel.
Each day I'll make new choices,
and if ever I have doubt,
that is when I'll ask for help.

Yes, that's how I'll work it out!
Then, one day, I'll wake and look,
and in the mirror I'll see
that choosing better day by day,
I made a better me.

Bubbles

The more self-care I practiced, the stronger my spiritual muscle became and the more I noticed the miracles, messages, and messengers. Now that I was looking back and connecting the dots in God's plan for me, I could see one big miracle messenger that God sent me to help me in my struggle. She came in the form of a fluffy little being with four legs.

I realized God sent me a puppy to help me through my struggles not once but twice in my life. The first time was when my parents were going through their divorce, and God sent my puppy Little Bit to help me. Now my new major life struggle was met with another fuzzy ball of unconditional love. My new messenger of light was named Bubbles. Just like before, God sent a dog. This time, the pup wasn't for me; she was for my daughters, but she was heaven-sent nonetheless.

When we first got her, I thought there was something familiar about this brand-new puppy, but I couldn't quite place it. Bubbles, as my girls named her, is a continual source of unconditional love. As a puppy, she was adorable, cute, and cuddly. As she got older, which coincided with my energetic muscle growing stronger, I began to see that Bubbles was just like my Little Bit. I know all dogs are love, but the similarities were uncanny. Her temperament, how she snuggled, and even the expressions on her little puppy face reminded me of my Little Bit. Bubbles looks nothing like my puppy from childhood, but the similarities in personality and behavior are remarkable.

One day something happened that surprised me but seemed to confirm my theory that Bubbles and Little Bit came from the same spirit. I was cleaning out some of the clutter in my garage, when I happened upon an old box of childhood things my mom had saved for me. With a rush of nostalgia, I decided to open it up to see what treasures were inside. I was excited to see that it had some of my old toys and stuffed animals. I found Little Bit's favorite toy as I dug a little deeper. I pulled it out and showed my daughters the toy and an old picture I found of Little Bit sleeping with that same toy. It was cute.

Not wanting to shove the toy back into an old box to be stored again, I put it in the basket with all the other dog toys. I put it at the bottom of the pile on purpose. Part of me didn't want the cute little mouse stuffed animal to get messed up even more. The toy was already missing parts of the ears and nose because Little Bit had chewed them off. I kind of hid the toy. Guess what Bubbles did. She scavenged to the bottom of the pile and found the toy. She had not been watching while I put it in the basket either. Bubbles had been in the yard when I put the toy in the basket. When she came in, it was as if she zeroed in on the vibration or smell of the toy or the memory of it and went straight to finding it. That toy is now Bubble's favorite toy too.

The last similarity between the two dogs that makes me believe Little Bit has returned to me as Bubbles is the rib deformation. Remember that Little Bit had a concave shape on one side because she had broken ribs from when the horse stepped on her? Well, Bubbles was never near a horse. She was just born with an oddly shaped rib on one side.

I feel sure that God sent me angels in furry form at the most challenging times of my life to help me, and I genuinely believe that our childhood pets find a way to come back to us later in life. I believe they are angels in a furry form sent to shower us with love and help us heal. Our Bubbles does that, just as my Little Bit did. Bubbles is a fluffy little messenger of light that speaks to me every day of pure love.

Chapter 19

Finding My Stride

Finally Really Healing My Perception of the Past

What happens when you start using the tools of self-care? You find more tools to add to your tool belt. What happens when you use the tools in the tool belt and start asking for help in feeling better? You get it.

Anything we ask for in prayer with faith, we receive. Right? That's what Jesus said, and I believe him. And asking for help is not weak. It takes great courage. It takes great strength to face your fears. Everyone needs a little help sometimes, and because of free will and the law of magnetic attraction, if we don't ask for it, we don't receive it.

Asking for help is the first step in healing, and I asked. I followed my guidance. I practiced self-care. I ran, I walked, I wrote, and I prayed. In all of that, I got answers. I received messages of light from everywhere. One particularly impactful message came from my friend Chris. She called me one day because she was worried about me. I'd had a moment of frustration and anger that she and several others saw during a meeting for one of my volunteering duties, and it had not been pretty. My lack of composure had been ugly enough to prompt a wellness check after the fact, so this angel on earth called me. She didn't have to. She wasn't my best friend. Chris just cared enough to make an effort. We had a deep conversation, which consisted of me basically sobbing and complaining about what a mess I was and how embarrassed I was to have lost my calm in front of her and the other boosters. Then she told me about a fabulous therapist she knew in the area. The timing was perfect, and I realized therapy could help me navigate some of my internal struggles. I recognize a message of light now when I hear one, so I made an appointment with Ms. Sharon.

When I began approaching all self-talk the way Ms. Sharon, my incredibly wise therapist, taught me, I started to forgive myself. Whenever I had a trigger come up, I had to take a deep breath to calm my nervous system first and then pretend to be talking to a two-year-old me. I was to treat myself with the same kindness I would have shown to any small two-year-old child who was learning about life. This approach got my attention and seemed like it would be helpful.

Then, as if to highlight the concept, I got another message of light on the way home from the therapist's office. In the seminar I was listening to on cassette, Abraham-Hicks said something to the effect of "You don't berate a toddler who falls while learning to walk." Abraham-Hicks was right. The child will fall down. It's a given. It's part of the learning experience. You don't automatically assume the child will never walk. You don't criticize the toddler for ineptitude. Instead, you encourage that child to keep trying. I loved that. It gave me permission to forgive my past mistakes and keep trying to be a better version of myself.

Think about it. Even if your soul is thousands of years old, it's in a body that is most likely less than one hundred years old. Compared to God's existence, we are infantile. It's the difference between our thousands of years over many lifetimes of wisdom and experience versus God's trillions of years of wisdom and experience. We are all just toddlers learning to walk. Furthermore, Jesus never calls us adults in the Bible that I know of. I am fairly sure he tells us we are all God's children.

These messages made a difference in my mindset. I was able to connect with and console my inner child. Children make mistakes, and we love them anyway. I began to offer myself the same kindness I would have offered a toddler. Whenever I found myself in a moment of self-judgment, I had imaginary conversations with the two-year-old me. I talked to the childlike version of myself the same way I would have spoken to my daughters when they were two years old, with love and compassion. Somehow, this approach helped.

The approach helped so well that something changed. Once, when I caught myself focusing on one of my traditional negative thoughts, I remember thinking, *If anyone said that to my child, I would have to hurt 'em!* Yet there I was, saying those hurtful things to myself. That moment made all the difference. I caught myself. I recognized the behavior, and I altered it by taking a deep breath and talking to myself with kindness and compassion. And guess what. My two-year-old grew up to be healed.

The Half-Marathon Redo

Another thing that helped me to heal was redoing the Austin Half Marathon I'd failed at the year before. Yes, I'd committed to doing it over again, so I did. It was a real face-your-fears event, and I almost chickened out at the last minute. I had a panic attack and told Ron I couldn't do it. I wasn't going to go! I suddenly had no desire to put myself through another spectacular failure. But my amazing husband would not let me quit. He allowed me to cry it out and vent all of my insecurities. Then he reasoned with me. Ultimately, Ron, Kira, Aja, and I got on a plane together and headed for the race, and the fear was overcome.

That time, I got my finisher's shirt. I got my medal, and I got my confidence back. This time, the half marathon was about proving I could do it. I didn't post or talk about it (much). I just ran it. I'd learned the lesson about external validation, and it can be applied in all areas of life. Don't talk about endeavors to get attention. If you're going to do anything, just do it for yourself. This time, I wasn't running on external validation. I wouldn't have to pay anyone back for energetic investment in my efforts. Divine energy is always interest-free.

Because of that approach, everything shifted. I didn't have to look for a picture of myself running to post online, and I wasn't going to. This time, someone else did it for me. Prissy posted a picture for me. She was there in the crowd with Missy, supporting me, because that's what friends do, and she took pictures of me not only running but also finishing.

How funny. When I ran to impress others, I did all my own marketing on social media to get external validation. This time around, I ran for myself, and Prissy posted my victory with words of friendship that brought me to tears of joy. At the time, I was humbled by her post rather than exalted, as I once had thought I wanted to feel. I was in awe of the love of friendship, which felt much better than anything I felt along the lines of validation for physical achievement. How exhilarating to see the shift! The best part of the whole experience was that we had a celebratory brunch after the race, and I was surrounded by family and friends. Life was good.

When I got home from that trip, I turned inward instead of looking to others for congratulations and validation. I did my thing; I went walking outside. I played my music, and I talked to God. I was basking in the awe of the dramatic change I was beginning to notice. I felt content and fulfilled. I recognized that the changes I experienced happened because I'd honored a commitment to myself, and in doing that, I began to trust myself. I thought about how blessed I was to have had the opportunity to see myself and my world in a different light. It was as if the sun had risen with a brilliant, colorful display of light and beauty after a long dark night of fear and misery. I wondered if this was the sunrise I had seen in my vision at the beginning of this story.

And just like that, I was back in the vision. I felt like a child again. I was gliding in the exhilaration and freedom of a child riding a bike. I was on an open road that I designed with plenty of time to spare and an entire world in front of me to explore. I was experiencing faith again. I trusted that God and my angels and guides would take over for me when I let go of the handlebars. I felt the freedom of choice and the magic of miracles flowing through my veins. It was the dawn of a new day for me. The world was transforming into a magnificent, magical playground complete with spinny swings and rainbow slides. This was it. It was really happening. The work I was doing was paying off. At that moment, I got a blast of incoming information from God and my angels and guides. This is what the message said:

The Choice to Be Made

> The choice to be made is in our focus. We must concentrate fully on what we want to see. We want to watch the heavy veil of darkness fall away, revealing the beauty waiting for us. The overwhelming feeling of joy is available to us whenever we choose to allow it into our lives. The feeling of being one with love and leaving behind the fear of being undeserving of it is an incredible experience.

It is the feeling of being able to look at the world with the clarity of knowing that there is nothing but beauty and perfection at this moment. We have no problems, because we've given them to the ultimate Problem Solver. We have no fear, because we are protected by infinite power. We have no sadness, because we are consumed with the irrepressible joy of connection to the divine self. In this moment, we are indeed one with God. We have removed all our fabricated boundaries and have spiritually merged with the Creator of all things. We are filled with and surrounded by beautiful light. It illuminates all the artistry within and around us that we could not see before. Everything is brighter. The illusions fade away, and our world transforms into the colorful, savory experience it was intended to be. This is where we are meant to be: in a space where we can truly experience the gift of life in this moment.

When we purposefully choose to take time to focus on love and beauty, there is no distance between the Creator and us. We realize that not only does God love us, but God's love is unconditional. We know he is always with us, but now even more, we understand he is within us. When we choose to connect with the love within, faith is renewed, and peace is experienced fully and completely.

When we connect with God, fear and ego fall away, making room for confidence and compassion.

A Not-So-Ordinary Day

My self-care approach was working. I began to ascend the spiral staircase again. I was in a better place emotionally and spiritually. My empathic ability seemed to be under control too. I could still sense others' energy and emotions, but I didn't absorb as much of their energy as before. I was faithfully using the technique I'd learned of flowing divine energy through me and out into the world. Remember, God's energy gets on you; you don't get your human energy on God. And whatever energy I did absorb I was more equipped to process. I used my Reiki to clear it out of my system because I was more conscious of energy itself. You don't think to clear energy if you aren't aware it's there. I wasn't creating as much of my own fearful energy as before because I'd learned to console the scared two-year-old who lives within me. It was a new dawn in my consciousness. I found myself more centered and balanced than ever before. I moved from the vibration of hope, which was doubtful, fearful, and chaotic, to a place of faith, which was confident, powerful, peaceful, and fluid. Thank God for that because I was about to be tested on every lesson I had ever learned.

It was an ordinary Sunday afternoon. The day was so average that I can't even remember what my family and I were doing when we got the call. We needed to get to the hospital right away. Tony, my brother-in-law, was being admitted. We had no idea how bad it was, but on the long drive to the hospital, I knew that something was about to change dramatically.

Tony was a protector and problem-solver for all those in his life. He was an all-around decent person, and he always went above and beyond to help people. He was a true messenger of light.

We almost lost this incredible person that day, but I think Tony saw how sad we all were and decided to stay. I believe he made a pact with God that night, asking God to let him get back into his body because the people who cared about him were obviously lost without him.

It was a long, hard road, but Tony was determined to improve after his stroke, and he did. He completed rehab at a facility and then continued his therapies at home. He was inspiring, and so were his family. They were by his side every step of the way. It was beautiful to see the love, support, and selfless dedication he inspired from his loved ones. The good he did in the world with his life, his good karma, was impressive. There was an outpouring of love too extensive to mention here. It seemed everyone he'd ever helped suddenly appeared and offered to help him in return. Love and kindness still overwhelmingly exist in this world. There are messengers of light everywhere!

Some unforeseen miracles happened to me due to those difficult circumstances. I was called to use my nursing knowledge again, and I realized how much information I still had in my memory banks, even though I hadn't worked in the field for a while. I was able to help our family navigate the medical world in a time of crisis. I liked to say I was the translator, because I could explain what was happening medically in ways Tony's family and friends could easily understand.

I was also able to offer comfort and spiritual support to the people who were struggling. It was miraculous that the empath in me was able to navigate the energy of the fear around me without absorbing too much of it. Hospitals are brutal energetically, but somehow, my spiritual muscle was strong enough to manage it. I was able to maintain my energy and my focus to offer support without feeling drained myself. It was a miracle for me to see how I went from being a person who needed constant help to a person capable of giving support to others. It was a blessing to be there for them, and it felt good to be of service. At that moment, I realized that in helping others, I was also helping myself. This time, I had that realization while I was energetically stable enough to embrace it. Remember, you can't flow love through you without getting it on you. The reward of being of service reminded me of a message of light I had gotten long ago. You may remember these words: "You are all one! You are connected. You cannot perform any action without also affecting the group as a whole."

I actually understood what that meant. It looked as if I had made another trip around the staircase! I understood that we are all connected and that helping someone else also meant helping myself. The difference this time was that I wasn't already depleted of energy. This time, God didn't have to trick me into helping myself by presenting someone else to serve. You may recall that whenever I had been low on energy or self-love in the past, God had brought me someone else to help, which forced me to charge up with divine energy to replenish what I'd lost to my negative thinking. This time, I was already filled with God's love and energy, so I was in overflow.

I learned much from this experience. It profoundly changed my life in ways I never anticipated. Tony asked me for Reiki as part of his approach to healing, and I was happy to oblige. The treatments allowed him to relax and release all the chaotic energy he'd absorbed from the hospitals. He was able to focus on what he wanted to do, which was heal. Because God's timing is always perfect, I just happened to have been working on breathing exercises to go with the Reiki so my clients would have a way to maintain energy on their own. So we added what I'd learned about the vagus nerve and breath to the Reiki treatments. Would you believe his recovery process sped up, even after the therapists thought he had plateaued? By purposefully engaging the biochemicals designed to heal the body, he continued to heal. By his practicing the breathing exercises before and after his therapy sessions, his brain began to rewire itself at a much faster pace. It was a miracle to see this man regain so much strength and mobility. Now, I am not going to tell you it was just the Reiki or the breath work that caused this change. It wasn't just the treatment of the doctors and the therapists that helped him improve. It was all of those factors, combined with Tony's determination, free will, and the power of prayer, that made the difference.

I didn't know it at the time, but Tony was giving me a message of light. In his willingness to apply and practice the skills I shared, he taught me that they worked in remarkable ways. The skills I had learned and was practicing so that I could help myself and my Reiki clients move from surviving to thriving were valuable in this way too. He showed me the miracle of his healing. In doing so, he inspired me and confirmed I was on the path God intended for me. It was my first glimpse of the benefits of true integrative wellness, which is the combination of spiritual, medical, and therapeutic approaches to amplify health. I found my passion.

The sense of fulfillment I experienced in being of service overflowed my energetic reserves instead of just filling them back up. This time, when I helped the people around me, I could feel the good that was coming from it. This time, I was making the biological chemicals that let me experience the fulfillment that comes from service to others, because I was already serving God and myself through self-care.

Learning to Love Myself

I'd learned to be kind to myself. I'd learned to forgive myself by treating myself with the same compassion I would have offered a small child. I was learning to trust myself by making commitments to myself and honoring them. I'd begun that process by running a half marathon for myself instead of for external validation from others. I continued to honor myself and God, who lives within me, by consistently taking time for self-care even after the marathons were over. So it stands to reason that the next step in my conscious evolution was learning to love myself.

As I continued to share the love I was flowing with my family and helping when I could with Tony's recovery, I continued to progress. I was still doing my breathing exercises, meditating, walking, praying, journaling, and being of service (first to myself and then to others). I was right on track. In doing all of those things, I was rebalancing my body chemistry. I was making serotonin, oxytocin, and all the other good chemicals again.

By consciously making the biochemicals needed, I could embrace the emotion of love. In my doing so, a remarkable thing happened. When someone said, "I love you," I actually felt love, instead of the sadness those words once had provoked. I could really feel the emotion of love. Talk about a miracle! You see, you can't experience love or trust completely without enough oxytocin in your body.

I think that in the times of my life when I was feeling really down, I confused *need* with *love*, or maybe I never had noticed the difference between their vibrations until then. I definitely noticed a clear difference now. In the past, when I'd told others I loved them, I'd felt I would fall apart if they didn't say it back. That's need, not love. Worse, when people did tell me they loved me, I couldn't believe them. I wasn't able to receive love without feeling unworthy of it. How could I? I wasn't making the right biochemicals!

With my biochemistry getting back on track, it was much easier to find compassion for myself, but there was a trick to learning to love myself. I had to start by finding an example of love to use as a guide. I decided to use the unconditional love of my mother as a template. I imagined my higher self as my mother and my human self as a child, and I consoled myself according to how Ms. Sharon had taught me. It was another perspective on how to care for my fearful energy vampire of an inner child. Who would know better how to do that than the woman who actually had done it?

That was the trick: I found a frame of reference. I had to tap in to the highest vibration of love I knew: the love between a mother and a child. That love is transcendent. There is an unspoken bond between a mother and her child that exists regardless of our attention to it. There is a connection, a love free of conditions. There are no wrongs or grievances, only love. In the love between a mother and a child, disappointment is quickly overridden by support, and judgment is easily replaced with love. A mother understands what is in her child's heart better than anyone. She wants nothing more than that child's happiness and fulfillment.

I began to feel the depth of that connection in a new way as I healed.

Under all of my self-judgment and negative self-talk was a sweet, well-meaning child with a heart full of love. I found my authentic self, and she had a message of light for me: "When you flow from a place of love, you cannot get it wrong."

When I acted in alignment with my authentic nature, I discovered that the rewards for flowing in authenticity are the feelings of love and alignment. How cool is that?

The Difference between *Insane* and *Crazy*

Guess what happens when you get into alignment with higher consciousness. You recognize insanity. After all those years, I finally really understood the definition of *insanity*. You know it, right? *Insanity* is repeating the same action and expecting a different result. According to that definition, I had been insane for most of my life. I was always trying a variation of the same thing, thinking it would make me happy: external validation. I did the "Poor me" thing and the "Hey, look at me" thing, but both of those approaches yielded the same result: pain. Then the pain led me to the insanity of self-medicating with alcohol—which caused more pain. I could clearly see the spiral of insanity from my higher state of being, but I couldn't see past my suffering while I was in it.

Because I recognized my insanity, I was able to make the necessary changes. Without identifying that a problem exists, you can do nothing about it. If you ignore it, it doesn't go away. It gets bigger, just like a dust bunny. I was done with that mentality. I decided not to be insane anymore. I chose instead to be crazy.

I know what you're thinking: *How is being crazy any better?*

Here's the difference: insanity involves running around in circles and essentially never doing anything differently, while craziness is all about being different. It's about forward motion. *Crazy*, in this context, is the courage to be crazy enough to try something new and different instead of regurgitating old emotions and repeating the same patterns and poor choices.

Wouldn't it be crazy to live a life of happiness and fulfillment? Wouldn't it be crazy to live in a world where magic and miracles are part of everyday life? Well, that's the life I signed up for, so call me crazy! I'll take it as a compliment!

It was an "Aha" moment for me when I recognized my insanity and decided I was going to be crazy instead. I would try something new— anything other than indulging in my old thoughts and behaviors. I would no longer repeat the insane action of consuming alcohol and expecting it to ever go well. It was as simple as that. The alcohol option was off the table, and I was sincerely happy with my decision. No one wants to be insane!

I recognized the problem (my insanity), found a simple solution (to be crazy instead of insane), and acted on it. I was crazy enough to choose a life free of alcohol in a world where alcohol is as free-flowing as water. I decided to look at all I could do in this world with a clear mind and healthy body, and a fantastic thing happened: the less I focused on the problem, the less power it had over me.

The option of alcohol—and the insanity that came with it—was off the table. The doorway in my mind was closed to that path. Because of my self-love approach modeled after my mother, triggers in my mind began to lose their power over me. They atrophied like an unused muscle, while at the same time, I worked to strengthen my core. In this case, I wasn't working on my body's abdominal and back region, as those words might suggest. I was working on the core of my spiritual well-being. I started spending the same amount of energy on self-care and meditation that I used to spend on ridiculing and judging myself. It was a much better use of my time and energy.

This takes us back to the difference between concept and application again. It's not enough to understand an idea. You must act on it for it to work. This is the difference between understanding that a particular approach works and actually using the method. It's the difference between imagining taking a deep breath and actually doing it. If you want to know what I mean, try it. Imagine taking a deep breath while you hold your breath. Hold your breath, and imagine how good it would feel to flood your lungs with oxygen, but don't do it; just think about it while you hold your breath. Did you feel that? That is thinking about something but not doing it.

Now think about taking a big deep breath, and do it. See the difference?

I knew for years that meditation and self-care were important. I encouraged everyone else to do self-care, but at times in my life when I was a mess, I wasn't practicing what I was preaching. When I finally decided to walk the walk instead of just talking about it, I got exponentially better. I actually healed. Guess what. When you do the work of healing, you actually heal! Who knew?

Riane did. Riane is wise. One day we were talking, and she simply said, "If you want to heal, you have to do the work." Boom!

She was right. It's not enough to know what work needs to be done; you must act. You must do the work of healing. So that was what I did. Thank you, Riane, for that life-changing message of light!

Now I can deal with the present more efficiently. I don't carry around the baggage of the past with me anymore. I traded my baggage for the present. Get it? I pictured an old beat-up suitcase magically changing into a gift box with a big red bow, a present. With the vision, I got another message of light:

> It's not about never getting stressed or angry, because that happens to everyone. When it happens, it's about looking at the issue, healing it, and then letting it go. Just because we have baggage doesn't mean we have to carry it around with us all the time.

Another Spin on Karma

The stories that accentuate the messages of light are a big part of the magic, and they are always touched with a flair of God's unparalleled sense of humor. One day I got a call from Kathy with a story to complement the previous message of light, and get this: it even involved baggage!

On the call, we got to talking about karma, and Kathy started telling me about her most recent experience with it. Kathy is a sweet, kindhearted, and loving person. She is definitely one of God's angels on earth, a true messenger of light. God's angels on earth come in human bodies with human emotions and physical energy limitations, so they are susceptible to having human moments. Shocker, right? Well, here's what happened.

Kathy had been traveling. The trip required multiple airports and plane changes—it was the kind of trip that takes all day. You can imagine how exhausting that was for her.

By the time the plane pulled into the gate at the airport, Kathy was ready to go home. As she told me the story, I imagined she had already gathered her belongings. I pictured her sitting at the edge of her seat, waiting anxiously for the Fasten Seat Belt sign to switch to the off position. She was sitting close to the front of the plane and was ready to bolt toward the exit door the minute she got a chance. There were only one or two rows for her to get past before she was home free. Kathy told me she thought it would be a quick and easy exit, until she saw the man getting out of the seat next to her.

When the Fasten Seat Belt sign went off, Kathy had a choice: she could be courteous and patiently wait for the old and weakened man to stand up, get his cane, gather all his belongings, and go before her, or she could jump in front of him quickly before he managed to make his way into the aisle. As she continued to tell me the story, the empath in me kicked in, and I could feel embarrassment with a twinge of shame coming from her. I was about to find out why: she said she chose the rude route and jumped in front of the old guy. She admitted that she did not want to wait for the extra time it would take for him to amble off the plane.

Then Kathy talked about her karma. She said it was instant. While she stood in line, trying not to make eye contact with anyone who had seen her jump in front of the elderly man, the one person in front of her began struggling with a bag in the overhead compartment. The guy struggling with the bag managed to get it free from the overhead bin but somehow did not control it as he brought it down. The bag went flying right into Kathy and knocked her upside her head, causing her to fall backward and hit her rear end on the arm of the chair beside her. As she was telling the story, the empath in me felt that she felt as if she had been slapped in the face and kicked in the rear by God for being rude. Then she basically said as much.

I took a deep breath and asked what message her guides wanted me to relay to her about what had happened. They said, "Even when you're being a jerk, you're still doing God's work."

Then they went on to explain what really had happened. Kathy's angels and guides had used her exhaustion to help someone else. They showed me what would have happened if she hadn't been rude, as she saw it. If she hadn't been standing in that exact spot at that precise moment, the elderly man would have been there instead. Can you imagine what would have happened to that frail little old man if he had been hit in the face and upper body with heavy baggage and knocked backward like that? I'll tell you what would have happened, because our guides showed me. They shared a vision of EMS responders taking over the plane to help the man. In my vision, I heard the flight attendants telling the passengers to have a seat, as there was an emergency, and it would be a while. In the vision, I felt both the pain of the man who was injured and the stress of the stranded passengers. Do you see?

Kathy had been in the right place at the right time. Despite her momentary frustration, her desire and purpose to be of service had been her primary and overriding vibration. Because she'd asked God to be of service to the greater good, she had been, even if her human mind couldn't see it.

Of course, it's not ideal to be a jerk in any situation, but if you say yes to God, he can use you to help the greater good, even on your bad days.

Tapping In

It was remarkable how easy it was for me to tap in to my higher self when I was working with a healthier vessel. This change enabled me to get in touch with another feeling I had long gone without: happiness.

What I learned about happiness and higher vibrations, such as joy, is incredibly profound: the higher the vibration, the clearer the communication.

Happiness is an extremely high vibration. I'd grasped part of this concept before. It is the reason I understood that the easiest way for me to tap in to divine energy was by walking or running outside. Running, walking, hiking, and other forms of exercise raise your metabolism and boost your spiritual vibration.

God, our guides, our angels, and our loved ones on the other side—everyone in the light—vibrate on the energetic level of happiness or joy. They vibrate at the highest frequencies of energy. Where they exist, there is no pain or grief. Those vibrations and emotions are only on the earthly plane. They are experienced by humans with the biochemistry of the physical body and by earthbound spirits who draw energy from humans around them. Negative emotions aren't experienced in what we call heaven, where the inhabitants are bodiless spirits that run on divine vibration. For that reason, it makes sense that when we are happy, we are more able to sense the communication they offer us, and it makes sense that our bodies would be better able to tolerate the high frequencies without toxins polluting them.

When I started my new life, creating a more balanced biochemistry free of the toxins of alcohol, I began to consistently vibrate on a higher level. I could even tune in without running, walking, or meditating, although I did most of those daily. Most times, it took only a few deep breaths for me to connect with my higher consciousness.

I intentionally connected to that feeling, that higher vibration, almost always. I began to have visions and dream again. Friend, the timing couldn't have been more perfect, because as they say, life was about to get real.

This time, I was ready.

Chapter 20

Magic and Miracles Abound

The Phone Call

It was a Saturday morning in September. It was a beautiful day, and I was enjoying it to the fullest. I had just returned from a walk.

By then, I had overcome the compulsion to run. I was no longer running from myself. I was in a healthy place, and I recognized my mother's wisdom "Too much of a good thing is still too much of a good thing" as valid. By then, the running was starting to take a toll on my body. My feet were becoming deformed, and my hips hurt nearly every day. Worse, I started to walk like an old person because I was always stiff and sore. I had to learn to practice moderation in running out of necessity. In fact, I was trying to practice moderation in all things, except for alcohol. I had a zero-tolerance policy for the peace destroyer. I finally had conquered my insanity on that subject.

When I got home from my walk that morning, my house was empty. Ron had gone to the grocery store, Kira and Aja were at cheer practice, and Riane was living on her own by then. Embracing the quiet in the house, I decided to call my mom. I would have usually called her on a Sunday, but this was a rare and perfect opportunity to speak to her without distractions. When she answered, I could tell she was driving. I asked her what she was up to, and she said she was on her way to work. I wasn't surprised she was working on a Saturday. My mom was dedicated to everything she did. She always put in 110 percent, and she didn't know how to do anything halfway.

The Messages of Light

She must have just gotten into the car, because we talked for a long time while she drove. We had an enjoyable conversation. It was the best talk we'd had in a long time. The slight rift we had been experiencing since her near-death experience had long since vanished. We were really connected, and I was feeling the love. We talked about everything and nothing. I gushed about Kira, Aja, and Riane and their most recent accomplishments. She spoke to me about what she was up to and whom she loved spending time with, whether in person or on the phone. She talked about her sister Helen, her friend Deb, her work, and her coworkers and what they meant to her. My mom got to the office right about then, and she had to get off the phone because she didn't have a hands-free device. My mom couldn't carry what she needed while toting a phone in hand.

I was surprised when my mama asked if she could call me right back, because she was going into the office. She didn't usually like to talk on the phone while she was there. Since it was Saturday, we wouldn't interrupt the quiet office vibe by being on the phone.

She did call me right back, and I was thankful because the conversation after that was probably the most important conversation we ever had. I wish I could remember every detail, but here's what I do remember from that day. For some reason, I apologized again for not being the best daughter I could have been and for all the times I had let her down.

That day, I told her how long I'd been sober. Until then, she had been afraid to ask, and I hadn't wanted to share, because I was still afraid of failure. Besides, I hated empathically feeling the twinge of doubt I had conditioned into my loved ones regarding alcohol. They had heard me say that I would stay sober many times, and I'd failed them every time before. So this time around, I didn't tell anyone I had stopped drinking. I just stopped. Instead of talking about alcohol and how bad it was for me or how far I had come since quitting, I did something else: I occupied my time by being of service to myself. I know this might sound selfish, but it worked for me. I decided to put myself and my desire for wellness first. And this time, I actually honored that commitment. I remembered the message of light I'd received many years before about priorities, and I decided to actually apply the concept for myself and stick to it. I would be number one on my list of priorities. Why? Because we can't serve from an empty cup. How could I be of service to others, when I hadn't fully learned to serve God, who lives within me? The Bible says, "But seek first His kingdom and His righteousness, and all these things will be given to you as well" (Matthew 6:33 NIV).

To me, the kingdom of God is within us. We are living, breathing extensions of God. I believe that when we honor ourselves and the love that we are, we honor God, who lives within us. So call me selfish, but I started honoring my indwelling God energy, and it grew. I was stronger than ever before, and it was because I was fortified by the divine energy that had been within me all along.

The moment I told my mom of my new life free of alcohol, I could feel her relief as if it were my own. It was the first time I told anyone about my sobriety without the empath in me feeling doubt and disbelief coming from the person I spoke to. Instead, I thought I heard joy in her voice. She wasn't hesitant or suspicious. She wasn't just nodding and agreeing with me, humoring me, while all along expecting my impending failure. She believed in me. She could sense that something had changed in me and that it would last.

I told her how I'd redirected my focus and that I was crazy enough to begin dreaming again. I told my mom that I would either start my own business or go back to nursing school. Being in the hospital and the medical environment for the past months during Tony's recovery process had awakened the part of me that loved nursing, and I had been reminded that I was rather good at it too.

My mom said she knew I would start a business. She told me she had seen it in a vision. She said, "I knew you would do it. I just thought it wouldn't be until after I was gone," and we laughed.

We talked for quite some time about everything we needed and wanted to talk about. At one point, I asked, "Mom, are we OK?" I still carried some guilt about not being with her while she struggled with her health.

She said, "Of course we're OK! Christi, I love you!" She said she had known I was in no place to help her, when I had been struggling so long to help myself. Then she asked me in return, "Are we OK?" As if she had anything to feel bad about!

I answered, "Yes, Mama! You're the best mom ever. I love you!" At that moment, everything was healed.

We laughed at our silliness and basked in the warmth of our connection. I had a moment when I was filled with so much love that all my doubt, insecurities, guilt, and shame dissolved and were replaced with peace. That's a mother's love for you!

Just about that time, Ron came home with a carload of groceries that needed unpacking, and it was almost time for me to leave to go pick up the girls from practice. My mom and I said, "I love you," to each other and ended the call.

For the rest of the day, I couldn't shake the feeling that there had been something unusual about that call, even for us. But per my tendencies, I pushed the thought to the back of my mind to deal with later. I knew it wasn't something I wanted to face yet.

The Dream

That same night, I had a dream. I was walking down the hall in the hospital. The hallways were dark and quiet. As I passed a patient room on the right, I saw my mom. She was in a hospital bed. I knew it was a dream because she was curled up in the fetal position and on a ventilator. That would not have happened in the real world of medicine that I knew. In my dream, I dropped what I was carrying and screamed, "That's not what she wants!" Then I woke up.

I knew my mother's wishes and advanced directives even in a dream. She wanted no artificial life support. I couldn't go back to sleep that night, because I couldn't stop thinking about it. I was bothered by the dream because I was afraid it was prophetic somehow. Sometimes my dreams told me things I was too oblivious to see with my conscious mind. Something was up, and I knew it.

The next morning, while I was getting ready to go with Ron to the hospital to see Tony, I saw an infomercial about a car cane, a nifty gadget to make it easier for people with limited mobility to disembark their vehicles. My conscious mind thought, *Oh! I should get that for my mom for Christmas!* but just as I finished forming the thought, I heard in my deaf ear, "I don't need it."

I could hear my mom in my head. That had happened once before, and it hadn't been good. The last time that had happened had been three years earlier, when she actually had been on a ventilator. I didn't want to think about it. As I brushed the words from my consciousness, I listened to my mom's voice say, "I'll just think about that tomorrow," mimicking Scarlett O'Hara from *Gone with the Wind*. She used to tease me because I was a procrastinator and had been confrontation-avoidant my whole life.

I kept telling myself to call my mom that day, but something kept me from it. Fear. Denial. Maybe deep down, I knew she wouldn't answer, and not knowing for sure what was going on with her would have been torture.

On Monday, I got the call. My mama had crossed over in her sleep. They said she looked peaceful, and I knew she was, because I could feel her fully. It wasn't like before, when I had to be close to get a good signal. She was in the light, and she was happy enough to tease me. The signal was clear enough for me to hear that she wouldn't need a car cane. I could feel her vibration, and nothing about it was dark, heavy, or sad. My mom was having her own personal freedom party. I could almost see her doing a happy dance. She was free of the body that had betrayed her.

Road Trip through Time

The next thing I knew, Ron and I were driving to where my mom lived. Kira and Aja stayed behind until we knew when the funeral would be. By then, the girls were in high school, and classes had just started a week before. Missing a lot of class at that time would have started them off on shaky ground for the school year. Riane was in Austin and planned to drive down to my mom's small town soon. This drive was just Ron and me, or so I thought.

The drive was strange. As we drove along the open road, I was quickly entranced by the swiftly changing scenery, and the steady hum of the engine lulled me into a calm and serene state. I felt as if I had been transported back in time to a road trip from my childhood. My mom and I had road taken trips often when I was growing up. It had been a beautiful mother-daughter bonding time. Those trips had been special, and I always had felt safe, loved, and connected to her.

The Messages of Light

As I peered out the window at the passing scenery, I could feel my mom there with me. She was still with me in spirit, and she was about to send me her first message of light from the other side. It was as if we were together, talking just like we used to on our road trips. It was one of those "Remember when" conversations. I was looking out the window at the scenery of the desert road, and she took me back to one of her favorite road-trip memories. We were driving to visit family in Lubbock, and I was probably around three years old.

My mom showed me the details of that moment from her perspective. It was nighttime in the vision. My mom was driving, but I felt as if I were behind the wheel, as if I were having my mom's memory. I was enjoying the quiet of the dark night, and I looked in the rearview mirror and saw the golden glow of the moonlight shining on my little girl's head of long blonde hair. My baby was snuggled up with a stuffed bear and looking out the car window at a giant silver full moon. She was mesmerized, and there was such a look of wonder on her little face that it made my heart leap.

In the vision, I could feel my mom's love for that little girl—and she was me. My mom was basking in that love. I was seeing and feeling everything from my mom's perspective, as if I were her. It was kind of a *Freaky Friday* moment in the coolest way possible.

Then, suddenly, I wasn't looking at the vision from my mom's perspective anymore. I was in my own memory of that moment just in time to ask her in a cute little voice, "Mama, why is the moon following us?"

I felt my mom's response even before she answered my question, and it had nothing to do with the moon. I felt a flash of emotion coming from my mom. It was a combination of humor and deep, abiding love. At that moment, she was basking in the innocence and wonder of my childhood. She was so happy she giggled a little bit, and I felt so much love that I didn't care about the moon anymore. Instead, I just soaked up the look of adoration on her face, memorizing every detail. I could feel that at that moment, she just wanted to scoop me up, hug me, hold me, and tell me all about the wonders of this magical world. I felt her love for me, and it was so strong she was overflowing with it.

In the moment of the memory, all my cares faded away. I was a small child again, I was on a new adventure on the open road with my mom, and all was right with the world. I can still see it and feel what I felt back then just by thinking about it. It is just as real to me now as it was when it happened all those years ago.

Time travel is possible, and I manage to do it all the time. I get so enthralled in the memory; I feel as if I were actually there.

How cool is it that my mom taught me that perspective on the concept of time travel from the other side of the veil? She was already busy taking over her expanded role as a spiritual guide. She always had been a spiritual guide on earth, and now she was actually a spirit guide—and she was good at it!

And the Magic Continues

When we arrived at my mom's apartment, Deb, my mom's best friend, met us out front. Deb and Teresa, the lady who took care of my mom's household duties, were there together, sharing stories to honor my mom. I was glad because I got to meet Teresa and thank her for all she had done for my mom. My mother had been able to keep her independence partly because Teresa did all the cleaning and shopping for her. Her help was invaluable to my mom. There are no words to express my appreciation for what she did for her. Teresa also delivered a beautiful message of light to me that day: she told me I had my mom's eyes.

In my entire life, I never had noticed that I had her eyes—probably because her eyes were green, and mine were blue. But apparently, I do have her eyes, not the color but the shape. That was the best compliment ever because I think my mom's eyes were the most beautiful thing about her. How could they not have been? Her beautiful spirit shone through them.

Deb was already set up in my mom's room since she'd arrived the night before, so Ron and I slept on the couch. Then the woo-woo stuff started happening. That night, my mom's phone rang at 3:00 a.m. Of course, there was no one on the line. It was odd, but I knew it was my mom's way of making her presence known.

It was surreal to be in my mom's apartment, especially late at night, without her physically there. I could feel her energy stronger than ever, but sensing her energy in that new way made me sad about my loss. I sobbed for a moment quietly in the darkness. Then I took a deep breath and thought about my mom and what she wanted. How could I complain, when she was happy and free? As I breathed, I focused on my mom and her peace. Suddenly, I could feel her there, consoling me, and I could hear her voice clearly in my mind: *"Christi, I'm OK. I'm better than OK! I'm free. Be happy for me! I love you so much. You can do this. I'll be right here when you need me."*

I drifted back to sleep that night in my mother's arms, and it felt good. Different but still good. I felt more grateful for my ability to talk to spirits in that instant than I ever had in my entire life. All my years of practicing and talking to those on the other side had led to that moment and that amazing gift of connection: the blessing of a mother's love transcending time and space, coupled with my ability to experience and receive it. Talk about a message of light.

Honoring My Mama

The next morning, I awoke with inspiration. I set about honoring my mother in a special and unique way. Anyone who knew my mom knew to associate her with butterflies. She loved them because they were symbols of transformation and miracles. There were butterfly decorations everywhere in her home. Her username on her email account had butterfly in the name. She also had a butterfly tattoo on the back of her shoulder. So I thought a butterfly release would be appropriate to commemorate my mom's transformation into spirit. I'd attended a butterfly release at M. E.'s memorial many years before, and the beauty of the experience had stuck with me. It inspired me to honor my mother in the same way.

The only butterflies I could find for the release were called painted lady butterflies. In the back of my mind, I thought my mom would probably have laughed about their name, though others might think their name inappropriate for a funeral. The term *painted ladies* was once used to reference women in the oldest profession. My mom also had used it to guide me at the times when I wore too much makeup as a teen, saying things like "You don't want to look like a painted lady, do you?" Ah, good times and another flash down memory lane. It was as if my mom were there reminiscing with me.

There was no real dilemma about the butterflies; I had to take what I could find, and no one besides me and my mom would know what kind of butterflies they were anyway. The butterflies were beautiful, so I ordered them.

In the energy of connection, even setbacks can be viewed as miracles, and we had a few. The next morning, the funeral director told us it would be a day longer than initially expected before we could hold the farewell service. The crematorium was undergoing a cleaning of the facility, so we would have to wait, but my mom would be the first one through once it was all cleaned out. I love it! Of course my mom would get the red-carpet treatment. Everyone who knew her can attest that my mom was like spiritual royalty. Even people who knew her well enough to be on a first-name basis still called her Ms. Robin. There was just something regal about her. My grandmother Evelyn and great-grandmother Helen were that way too.

I can attest to that not just because I knew them when they were alive but also because the energy I sense when they visit me feels powerful and holy. And of course, my grandmothers were visiting then. I could see my grandmother and my great-grandmother smiling, and there was so much love coming from them it was incredible. I could see their excitement at welcoming my mother into the ranks of our ascended ancestors in heaven. I loved that they were conspiring to make my mom feel special for her arrival into the light. They were probably the ones who told the crematorium it was time for a cleaning!

The change in plans couldn't have worked out better, because that night, I got a call from the company that had promised me the butterflies in time for our ceremony. They were completely sold out of butterflies and called to let me know the order had been canceled. Ordinarily, that development would have caused wild hysterics on my part, but I was calm. I figured my mom was up to something from the other side. So instead of losing my marbles, I just looked for another option for butterflies. Luckily, because of the cleaning at the crematorium, I might still have a chance to get them there in time.

I ran another internet search, and this time, monarch butterflies came up. Those seemed better than painted ladies. Monarch butterflies have a name more befitting the regal energy of my mom. This was meant to happen, and I knew it. I placed the order.

Within an hour, I got a call from the butterfly company. They weren't calling to cancel on me like the other company; they were calling to offer up another miracle. This time, the box I'd ordered to house the butterflies before the release was out of stock. My original choice featured multicolored pastels with spring flowers on top. It was pretty, and it was the only one I could find that was a reasonable choice, because they didn't have solid purple or lavender, as I'd hoped. Or so I thought. The woman on the other end of the phone offered a list of substitutions, starting with a white box adorned with purple roses. Can you believe it? It couldn't have been more perfect. Purple is the color of the crown chakra. It is the color associated with transformation, and of course, it is the color associated with royalty. The crisis was averted miraculously. The butterflies would arrive by 9:00 a.m. on Friday morning, with the service being scheduled for 10:00 a.m. That would be exactly enough time for the butterflies to reanimate after the dry ice from shipping.

Planning my mother's funeral, was a full circle experience. Since my wedding planning adventure, I had learned that things work out whether or not I choose to stress. So, I decided to flow in faith.

More Miracles

The miracles were flowing. That afternoon, Ron and I drove to pick up Kira and Aja from the airport. On the way, I had another conversation with my mom, who was already on the higher plane.

It occurred to me that at that moment, her body was being cremated. Naturally, I asked her what she thought about that. Her response was comical and true to her personality: "That body? Burn, baby, burn!"

She was happy to be rid of the body that had betrayed her. She was free of the vessel that had caused her so much physical pain and illness over the recent years. She was free!

I laughed to myself and peacefully looked out the window, taking note of how beautiful the clouds looked that day. Then I heard my mom say, "Take a picture!" I knew there was a reason. The last time I'd gotten the random inspiration to take a picture, with Yvonne and her mom, it had resulted in a miracle, so I did. I took a picture of the beautiful blue but cloudy sky. It wasn't until after I took the picture that I noticed the cloud's shape was undeniably a butterfly. It wasn't perfectly shaped, but the more I looked, the more obvious the butterfly became. I was excited. It seemed unbelievable, even with all the miracles already flowing, but it happened. Now I have photographic evidence of my mom sending me messages from the other side. The messages prove to me her continued existence if I ever have a moment of doubt. Take a look for yourself. What do you see?

Butterfly in the clouds

I had no doubt my mom was sending me a message of light. Do you see her there? I didn't see her at first. I spent months focused only on the butterfly, but then one of my dear friends, Stacey, saw it and pointed it out. Stacey not only had been a friend of mine since our kids were little but also was one of my Reiki students who had done the training to become a Reiki master. Her spiritual connection was strong, and as with many of my students, her abilities surpassed mine in many ways. This brilliant lightworker pointed out the most important part of the picture. The butterfly is obvious, but look closer. See the woman in the middle?

The Messages of Light

See the woman of light inside the butterfly? You can't miss her. Her wings seem to extend from her shoulders. Her body of light curves like a mermaid through the middle of the wings, and there is light shooting out of her feet. My mom even did her hair the same way—see it shining in the light as if it's blowing in the wind? There is a woman made of light sprouting wings made of clouds in this picture. Can you believe it?

When I finally saw the whole picture, I laughed out loud from the sheer joy I felt at realizing that extraordinary miracle. I actually have a picture of my mom from the other side! It was an amazing feeling to see that she was there in my life, still active and involved. Wow, what magic they can do from the other side! Honestly, what is the chance a cloud formation would look like a butterfly at the exact moment I was talking to my mom? And the lady of light in the center! What!

During the car ride to the airport, just as I was basking in the glow of the butterfly-in-the-cloud miracle (I hadn't seen my mom in the butterfly yet), I heard again, "Take a picture!"

I thought, *Of what?*

Just then, I saw it. There was a butterfly emblem decorating the back window of the car directly in front of us. I was in awe again.

Butterfly on car window

After that, there was no question that my mom was sending me messages of light from the other side. I felt her with us the whole time because the miracles and messages continued.

And Miracles Continued to Flow

Once Ron and I got back from the airport with the girls, Riane joined us, and we spent the rest of the day going through my mom's belongings and telling stories about her life. Deb and the girls thoughtfully picked some of my mom's things that had special meaning to them, and I could see my mom smiling at each choice. She was centering her energy over each of them. I visibly noticed a pink glow to their auras whenever my mom was near them, which was all the time. I wondered how pink I was, because I could still feel her all around me. The feeling of warmth and peace I felt can only be described as the sensation of relief and serenity you have after a good joyful cry. It's the way you feel after watching a really good, heartwarming tearjerker movie, the kind of movie that leaves you with a renewed sense of hope and faith in humanity. It's like that, only a thousand times better.

The morning of her funeral was when I felt her the strongest. I was alone in the bathroom of our hotel (there wasn't room for five of us in my mom's apartment), and I was talking to my mom, telling her that I had no idea what to say when it came time for me to speak at her funeral. I wanted to offer words that would honor my beautiful mother, and nothing was coming.

Just as I thought there was no way I could find the right things to say, words began popping into my mind. I felt the rush of the exhilaration of connection, and I noticed the hair on my arms standing up. I had total-body goose bumps, and I could feel my heart rate begin to rise. I experienced all the physical signs of incoming, a.k.a. divine inspiration, and I realized it was my mom helping me with my dilemma.

I grabbed a pen and the hotel notepad since they were the only things handy at the time, and I wrote the words as they came to me. I found it challenging to keep up, as the words were coming more quickly than my hand could write while flipping pages on the tiny notepad. Eventually, the words stopped flowing just as I reached the final sheet on the pad. When I was done writing, I looked at the scattered pages and asked aloud, "Now what?"

Suddenly, in my mind, I could see different phrases begin to highlight in gold on the page, as if indicating the order of placement in the poem. This was just how it had happened when I'd received the inspiration for "You May Think" all those years ago. By then, one of my girls had given me a spiral notebook from her backpack so I could transcribe the message. I couldn't help but notice how my writing had come full circle. I was back to the trusty spiral notebook for probably the most important message of my life.

As I read the words in their intended order, I heard my mom's voice in my mind. No doubt this message was straight from the Source! I was getting the words straight from my mom, who was merged with God, the Source of all energy. This is what she said:

> I love you all.
> I am not gone, only changed.
> I can feel the pain of your loss,
> but I am still here with you.
> When you think of me, I am near.
> When you speak to me, I can hear you.
> When you remember me, remember this:
> I lived! I continue to love,
> and yes, I can feel that I am loved by you!
> My life was a full one.
> I found beauty and bliss in the eyes of my girls.
> I found warmth and comfort in the embrace of my friends.
> I had adventures that left me breathless!
> I had pain and sorrow too, but nothing I ever went through
> could overshadow the love and joy I found in being with all of you!
> There is nothing left unsaid, because you can still say it to me,

and when you see a butterfly,
know it carries my love for you, and that is my reply.
Please trust my love for you endures forever.
It is real and deep and true!
So remember me, and rejoice with me,
knowing that I am free!
And believe when I say, my loves,
that this is not the end.
It is just farewell for now.
We will be together again.

I was out of my body with pure light energy when we finally got to my mom's office, where we held the ceremony. I arrived late, but I was right on time for the butterflies, because they too were a few minutes late and needed time to reanimate. Kim and Karen, my mom's bosses, graciously had offered the space for the ceremony, and they went to great lengths to honor my mom. By the time I got there, they had food set out and pictures of my mom through the years in frames everywhere. I was so taken aback all I could do was laugh. I couldn't help it or control it. I must have looked like a madwoman, but the joy of knowing that my mother was so loved was so overwhelming that it took me a minute to stop.

The service was held in the backyard area of the spa. It was a magical space. It looked like a fairy wonderland complete with trees, wildlife, and a small stream running through the yard and beautifully cascading into a gentle waterfall. It was perfect.

My mother had wanted a Wiccan farewell. She felt a deep connection with goddess energy, the divine feminine. So Deb, her best friend, who was also Wiccan, helped us make it happen. We were in a circle around my mom's altar. Ron, Kira, Aja, and I marked the four directions in the ceremony. I was on the west side of the circle. I felt how much my mom loved that everyone had tried to wear the appropriate color corresponding with his or her position in the ceremony.

The Messages of Light

Altar

My mother's friend Deb officiated and was in the center of the circle, closest to the altar. She performed the ceremony, reciting *Charge of the Goddess*, and then we each said something to honor my mother. I was the last person in the circle. When it was my turn, I read the message my mother had sent, and it was well received. I could hear my mom's voice in my mind as I spoke, and I could feel her love all around me. Afterward, Deb picked up the box containing the butterflies, set to release them.

When she opened the box, all the butterflies flew out except one. Deb shook the box, trying to get it to fly, but it wouldn't leave. I suddenly said, "No, that's my mom! She wants to say goodbye to us!" How funny that I would blurt that out in front of a bunch of perfect strangers, but I did.

We then passed the container around to each person in the circle. All of us were saying our goodbyes to a butterfly in a box! I know it sounds funny, but it was so real. When it finally came to me, I said, "Hi, Mama! Thank you for waiting for me." I had been afraid she would fly off before the box got to me, since so many people were ahead of me.

Look at that! I still had doubt, even after all I had seen. But there was no reason for doubt. The butterfly waited. It stayed in the box until it got to me. When I looked at the butterfly, I saw my mom. I told her, "I love you so much. Thank you for waiting. You can go now. I understand."

At the moment I said, "I understand," the butterfly flew out of the box, and it circled me as if giving me a hug. Then it flew around the circle as if addressing and thanking all the guests again. Then it landed on Deb's shirt!

More specifically, the butterfly landed on my mom's shirt, which Deb was wearing for the ceremony. It was as if she were thanking Deb for being there for her. It seemed she was giving her best friend a hug too. You should have seen the look of shock on Deb's face when it happened. She felt the message of light for sure.

By that time, Ron had gone into the building to get my camera, and I was able to get photographic evidence of the miracle. Pictured below is the butterfly that waited for everyone to say goodbye and then landed on the shirt Deb was wearing.

Butterfly on Deb's shirt

From there, the miracles kept happening, and now I had the camera with me, so I began documenting the experience with my mom in her temporary new form, a butterfly.

The butterfly then left Deb and landed on the flowers on the altar next to my mother's ashes and picture. It was as if she were taking the time to appreciate her flowers.

The Messages of Light

Butterfly on flowers 1

My mom had commented once or twice when I was growing up that it would be interesting to be a fly on the wall at her own funeral. I guess she chose to be a monarch butterfly instead. Here she is, spreading her strong and powerful wings as if posing for the picture:

Butterfly on flowers 2

As if there weren't enough indicators that my mom was there with us, the same butterfly landed on my mom's picture and posed again. It was as if she were giving me a before-and-after photo of her in the same frame. Can you believe it?

Mom: Before and after

The entire experience was magical, surprising, and awesome in the truest sense of the word. It created an unbreakable faith in me that has filled me with joy ever since. I know there is more to life than what we have been living on this earth. The magic is real in this world, and there are many miracles to be found in it.

I am grateful for the pictures I was able to take of the experience, because without them, I might not believe it myself. Now, whenever I doubt the magic and mystery of this incredible universe God created for us, all I have to do is look back at this tangible, physical proof. There is no doubt in my mind, or in the mind of anyone else who was there, that my mother was with us that day. You decide for yourself. Do you believe in miracles?

Continuing Connection

My mom still sends me messages every day. I can still hear her voice in my head, and I can still feel her around me. She is always around because I think of her all the time. Is she here because I think of her, or do I think of her because she's here? I don't know if the chicken or the egg is first, but I know if she's in my thoughts, she is here in spirit. When I am sad, I can feel her warmth and comfort, and when I am excited, I can sense her cheering me on. She's not gone, just different, as she said. Our relationship has evolved and has even grown stronger in many ways. She has become my anchor on the other side, keeping me tethered to the light at all times. She keeps me consistent with my spiritual work. I keep my spiritual muscle strong. It establishes the connection that allows me to hear, sense, and sometimes even see my mom. You bet I'm going to keep it strong!

My mom has gotten highly creative in her means of communicating with me. Besides the fact that I can feel her when she's near and hear her voice when she speaks to me, she also found another way to reach me: in my dreams. The first of her adventures in communication with me in the dreamscape was awesome. It was so real. We were walking along a golden path out in a field of wildflowers. Every color of the rainbow grew up out of the ground around us. The indigo sky above was so infinitely expansive that I felt as if I were floating when I looked up. The place was ethereal and full of light and energy, and my mom was right there with me. When we hugged, it felt as warm and comforting as any hug I'd received from her on earth. I was happy to be with her again. I was buzzing with joy, and it wasn't just my own happiness I was feeling. I could feel and see that my mom was ecstatic. She exuded elation and pure bliss when she told me what she'd been up to since she left her body. She said she had been busy exploring the metropolis. There was a gleam of joy sparking radiantly from her eyes as she pointed off to something in the distance. Then a golden city of light materialized right before my eyes, as if she, by pointing it out to me, somehow lifted the veil obscuring my view of the magical city. She was beaming with delight when she showed me the metropolis she had been exploring and told me of her encounters and experiences since she'd arrived there. I was amazed.

To me, the metropolis, as she called it, looked like the land of Oz. The picture was complete with a yellow brick road leading up to a city and a giant castle with pointed rooftops. Instead of being green like Oz, it was all a brilliant, shimmering translucent gold. It was more beautiful than words can describe, and the energy of the place was magical yet serene. It was her heaven, and I could see she was happy there.

After she showed me where she'd been, she gave me a message of light when she said, "You know I would never have left you when I did if I hadn't known you could do this."

She was referring to my ability to communicate with those on the other side. She had known we would still be together even after she left the physical world. She'd had plenty of experience of her own in communicating with beings on the other side, so she had been sure she would still be able to reach me when she crossed over, even before she left her body.

We spent the rest of our time floating together on a tour. We journeyed through the colorful, shifting lights of the ethers, which reminded me of the aurora borealis, in an exchange of love that was so pure it needed no words. My mom stayed with me until it was time for me to wake up. Then she gave me another big mama-bear-type hug. It was as warm and comforting as a mother's embrace can be, and I woke up still feeling the weight of her arms around me.

Clarification on a Previous Communication

Months later, I got more insight into the vision in my dream of my mom's version of heaven. I realized why it looked the way it did. It was our first Christmas without her, and I was merging her Christmas ornaments with ours. There weren't many ornaments, because she had already given me most of the decorations from my childhood. She'd kept only the ornaments that were special to her, and there were few. When I came across a little red box, I had a flash of something in my mind. I had never seen that particular ornament before, but I remembered seeing something like it once in a dream. As I picked up the little golden ornament, the vision deepened. I took a deep breath to make the connection, I felt a whoosh of warmth come over me, and the download was complete. I understood. The ornament looked like the golden castle from my dream. It was the metropolis my mom had shown me when she visited me.

Suddenly, I was sure my mom was with me. I knew the rush of information that flashed into my mind came from her. How? Because in that flash, she explained why her heaven looked that way.

My mom's version of heaven came from the storybooks she'd read in the happy and peaceful moments of her childhood. This is important because as the oldest sister of four, she rarely had found quiet moments in her youth. My mom had spent a lot of time helping her younger sisters when my grandma was at work.

My grandmother Evelyn was a strong and powerful woman. She was a business executive in a time when women were seen as capable of holding only secretarial jobs. That meant my grandmother worked full-time at the office and spent weekends on the golf course and tennis courts with the other executives, who were all men. She was awesome. She did it all with four kids. My grandmother was a trailblazer for all the women who would choose to follow their dreams regardless of societal constraints. I am proud of her.

With my grandmother being a busy executive, my mom was responsible for helping out at home with her little sisters during the school year, but in the summers, she was free. My mom spent every summer with her grandmother, who was a second-grade teacher. G. G., as we called her, was off work during the summers, while school was out of session. That meant she was free to spend time with her granddaughters. My mom loved my G. G. and often referred to her as a second mother rather than a grandmother.

Having a schoolteacher as a babysitter meant there was no television as a pastime. I'm not even sure she had a television back then, but my G. G. had books—lots of them! My mom read many of them over the years, but the one thing she read every summer of her young life was *The Wizard of Oz*. She loved the magical world of Oz. In the stories, she found wonder, magic, and inspiration. It makes sense that she returned to the innocence and magic of her childhood in her heaven. She went to her happy place and then came back to tell me about it.

When I told my daughters about what my mom had shown me, explaining why her heaven looked like the land of Oz, they told me of another reason her heaven looked that way. My mom sent both of them their own downloads of information, and they both got the same information at the same time. It was part of another road trip we had taken with my mom. She showed them a vision of the time she, Kira, Aja, and I had gone to see the Broadway production of *Wicked*.

We found out that *Wicked* was playing in San Antonio, and my mom lived in Austin at the time, which was within driving distance. My girls were obsessed with the show, so we flew out to see my mom, and we took her to see the show with us. She loved everything about it. She loved being with her girls, she loved a good road trip, and she loved anything to do with *The Wizard of Oz*. I don't ever remember seeing her as excited as she was during that show. When it was over, she looked like a child filled with wonder. My mom, Kira, and Aja were vibrationally indistinguishable from one another. There was so much awe and joy radiating from them; it was contagious. Empathically, it was one of my most treasured experiences. I was both flowing in divine energy and absorbing pleasure from the joy of others. It is a beautiful and fulfilling memory for me.

So between the peace and sanctuary *The Wizard of Oz* stories had given her as a child and the return to the childlike wonder she'd experienced as an adult in attending *Wicked* with her granddaughters, the magic of Oz was just like the magic of my mom's version of heaven.

That experience of us all downloading memories and information was definitely my mom delivering messages of light. How would we have figured all of that out by ourselves if my mom hadn't been there explaining it to us? I knew she'd read those books, because we'd had two copies of them on the bookshelf while I was growing up, but I never knew what they represented to her until that download of information. And I knew she'd enjoyed the production of *Wicked*, but I never had realized the full extent of why she'd loved it so much.

Sending Signs

My mom found other ways to make herself known to me as she got used to her new existence. On her birthday, when I was writing to her on her Facebook page, she showed up. I was writing a long, heartfelt message,

The Messages of Light

telling her how much I love her and miss her. I was crying, when my computer started wigging out! No, I didn't short out the computer with my tears. It wasn't that. It was my mom. The screen changed, and everything went gray, except her picture and what I was writing. The exterior border was flashing white and blue, and it wouldn't stop.

Interestingly, when I minimized Facebook on the computer and opened up another page, I discovered that nothing else was doing that. It was just my mom's Facebook page. I could tell she was sending a message to make sure I knew she was reading every word I wrote. I could feel her there as I soaked up her warm and loving response.

I videotaped the experience. Unfortunately, I can't put a video on paper to show you, but the video does exist for any doubters out there!

My mom is nothing if not thorough. She even reached out to me through one of her clients and friends. Beverly messaged me via Facebook. We had never met before, but I could tell she was close to my mom when we connected. I could feel the familiarity in her vibration. Beverly messaged me out of the blue to relay a message of light. Sometime after my mom passed, Beverly spoke with a medium, and my mom popped in. Of course she did! That's my mama! It seems she's just as busy on the other side as she was here on earth.

My mom asked Beverly to make sure I knew that the poem I'd received for her funeral had been done just as she'd wanted it. Basically, the message was one of approval. I even heard her voice in my head say, "You did good!" as I read the rest of the message from Beverly. Now, keep in mind that neither Beverly nor the medium had been at my mom's funeral. So how could either of them have known about the poem? Could it have been a good guess? Anyone else might have remained skeptical, but I knew better. My mom was getting creative in her communications.

Then things got funny. In the same message, Beverly said that my mom also had said she likes to play with the lights and electricity to tell us when she's there. I laughed and agreed wholeheartedly, and I sent her the video of my mom playing with my computer, making the screen flash blue and white. Beverly laughed too, and we enjoyed a new experience together with my mom. Yes, she was there with us, and we both felt her. I am grateful to Beverly for going out of her way to share that with me. It was another confirmation of the miraculous nature of our existence.

My mom visited her boss Karen too. Not long after the exchange I had with Beverly, I had another one with Karen. She sent me a video of the most unusually behaving butterfly I had seen since my mom's funeral. This butterfly hovered about three or four feet above the ground outside Karen's window for a long time. It was as if the butterfly were communicating with her in its own way. It hovered there long enough for Karen to record it so she could send it to me. I know it was a message from my mom reminding Karen that she is loved and appreciated.

There were many more miracles and messages. My mom made her messages impossible to ignore. If ever I doubted the truth in energy and spiritual work, my doubt was eliminated completely by my mom's intervention. There is no doubt in my mind that my mother is with us. She proved to me there is life after death, and she is proof that energy never dies. It only changes form.

I am grateful for my ability to communicate with spirits. I used to think it made me strange, and maybe it does, but now I know what a fantastic gift it is to connect with the energy of the divine.

Looking back, I can see that every message I received and delivered from the other side led to this. All those years, I was strengthening my spiritual muscle so that when my mom made her transition, she would still be part of my life, and she is.

Chapter 21

Coming Full Circle

The Original Mission

Remember when I freaked out and gave up on writing my story? I know you're probably thinking, *Which time?* That was back when writing anything of value was a daunting task for me. You also may recall that my guides, in an attempt to save my sanity, instructed me to stop working on my book for a while instead of giving up on it completely. At that time, they also told me to make three copies of the original and to give two of the copies away. They never told me why. They only told me whom to give the copies to. You may also remember that the same guidance once said I would know when it was time to start writing my story again.

Well, it was time. How did I know? What signaled this revelation? Read on to see.

I hadn't thought about working on my story in years, but I found the manuscript one day while I was busy cleaning out my clutter. It was stashed in a leather briefcase alongside my scouting paperwork. The briefcase seemed to be calling to me. It was saying, "Clean me!" Just kidding. Just to be clear, inanimate objects don't speak—at least not to me! Anyway, the briefcase had been in the same spot for so long it was coated with a thick layer of dust and definitely needed cleaning.

Initially, it was the dust on the briefcase that got my attention. Once I noticed that my story was inside it, I got a flash in my mind's eye of a traffic light turning green. A message of light—a streetlight! I was so giddy at the sight that I laughed out loud.

I picked up the pages and began to go through them. The problem was that the pages were so picked through and out of order that I wouldn't have known where to begin even if I had tried. So I dusted the briefcase, put the pages back inside it, and put the briefcase back on the shelf. After that, I went about my business, trying hard not to think about it, but I was obsessed. I could think of little else, but did I do anything about it? No.

Well, God wasn't having that! There was a reason I'd found my story when I did, and apparently, I wasn't getting it. So God orchestrated a pivotal exchange. Kathy and I were talking, as we often did, and we got on the topic of what was next for each of us. We talked about her and her students, and we also talked about me. She could sense something different in my energy, and she wanted to find out what it was. I told Kathy I intended to follow through with what I'd told my mom that day on the phone. I told her I was contemplating going back to nursing school or starting a business in the integrative-wellness field. Kathy was almost dismissive of my plans. It's not that she wasn't supportive or interested in what I wanted to do next; Kathy was just more interested in knowing how I was progressing with my book. She wanted to know when I would start working on it again. How funny! It had been years since we talked about my book, and she brought it up right after I rediscovered my long-lost copy. The timing of the conversation couldn't have been more obvious. It was a message of light for sure. I laughed out loud, and when I told Kathy of the coincidence in the timing of her question, she laughed too. Then she said, "It's a miracle!"—something she and I were beginning to say often. Kathy and I were getting used to experiencing miracles by then, so every time there was a fortuitous coincidence in our lives, we said, "It's a miracle," and this was one of those times.

After that, I told Kathy about the green light in my vision, and she agreed it meant I should get to it. So when I gave her the excuse that my copy was a mess and I didn't know where to start, she insisted I take her copy. Hmm, do you think maybe God had seen that coming?

And as if God were working through her, when Kathy handed me the box containing the pages of my book, she also insisted I commit to finishing it. Kathy had always been one of my angels on earth. She was constantly pushing me outside my comfort zone, encouraging my spiritual growth, and this was no different.

Remember how my guides told me I would know when it was time to start writing again? Well, they were right. If I still had any doubt after the coincidences so far, it was about to be obliterated. Another well-timed synchronicity occurred. About a week after Kathy gave me her copy, I still hadn't started working on it, so I got another sign. God was on top of it. I had no doubt it was time to get to work when the last of the three original copies came back to me. I was sorting through some of my mom's personal papers, and voilà—there it was! Her copy of my manuscript was turned to the page with the message titled "Modern-Day Plague" when I found it. The third and final copy of the original three returned to me. By then, there was no denying I was being called back to my original mission. When I picked up my mom's copy, I could feel her urging me to get back to it too.

I knew it was time to write my story. It was finally time to finish my book!

A New View on an Old Message

It was the day I finally set aside the time to begin working on the mission again. I felt I needed inspiration to know where to start, so I used my tools. I meditated and connected, and I heard it again: "Write your story." But there was more to it this time. The message came in loud and clear: "You are the author of your story! Write your story!" Suddenly, after all those years of trying to write my story and believing I was supposed to write a book, I finally caught that there was another meaning to the original guidance "Write your story."

I laughed out loud as I realized the message was a reminder that I am the creator of my own experience. It was God telling me that I am the author of my own story. It's like the saying "You are the artist, and your life is the canvas." Had I taken the message too literally all those years ago? Maybe God was just telling me that I am responsible for the story of my life and that I should design it on purpose. What if I wasn't supposed to write a book at all? What if this whole experience was just designed to teach me how I attract energy, people, circumstances, and events into my experience with my vibration? I learned that regardless of the circumstances, no matter what happens in life, I am the one who creates the perceptions and perspectives with which I interpret my reality. All of my life experiences come from me and to me by my thoughts, words, and actions.

So when God said, "Write your story," maybe he meant I should take the time to decide what kind of life I want to live and create accordingly using magnetic attraction. I had been doing it all along, sometimes deliberately but primarily by default. Maybe God was telling me to be purposeful in my creations. What if God just meant for me to create a better perspective with which to view my circumstances? Maybe I didn't have to write a book after all! Ha! What if I had misinterpreted that key message of light, "Write your story," for all those years?

Maybe, but apparently not so. The loud and clear message I got from that contemplation was "The original message still stands! You're not getting off the hook that easily. Write your story."

So with new clarity and purpose, I set out to finally complete my mission. I wrote my story. Rather, I rewrote my story from my higher perspective instead of my needy and injured ego's view. This time, I decided I would leave out the dark and ugly stuff that was mostly a construct of my unhealthy ego. Those stories were just excuses to diminish the shame I felt over my perfectly human behavior, and they almost always cast blame on someone else.

It wasn't easy, especially when I first sat down to do the rewrite. I had no idea where to start. So I took a deep breath and connected to my higher self. Then, when I looked at the original copies, some of the pages and passages seemed to be illuminated. They were glowing. The bright passages and phrases were clues telling me where to start. This had happened twice before, so I knew exactly what to do. It was like the time I'd gotten the inspiration for the message "I Love You All" from my mom and the time I'd gotten "You May Think" from my papaw and the others. Each time, the phrases appeared to glow, directing me and guiding me through the process of delivering the messages of light. And it was happening again for the third time. It was a miracle—again! Another sign that all the experiences in my life had led to this mission.

The Miracles in the Messages of Light

This time, I wrote my story as I was directed while highlighting all the beauty and love in my life. From this perspective, I was able to see the miracles and the messages of light, which came in many different forms, always resembling coincidence. I was also able to perceive the messengers of light at pivotal times in my life. They came in all shapes and sizes. Many had two legs, a few had four legs, and some of them even had wings. Because of the experience of writing my story, I can recognize them all.

Reviewing my past allowed me to see every experience in a new light. I found a higher perspective, and through it, I found love and compassion for myself and everyone else. I realized that for my entire life, I had been looking to others to make me feel complete instead of understanding that I already was complete.

It wasn't until I wrote my story that I noticed just how present God had always been in my life. I was never alone, no matter how bad I felt. In fact, in the writing of my story, I saw that I was nurtured, loved, guided, and sometimes even carried through my trials. When I was at my worst, both heaven and the people on earth moved to help me.

Flowing from Love

The craziest thing happened. In living the experiences I wrote about in this text and viewing them retrospectively from a higher perspective, I healed. I made my mosaic. I took the broken pieces of my experiences and reassembled them in a beautiful, bright, and colorful way. I embraced the person I became as I redesigned myself, my perspectives, and my life from the vibration of love. I welcomed the energies of kindness and compassion and asked that they flow through me and out into the world.

I am my authentic self. I am love, and guess what. So are you!

From my true vibration, love, I began to thank my greatest teachers, who, believe it or not, were the most challenging people in my experience. For the first time, I was sincere in my appreciation for them because I could recognize and embrace the wisdom and expansion that resulted from our interactions. Sometimes it took a little extra effort to get from anger or pain to appreciation, but I did it. I started to savor the knowledge I obtained from the many lessons in my life, and I grew to revel in the miraculous ways they arrived at my experience. Do you know what else? In the act of appreciation, I discovered that growing doesn't always have to be painful. Sometimes growing is the most fun there is to be had!

Writing My Story

My childlike faith was renewed. The knowing of my youth returned. The pieces of my life's puzzle that I'd collected along my way fell perfectly and miraculously into place, creating a picture of a mystical and magical world. I was both the artist who painted it and the subject within the painting. In the writing of my story and in every wondrous experience I had on my journey, I collected colors for my artist's palette. I began with those created for me, but I also learned to create new colors with which to paint. Now I decide which colors to use, and I do almost all my painting myself.

I realized I have lived the life I designed every step of the way, good or bad. Writing my story taught me to be more mindful and purposeful in my creations so that I could actually enjoy them when they manifested.

Writing my story also allowed me to see how my abilities as an empath have allowed me all along to tap in to the feelings of every person involved in the critical situations of my life. Through this adventure, I was able to see that those feelings were communications from God, helping me to help myself and others. When I listened to my guidance, I began shifting my judgmental human view to a compassionate divine view in every situation possible. From this higher place, I see my story for what it is: a love story to God and my family, children, parents, friends, teachers, guides, and life.

I know now that everything I have experienced has had a message of light in it, waiting to be discovered, and I recognize now that I am getting surprisingly good at finding the miracles.

Writing this story has proven to me, to the point of utter certainty, that the wholeness and holiness I looked for throughout my many years of searching were within me all along. God has always been with me, living inside me. He is the small whisper to guide me when I am quiet and peaceful enough to listen. When it's too loud to hear the whisper because my subconscious mind is talking over it, God becomes the screaming anxiety in the center of my chest. God always lets me know when I start to miscreate. And when I get goose bumps and a feeling of giddiness or exhilaration, I recognize that is God essentially giving me a high five and cheering me forward because I am in alignment with my life's purpose and the highest and best good for all concerned. God is love and always offers us messages of light to guide us through the darkness. We just have to be willing to receive them.

The Journey through Life as an Empath

This grand adventure has led me to this place and this moment in my life when I can honestly say I love my life. I love all of it! There's nothing I would change if I could, because if I did, I would not be here right now, living my best life and striving daily to be the best version of myself I can be. I forgive myself for my human mistakes as I make them, and I learn from them instead of punishing myself for being what I came here to be: human. I know I am perfectly imperfect just as I am, and I'm good with that. I believe I am here on this earth doing precisely what I came to do, and I have been all along (even when I was being a jerk). I have answered the call to change my world, because that is the only world I truly have the power to change. I know that at every moment, I have a choice. I try to choose mindfully. I try to remember not only to ask for guidance but also to follow the advice of my guides when I do. I know I am still traveling up my life's spiral staircase. I understand that I still have much more to learn. I am excited about that now instead of afraid. I also know that life gets more wondrous and beautiful the higher up I go.

As I mentioned, I now see why it took so long to write my story. When I began, it wasn't time. I wasn't ready. I was busy living life, learning, growing, failing, and overcoming. I was occupied with having the life experiences that gave me what I affectionately call my "street cred." I understand now that every ounce of pain I experienced had a purpose. I know that every failure made me stronger. Every dark night had a sunrise in the morning. I don't want to be like anyone else. I'm perfectly happy to be me. I love this life—all of it. I have found that for every horrible experience and every painful moment in my life, God had the universe creating a beautiful, joyful experience equal in intensity but opposite in vibration for me. And I continue to have them!

I get to have wonderful, wondrous, miraculous moments and ecstatically joyful experiences every day just by doing what I love: helping people like me to find their own strength and power to heal. Beyond that, I get to help people design the lives of their dreams and watch as their wishes manifest into reality. I get to help others move from the vibrations of healing and surviving to the vibrations of creating and thriving. I get to help people find their childlike faith and, most importantly, remind them of their relationships with God and love.

I still have moments when I am 100 percent in my little human self. I have pain and misfortune, and sometimes I can be a real jerk, but those moments are fewer and farther between than ever before, and none of them make me feel like having a drink or berating myself.

Now, all these years later, I have stories and examples to share, and it is my deepest desire to use my experiences to help others. I want to be part of the shift in energy that is pulling our world out of the vibration of hell and into the vibration of heaven on earth. Each year, the veil between this planet and the spiritual realm gets thinner, and as it does, the magic gets thicker. It's time to use our empathic gifts to influence energy; to intentionally use the quantum cosmic energy to boost our designs for happy, healthy, loving, and fulfilling lives. It is already happening, and I know I will love seeing the old paradigms crumble as we design our world in beauty and light.

- Stress does not equal success. Chronic stress causes the nervous system to stay in fight-or-flight mode and limits everything from the immune system to the ability to experience happiness. The truest success is found in the feelings of joy and fulfillment.
- Hope is not faith. Jesus never said we should have hope that I know of. He said we should have faith. Hope is doubt. Faith is belief. With faith, we can move from the vibration of surviving to one of thriving. We can have freedom from the bondage of self-loathing and self-destruction when we realize the power of our free will.

- Sympathy is not empathy. Sympathy is feeling bad for the person you are focused upon. This is essentially adding weight to the person's already heavy load. Empathy is feeling what another is feeling and using that information to create a connection to help lighten the other person's load. It's the difference between "I feel sorry for you" and "I am here for you."
- Set priorities, not boundaries. Boundaries will attract that which we are trying to repel because of our attention to it. Be number one on your list of priorities, and the universe that God created will draw to you the people, circumstances, and events that are in your highest and best good.
- Worry is weight. When we worry about our loved ones, we add energetic weight to their already heavy burden. Instead, envision your loved one happy and fulfilled. Pray in the positive for the highest and best good for all concerned.
- Life is not a competition; it is a collaboration. When we work together, miracles happen. "Again, truly I tell you that if two of you on earth agree about anything they ask for, it will be done for them by my Father in heaven" (Matthew 18:19 NIV).

I want to help people learn to experience their own messages of light, and my street cred allows me to do that. Think about it: no one wants help from someone who cannot relate. And boy, can I relate! I haven't by any means been through every painful experience a person can endure, at least in this lifetime, but my ability as an empath helps me relate to all the rest. I have learned to flow divine energy powerfully through myself. I flow so much love onto the people around me that I rarely act like an energy-absorbing sponge anymore. I can still sense what they feel, but what's theirs is theirs, and what's mine is mine. Once I tap in to the emotions a person is experiencing, I ask God and my angels, ancestors, and guides for help, and together we sort it out.

Everything that was once bad in my life has reversed. I have shifted my focus from healing to creating.

Ron and I have never been better. He is the love of my life. I am blessed to have found such an amazing human being to grow with. He is loving, kind, and generous. He's an honest, good man, and I appreciate him more than he'll ever know. My connection with my daughters has grown and strengthened. I'm blessed to say we're closer than I ever could have imagined. We have more than mother-daughter relationships; we have become friends too. They are my heart and soul. Having my daughters has made my life worthwhile, and I am happy to see them grow into the kind and confident young women they are. I can't wait to see what they do next!

I have an excellent relationship with my dad and my other mother, Mary. They are a beautiful example of a lasting, loving relationship and an excellent source of love and support to me. I'm blessed to have them in my life. I know without a doubt that my parents would move mountains if I ever needed help, and I hope they know how much I love and appreciate them.

I have more friends now than ever before, and our relationships continue to flow in divine love. I am in better physical condition than I was when I ran half marathons, and mentally, I'm pretty clear and focused these days. Don't get me wrong; life is life, but I am really enjoying the good in it. Sometimes I like to say, "Life is life, but the coffee's good!"—because it is! Or even better, "Life is life, but my thoughts, beliefs, and expectations are good!" Maybe one of those sayings will end up on a T-shirt someday.

If you haven't guessed by now whether I went back to nursing school or started a business, I did the latter. I found my passion in integrative wellness. After suffering a stroke, Tony helped me and some fantastic friends—Kathy, Erica, Stacey, Tina, and Rocio—to start a wellness company geared toward society's youth. This is where I connect the dots. All the skills I learned and developed over the years though Reiki, nursing, the law of attraction, and my scouting experiences came together. Who knew my experiences over all those years would lead to this? God, of course!

We called it Happy Healthy Whole World, and it was well received by the community. Together we developed a curriculum for children based on being mindful and strengthening the vagus nerve. We offered regular workshops for kids as well as meditation classes and workshops for teens and adults. We were honored to have some amazing and brilliant people attend our classes, and we were blessed to have some incredible and inspiring guest teachers come in to teach classes as well. Deb and

Nydia taught us the chakras through yoga, and Suzie taught us about Eastern cultures and belief systems. My friend Lina from high school even came in from out of town to teach us kundalini yoga and introduced us to Paramdayal a local kundalini instructor. Crazy how it all comes together, huh?

The most incredible thing we did at Happy Healthy Whole World was develop a revolutionary breathing technique that can be used to rewire the brain and the thought processes that stem from it. The method clears the energy that no longer serves us as it replaces the energy within and around the physical body with divine energy. It's the same technique I teach now in all my classes and Reiki sessions. As a result of our endeavors, my already semiestablished Reiki business took off and began to thrive. When I got into alignment, the universe that God created to assist me sent me many more clients to keep the energy of prosperity going. It almost felt as if I were being rewarded for my efforts to contribute to the greater good.

I continue to work with individuals in private sessions, and thanks to Lidia, Traci, and Julie, I teach groups and organizations mindfulness, wellness, and stress-resilience techniques. In teaching integrative wellness, I combine what I know of the spiritual world with the science of the physical world to enhance overall health and wellness. I have been honored to present what I know in places I never imagined to people I never would have expected to teach. The original text included a list of all my accolades, achievements, and high-profile clients. Those too were thoughtfully omitted because writing them here would be boastful and feel like a drive for external validation. See? I learned! More miracles!

Another big miracle happened because of my continued faith. The impossible became probable, and the thing I had almost given up on—writing my story—is complete and just in time to be of service in the ever-changing energy of our times. The secrets to using our empathic gifts for healing and creating are here in these pages. God has turned up the volume on our empathic gifts. We can no longer ignore the voice of God when he screams at us from the inside. It's time we learned to listen to the whisper again. It's time to strengthen that connection between ourselves and God, the divine energy of creation. We have been praying, "Your Will be done on Earth as it is in Heaven" (Matthew 6:10 NIV), for two thousand years, and now is our opportunity to make it happen. When we flow from divine love instead of human need, we can create our own versions of heaven on earth. It's time to flow in childlike faith and wonder again. Magic and miracles are real.

Write Your Story

When I reflect on the blessings of my life and the miracles, messages, and messengers of light that have been with me all along, I am humbled and in awe. The writing of my story from a higher perspective changed my life for the better. God knew what he was doing all along. Am I surprised? No. Am I in awe? Always.

There is no limit to the bliss we can have in our lives. If you've experienced pain, know that out there is the equal but opposite vibration of comfort waiting to be found. Misery has a rock bottom, but happiness has no ceiling. So go for it! Write your own story!

This life can be anything you can imagine. Why not imagine the good stuff? Why not make it a love story? Connect with your inner power through God, the infinite Source of all creative energy. Rewrite all the pain of your past with compassion and understanding. That is where true healing begins. Find the messages of light all around you, and you will be filled with gratitude and awe. Experience the exhilaration of expansion as you grow, and then share the wisdom and compassion you've learned with the world. Bask in the awesomeness of the divine love that has been with you all along. Learn to appreciate everything—the lessons and the blessings. Learn to hear your own whisper in the silence. It is the small voice in the back of your thoughts expressing love and compassion for everyone, including yourself. And it sounds just like you. Learn to receive and interpret your own messages. Anyone can do it! Just ask, breathe, believe, and receive.

Learn to listen to your own guidance. It's flawless, but it's useless unless you actually follow it. Be of service, first to yourself (God in you) and then to others, serving from an overflowing cup. Nothing will bring you closer to God than being of service. The rewards for this service are the feelings of fulfillment, peace, tranquility, and prosperity that come from that connection to God. Become who you came here to be. Embrace your authentic self, and watch the magic unfold in your life. Miracles happen every day, and they can happen for you!

Today, at this moment, as you're reading these words, make no mistake: you are being called to your own higher purpose. Wake up! It's time. This is the sign you've been waiting for! Will you be the author of your own story? Will you be the artist formulating new colors with which to paint? Will you do what you can to save this world? Will you start by healing your own world? Will you commit to designing a new one to enjoy and appreciate living in? Will you look for and listen to the messages of light offered to you by God? Will you say yes to the call and be a messenger of light for others?

Remember, we are all messengers of light, and it's up to us to say yes to the call. When enough of us awaken and shine the light of love on one another, we form a matrix of love and light over this planet we call home. When we shine the light, the darkness will dissipate. So I urge you now: shine brightly. Write your story! Fill the pages of your life with love, beauty, and compassion. Purposefully seek out the feelings, thoughts, circumstances, and events that bring you experiences of love, peace, comfort, and joy. Live in the freedom and wonder of childlike faith. Be the conscious, intentional creator of a history that is worth repeating. The time is now! Wake up! Heal your world, and help to design a new one that you can love. Rise and shine!

> For you were once darkness, but now you are Light
> in the Lord. Live as children of Light.
> —Ephesians 5:8 NIV

Namaste. The light within me honors, respects, and adores the light within you!

With love and appreciation,
Christi

The Beginning

CPSIA information can be obtained
at www.ICGtesting.com
Printed in the USA
LVHW102051270822
727003LV00012B/147/J